初級全民英檢必備

嚴雅貞・張淑如　編著

基本1000單字書

內附MP3光碟

三民書局

國家圖書館出版品預行編目資料

Vocabulary 1000:基本1000單字書 / 嚴雅貞,張淑
如編著.－－初版八刷.－－臺北市：三民，2018
　　面；　　公分

ISBN 978–957–14–4344–7　（平裝）

1.英國語言－詞彙　2.小學教育－教學法
3.中等教育－教學法

523.38　　　　　　　　　　　　　　94013939

© **Vocabulary 1000**
——基本1000單字書

編 著 者	嚴雅貞　張淑如
發 行 人	劉振強
著作財產權人	三民書局股份有限公司
發 行 所	三民書局股份有限公司
	地址　臺北市復興北路386號
	電話　(02)25006600
	郵撥帳號　0009998–5
門 市 部	（復北店）臺北市復興北路386號
	（重南店）臺北市重慶南路一段61號
出版日期	初版一刷　2006年8月
	初版八刷　2018年4月
編 　 號	S 806870

行政院新聞局登記證局版臺業字第○二○○號

有著作權·不准侵害

ISBN　978–957–14–4344–7　（平裝）

http://www.sanmin.com.tw　三民網路書店

給讀者的話

　　本書係參考教育部頒訂之「國民中小學英語最基本一千字詞」所編寫而成，全書依字母排序，以二十個單字為一回，方便您分階段學習。而且，每個單字均附有 KK 音標、詳盡的中文釋義，以及精心編寫的例句，在重要單字部分甚至還有重點文法的說明、常用片語、與容易相混淆單字的比較，以及該單字的同義字、反義字，可以說是目前坊間補充最為完善的一本單字書。此外，每十個單字之後更有十五題的練習題，讓您能夠即時練習、活學活用、加深記憶。

　　本書除了有豐富的內涵，更附有朗讀光碟，由發音純正的美籍專業錄音員所錄製，讓您知道每個單字最正確標準的發音，隨口說出最標準的英語，保證讓您從此單字牢記不忘、學習英語輕鬆自在、應付考試得心應手，就像派一樣容易 (as easy as pie) 喔！

略語表

V	原形動詞	*n.* [U]	不可數名詞	*interj.*	感嘆詞
v.	動詞	*adj.*	形容詞	*abbr.*	縮寫
v.t.	及物動詞	*adv.*	副詞	*aux.*	助動詞
v.i.	不及物動詞	*conj.*	連接詞	*art.*	冠詞
n.	名詞	*prep.*	介系詞	*phr.*	片語
n. [C]	可數名詞	*pron.*	代名詞		

contents

Unit 01

A

1. **a few**
[ə`fju]

phr. 一些，一點

· I have **a few** good friends in the U.S. （friend 為 *n.* [C]）
我在美國有一些好朋友。

單字	後面必接	中譯	比較
few	*n.* [C]	幾乎沒有	
a few	*n.* [C]	有一些	數量較 few 多
little	*n.* [U]	幾乎沒有	
a little	*n.* [U]	有一些	數量較 little 多

2. **a little**
[ə`lɪtḷ]

phr. 一些，一點

· We still have **a little** water to drink. （water 為 *n.* [U]）
我們還有一些水可以喝。

· Tom felt **a little** tired after work. （tired 為 *adj.*）
下班之後，湯姆覺得有點累。

注意
a little 後可接不可數名詞 *n.* [U] 及形容詞 *adj.*，而 a few 後面只能接可數名詞 *n.* [C]，兩者務必區分清楚。

3. **a lot**
[ə`lɑt]

a lot of/lots of + N
許多～

phr. 許多，很多

· Sarah ate **a lot** at the night market.
莎拉在夜市吃了很多東西。

· There are **_a lot of/lots of_** books in the library.
圖書館裡有許多書。

4. **a.m.**
[e`ɛm]

abbr. 上午 = ante meridiem（拉丁文）的縮寫 = before noon

· Amy was playing the piano at 10:00 **a.m.** this morning.
今天上午十點整的時候，艾咪正在彈鋼琴。

A

單字	拉丁原文	英譯	中譯
a.m.	ante meridiem	before noon	上午
p.m.	post meridiem	after noon	下午

◎ a.m. 及 p.m. 兩者用法相同，通常加在表幾點幾分的數字之後，如 6:00 p.m. 指下午六點。

---

5. **able**

[`ebl̩]

be able to + V

有能力～；能夠～

adj. 有能力的；能幹的

· I believe that Suzanne *is able to* do the job well.

我相信蘇珊有能力將這項工作做好。

· Allen is an **able** businessman; he has made lots of money.

艾倫是個能幹的生意人，他已經賺了許多錢。

---

6. **about**

[ə`baut]

prep. 關於；對於

· Tell me more **about** your friend, Bill.

多告訴我一些有關你朋友比爾的事。

prep. 大約（在某時、某地）

· It's **about** five o'clock now.

現在大概是五點鐘左右。

---

7. **above**

[ə`bʌv]

prep. 在～上方

· Many birds are flying **above** the Snow Mountain.

許多鳥兒正飛越過雪山上方。

注意

(1) 就相關位置而言，above 指「在～上方」，反義字為 below。

(2) above 除了可以指「位於～之上方」之外，還可以指：

prep. 程度上大（高）於～

· It's hot today. It must be **above** thirty degrees centigrade.

今天很熱。一定有攝氏三十度 (30°C) 以上。

A

adv. 上面；在上面
· The dark clouds **above** cover the sky; it is going to rain.
上方的烏雲遮蓋了天空，快要下雨了。

8. **afraid**
[ə`fred]

be afraid of
+ N/Ving 害怕～

be afraid that +子句
害怕～；恐怕～

adj. 害怕的；恐怕的
· Little Jeff is **afraid** because it is dark outside.
小傑夫很害怕，因為外面很黑。
· *Are* you *afraid* of mice?
你會害怕老鼠嗎?
· The bad man *is afraid* of being caught by the police.
這個壞人害怕被警方抓到。
· I'*m afraid that* I cannot lend you money.
我恐怕無法借你錢。

9. **after**
[`æftɚ]

prep. 在～之後（後面接 N/Ving） ↔ before [bɪ`for] 在～之前
· I can't go out **after** ten p.m.
我不能在晚上十點鐘之後出門。
conj. 在～之後（後面接子句）
· Sophia wants to become a super movie star **after** she grows up.
蘇菲亞想要在長大後成為一個超級電影巨星。

10. **afternoon**
[ˌæftɚ`nun]

n. [C][U] 下午
· We are going to see a movie in the **afternoon**.
我們下午要去看電影。

比較

單字	中譯	時間片語
morning	早上	in the morning
noon	中午	at noon
afternoon	下午	in the **afternoon**
evening	傍晚	in the evening
night	晚上	at night

Exercise 1

A

I. 字彙翻譯

1. 上面 _____
2. 上午 _____
3. 關於 _____
4. 一些 (+ *n*. [C]) _____
5. 一些 (+ *n*. [U]) _____

II. 字彙填充

_____ 1. I plan to go shopping with my classmates this a_____n.

_____ 2. She is not a_____e to see anything for it is too dark around.

_____ 3. A_____r two p.m., it stops raining.

_____ 4. A l_____t of people like to sleep late on Sunday.

_____ 5. Don't be a_____d. I am here with you.

III. 字彙選擇

( ) 1. We still have _____ bread. Do you want some?

    (A) a few   (B) a little   (C) many   (D) a lot

( ) 2. I am _____ that I can't help you because I am too busy now.

    (A) afternoon   (B) able   (C) afraid   (D) again

( ) 3. A _____ children are playing in the park.

    (A) afternoon   (B) little   (C) lot   (D) few

( ) 4. Frankie went to bed _____ he finished his homework.

    (A) after   (B) a.m.   (C) about   (D) above

( ) 5. Ben is _____ to speak English and French.

    (A) able   (B) afraid   (C) a few   (D) a lot

A

11. again
[ə`gɛn]

adv. 再，又；再一次
- You make the same mistake **again**. Be careful next time.
  你又犯了同樣的錯誤。下次小心一點。

12. age
[edʒ]

n. [C][U] 年齡；年紀
- When I was your **age**, I liked to read comic books.
  當我在你這個年紀時，我喜歡看漫畫。
- What's your **age**? = How old are you?
  你幾歲?

13. ago
[ə`go]

adv. 在～以前
- A monster lived in the lake long time **ago**.
  很久以前，有個怪物住在這湖裡。

比較

單字	中譯	用法	例子
ago	在～以前	一段時間 + **ago**	two hours **ago**
before	在～以前	before + 某個時間	before two o'clock

14. agree
[ə`gri]

agree with + sb
同意～

v.i. 同意，贊同 ↔ disagree [,dɪsə`gri] 不同意
- Jason asked me to help him, and I **agreed**.
  傑森要求我幫助他，而我同意了。
- Give it up. Your parents will not *agree* with you.
  放棄吧。你的父母不會同意你的。

15. air
[ɛr]

by air
搭飛機；經由空運

n. [U] 空氣
- The **air** in the country is much fresher than that in the city.
  鄉下的空氣比城市的新鮮多了。

n. 天空；空中 (the air)
- The birds are flying in the **air**.
  鳥兒們正在天空中飛翔。
- The rich man goes traveling *by air* once a year.
  那個有錢人一年搭乘飛機旅遊一次。

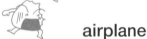
A

| on (the) air 實況轉播 | · This program is *on air* now, so listeners can call in anytime.
這個節目正實況轉播中，所以聽眾可以隨時打電話進去。 |

16. **airplane**
[`ɛr,plen]

n. [C] 飛機 = plane [plen]
· An **airplane** flew down and slowly landed on the runway.
一架飛機往下飛並緩慢地降落在跑道上。

17. **airport**
[`ɛr,port]

n. [C] 機場
· My plane will arrive at the **airport** at 10:00 a.m.
我的飛機將在早上十點抵達機場。

18. **all**
[ɔl]

adj. 所有的，全部的
· David ate **all** the apple pies and left nothing for Mary.
大衛把所有的蘋果派都吃完了，一點都沒留給瑪麗。
pron. 所有（人）（物）
· Do **all** of us need to join the party?
我們全部都得加入這個黨派嗎？
· **All** for one, and one for **all**.
[諺語] 我為人人，人人為我。

比較

all of us	**all** of you	**all** of them
我們全部	你們全部	他們全部

19. **almost**
[ɔl`most]

adv. 幾乎；差不多
· My dad takes exercise in the park **almost** every day.
我爸爸幾乎每天都在公園做運動。
· It was **almost** ten p.m. when Maria got home from the party.
當瑪麗亞從派對回到家時，差不多是晚上十點了。

20. **already**
[ɔl`rɛdɪ]

adv. 已經；先前 ↔ yet [jɛt] 尚未
· James has **already** finished his homework.
詹姆士已經做完他的家庭作業了。

Exercise 2

I. 字彙翻譯

1. 空氣 _____   2. 所有的 _____   3. 飛機 _____

4. 已經 _____   5. 年齡 _____

II. 字彙填充

_____ 1. Don't say that a_____n. You are repeating your words.

_____ 2. Arrive at the a_____t early before you take the airplane.

_____ 3. I can't a_____e with him because I don't believe his words.

_____ 4. A_____t every student in my class is cute and kind.

_____ 5. There were not so many cars in this city twenty years a_____o.

III. 字彙選擇

( ) 1. When I got to the train station, the train had _____ left.

　　(A) already 　　　(B) agree 　　　(C) all 　　　(D) always

( ) 2. Children at this _____ like to spend time with their friends, not their family.

　　(A) ago 　　　(B) age 　　　(C) airport 　　　(D) airplane

( ) 3. Don't lie _____ , or nobody will believe you.

　　(A) all 　　　(B) agree 　　　(C) air 　　　(D) again

( ) 4. When Nancy arrived at the park, _____ her friends had gone.

　　(A) afraid 　　　(B) already 　　　(C) agree 　　　(D) all

( ) 5. Is the _____ clean in Taipei?

　　(A) able 　　　(B) age 　　　(C) air 　　　(D) America

Unit 02

A

1. **also**
[ˋɔlso]

adv. 也；同樣地

- I like ice cream, and Janet **also** likes it.
  = I like ice cream, and Janet likes it, too.
  = I like ice cream, and so does Janet.
  我喜歡冰淇淋，珍妮也喜歡。

注意

　　also, so 和 too 都可以表示「也」，但使用的方式不同，also 是擺在主詞之後，動詞之前；too 固定擺在句尾，而 so 則是用於倒裝句，使用時要特別注意。

2. **always**
[ˋɔlwez]

adv. 總是；一直

- My mom **always** cooks delicious dinner for us.
  媽媽總是為我們烹煮美味的晚餐。

比較

頻率副詞	**always**	often	usually	sometimes	seldom	never
中譯	總是	通常	經常	有時	難得	從不
機率 (%)	100	99〜70	69〜40	39〜10	9〜0	0

3. **America**
[əˋmɛrɪkə]

n. 美國；美洲

- New York is the biggest city in **America**.
  紐約是美國最大的城市。

4. **American**
[əˋmɛrɪkən]

adj. 美國的；美洲的

- Jeff loves **American** food like steaks and hamburgers.
  傑夫喜歡美國的食物像是牛排和漢堡。

n. [C] 美國人；美洲人

- **Americans** celebrate their Independence Day on July 4th.
  美國人在七月四日慶祝他們的獨立紀念日。

5. **and**
[ænd]

conj. 和，與；同；而且

- Both my father **and** mother love me very much.
  我爸爸跟我媽媽都很愛我。

注意

　　and 前後必須連接兩個子句或同詞性的詞。

conj. 加

- Three **and** seven is/are ten.
  三加七等於十。

6. **angry**
[ˋæŋgrɪ]

be angry with + sb
對～生氣

adj. 生氣的，發怒的

- Jammy is **angry** because I ate her cake.
  潔美因為我吃了她的蛋糕而在生氣。
- Don't **be angry with** him. He didn't mean it.
  不要生他的氣。他不是故意的。

7. **animal**
[ˋænəml̩]

n. [C] 動物

- We can see many **animals** like tigers and monkeys in the zoo.
  我們可以在動物園裡看到老虎和猴子等許多動物。

8. **another**
[əˋnʌðɚ]

adj. 另外的；另一個

- Do you have **another** shirt? I don't like this one.
  你有另一件襯衫嗎? 我不喜歡這一件。

pron. 另一個（代替前面出現過的可數名詞）

- After finishing a candy, the boy asked for **another**.
  吃完一顆糖果之後，那男孩要求再來一顆。

比較

another	*adj.* 另外的；另一個 *pron.* 另一個（代替前面出現過的可數名詞） ◎通常指無特定範圍內的另一單獨個體。
	· The dress is too big; I want **another/another** one. 這件洋裝太大了。我想要另一件。

A

other	*adj.* 其他的　*pron.* 其他（人）（物）
	◎前面已提過部分個體，其餘剩下的就可用 other + N 或 others 表示。
	· Some people like apples, but <u>others/other people</u> don't. 有些人喜歡蘋果，其他人則不喜歡。
the other	*adj.* 另外的　*pron.* 另一個（人）（物）
	◎通常指兩者之間的「另外一個」。
	· There are two cakes here. I would have one and you could eat <u>the other</u>. 這裡有兩塊蛋糕。我吃一個，另一個給你吃。

9. **answer**
[`ænsɚ]

n. [C] 答案；回答；回應 ↔ question [`kwɛstʃən] 問題
· Nobody knows the **answer** to that difficult math question.
　沒有人知道那個數學難題的答案。

v.t. 回答；回應 ↔ ask [æsk] 詢問
· Who can **answer** me this question?
　誰能回答我這個問題？

v.i. 回答；回應
· I knocked the door but nobody **answered**.
　我敲了門，但卻沒有人回應。

10. **anyone**
[`ɛnɪˌwʌn]

pron. 任何人 = anybody [`ɛnɪˌbɑdɪ]
· The old lady doesn't like **anyone** who gets into her garden.
　這位老太太不喜歡任何進入她花園的人。

Exercise 1

I. 字彙翻譯

1. 美國人 _____
2. 動物 _____
3. 總是 _____
4. 任何人 _____
5. 另一個 _____

II. 字彙填充

_____ 1. The teacher was very a_____y with Johnny because he didn't finish his homework.

_____ 2. There is only one student who can a_____r the question.

_____ 3. John grows up in A_____a, so he can speak English very well.

_____ 4. Jim loves to eat chocolate, and Jay a_____o likes it.

_____ 5. There are three children in my family. I have a brother a_____d a sister.

III. 字彙選擇

( ) 1. Linda likes little _____ such as dogs and cats very much.

　　(A) always　　　　(B) airplanes　　　　(C) animals　　　　(D) answers

( ) 2. Tom _____ Bill are good friends. They like to play cards together.

　　(A) and　　　　(B) any　　　　(C) animal　　　　(D) another

( ) 3. Take _____ apple. This one doesn't smell good.

　　(A) other　　　　(B) another　　　　(C) any　　　　(D) always

( ) 4. Steven is _____ late for school; he gets up late every morning.

　　(A) any　　　　(B) and　　　　(C) also　　　　(D) always

( ) 5. Many young people like to watch _____ movies.

　　(A) America　　　　(B) American　　　　(C) angry　　　　(D) anyone

11. **anything**
[ˋɛnɪˌθɪŋ]

pron. 任何東西；任何事情
- Larry is a lazy man. He doesn't do **anything** all day.
  賴瑞是個懶人。他一整天都沒做任何事情。

12. **apartment**
[əˋpɑrtmənt]

n. [C]（一戶）公寓房間；公寓大樓
- You had better clean your **apartment**; it's so dirty.
  你最好清理一下你的公寓房間，它很髒。
- I live in an **apartment**, not a house.
  我住公寓大樓，而非住宅。

13. **appear**
[əˋpɪr]

appear to + V
看起來～

v.i. 出現 ↔ disappear [ˌdɪsəˋpɪr] 消失
- It is late now. I don't think Peter would **appear** tonight.
  現在已經很晚了，我想彼得今晚是不會出現了。

v.i. 看起來～
- The cat *appears* to be hurt; we should take it to a doctor.
  那隻貓看起來好像受傷了，我們應該帶牠去看醫生。

14. **apple**
[ˋæpl̩]

Adam's apple
喉結

n. [C] 蘋果
- People think the "forbidden fruit" in the Bible is an **apple**.
  人們認為聖經中所提到的「禁果」就是蘋果。
- He is a man; of course he has an *Adam's* **apple**.
  他是個男人，理所當然會有喉結。

15. **arm**
[ɑrm]

n. [C] 手臂
- Tim fell from a horse and broke his **arm** yesterday.
  提姆昨天從馬上摔了下來，摔斷了手臂。

【注意】
    arm 指的是從肩膀 (shoulder) 到手腕 (wrist) 的部分，而 hand 則是指手腕之後主要為手掌 (palm) 的部分。

16. **arrive**
[əˋraɪv]

v.i. 到達；到來
- Our teacher asks us to **arrive** at school on time every day.
  我們老師要求我們每天準時到校。

A

arrive 為不及物動詞，所以後面要接地點名稱時必須先加介系詞，而所應加的介系詞隨地點種類的不同而異，例如：arrive at school/the park, arrive in the big city/country (at 後面接小地方，in 後面則是接城市或國家等大地方)。

---

17. art

[ɑrt]

n. [U] 藝術

· Are you interested in **art** like dancing or painting?
  你對於像舞蹈或者繪畫之類的藝術有興趣嗎?

---

18. as

[əz]

conj. 和～一樣；如同

· The mountain is not so high **as** we have thought.
  這座山不像我們想地那麼高。

conj. 當～時 = when [hwɛn]

· **As** he was going to bed, the telephone rang.
  當他正要上床睡覺的時候，電話響了。

conj. 因為 = because [bɪ`kɔz]

· I didn't go to school **as** I caught a cold.
  我沒去上學，因為我感冒了。

adv. 和～一樣；如同

as...as...
像～一樣～

· Cathy can not run *as* fast *as* Penny.
  凱西無法跑得像潘妮一樣快。

prep. 身為

· **As** a student, you must listen to the teacher.
  身為一個學生，你必須要聽從老師的話。

---

19. ask

[æsk]

v.t. v.i. 詢問 ↔ answer [`ænsɚ] 回答

· If you have any question, you can **ask** your teacher.
  如果你有任何問題，你可以問你的老師。

v.t. v.i. 要求；請求

ask + sb + to + V
要求／請求某人～

· My mom *asked* me *to* come home before nine o'clock.
  我媽媽要求我九點以前回家。

A

20. **aunt**
[ænt]

n. [C] 阿姨；姑姑；舅媽；嬸嬸

· **Aunt** Polly was very angry because Tom broke her window.
波莉姨媽很生氣，因為湯姆打破了她的窗子。

休息一下喔！

Exercise 2

I. 字彙翻譯

1. 詢問 _____   2. 出現 _____   3. 藝術 _____

4. 手臂 _____   5. 和～一樣 _____

II. 字彙填充

_____ 1. An a_____e a day keeps the doctor away.

_____ 2. My a_____t is a kind woman. She always gives other people a hand.

_____ 3. You can borrow a_____g you like in this room.

_____ 4. All of you should a_____e at the bus stop on time, or you won't be able to catch the bus.

_____ 5. Clancy and I are neighbors (鄰居). We live in the same a_____t.

III. 字彙選擇

(   ) 1. The mother held her baby in her _____.

     (A) always   (B) arts   (C) arms   (D) aunts

(   ) 2. Is there _____ who can help me move the big stone?

     (A) anyone   (B) anything   (C) another   (D) American

(   ) 3. Music and movies are both part of _____.

     (A) art   (B) arm   (C) answer   (D) aunt

(   ) 4. Don't _____ me anything about David. I haven't seen him for a long time.

     (A) answer   (B) ask   (C) agree   (D) able

(   ) 5. Jenny will move to her new _____ next month.

     (A) anything   (B) apple   (C) art   (D) apartment

Unit 03

B

1. **autumn**
[`ɔtəm]

n. [C][U] 秋天（英式用法）＝ fall [fɔl]（美式用法）
- The weather is cool in **autumn**/fall.
 秋天的天氣很涼爽。

2. **away**
[ə`we]

adv. 有～之遠；遠離～
- The hotel is not very near. It's at least five miles **away**.
 旅館不是很近。它至少有五哩之遠。

away from + N
離～有多遠
- The house is not far *away* *from* here. You can go there on foot.
 那棟房子離這兒不遠。你可以走路過去。

right away
馬上
- I called 119 *right* *away* when I saw the house on fire.
 當我看到那棟房子著火，我就馬上打了一一九。

3. **baby**
[`bebɪ]

n. [C] 小嬰兒
- The newborn **baby** is so cute that all of us like her.
 這個剛出生的小嬰兒好可愛，我們都喜歡她。

4. **back**
[bæk]

adv. 向後；後退地
- I stood **back** to look at the big picture.
 我向後站，以便看那張大圖。

adv. 回原處；往回
- Put the book **back** on the desk.
 把書本放回書桌上。

n. [C] 背部；後部 ↔ front [frʌnt] 前面
- Ben patted me on the **back** to wake me up.
 班輕拍我的背，將我叫醒。

in back of + N
在～後面
- There is a beautiful garden *in* *back* of the house.
 這房子後面有一個美麗的花園。

in the back of + N
- I sit *in* *the* *back* of the bus, so I can see everyone on the bus.
 我坐在公車的後端，所以我可以看到公車上的每一個人。

在～的後面

注意

　　in back of 和 in the back of 的差別在於前者指的是在範圍外部的後面（如：我家的後面有山坡），而後者則是指範圍內後面的部分（如：飛機的後端是行李艙），兩者不可搞混。

5. **bad**
[bæd]

原級	比較級	最高級
bad [bæd]	worse [wɝs]	worst [wɝst]

adj. 不好的；壞的 ↔ good [gʊd] 好的；有益的

- Reading without enough light is **bad** for your eyes.
  在沒有充足光線的情況下閱讀,對你的眼睛不好。
- Huck is a **bad** boy. He always makes fun of other kids and laughs at them.
  哈克是個壞小孩。他總是捉弄其他孩子並且嘲笑他們。
- We stayed home for the **bad** weather.
  因為天氣不好，所以我們待在家裡。

6. **bag**
[bæg]

a bag of + N
一袋～

n. [C] 袋子；提袋；旅行袋

- Laura is shopping in the supermarket with a **bag** in her hand.
  蘿拉正在超級市場購物，手裡提個袋子。
- Hank brought *a **bag** of* dirty clothes home to wash.
  漢克帶了一袋髒衣服回家洗。

7. **bakery**
[`bekərɪ]

n. [C] 麵包店

- Yvonne likes to buy bread and cookies in that new **bakery**.
  伊帆喜歡在那家新開的麵包店買麵包和小餅乾。

8. **ball**
[bɔl]

n. [C] 球；球狀體

- A few boys are kicking a **ball** to each other in the park for fun.
  幾個小男孩在公園裡，互相踢著球取樂。

B

9. **banana**
[bə`nænə]

n. [C] 香蕉

· **Bananas** are sweet fruit with yellow skin and white meat.
香蕉是有黃色果皮以及白色果肉的香甜水果。

10. **band**
[bænd]

rock band
搖滾樂團

n. [C] 樂隊；樂團

· Johnny was a drummer in a **band** when he was sixteen.
強尼十六歲時，在樂團擔任鼓手。
· The famous American *rock* **band** is coming to Taiwan.
這個著名的美國搖滾樂團即將來到台灣。

休息一下喔！

Exercise 1

I. 字彙翻譯

1. 麵包店 _____
2. 球 _____
3. 遠離～ _____
4. 不好的 _____
5. 背部 _____

B

II. 字彙填充

_____ 1. Bill loves music, and he plays the guitar in a b_____d.

_____ 2. If you feel hungry, you can eat the b_____a on the table.

_____ 3. Mary is only a little b_____y. She can do nothing but eat and sleep.

_____ 4. Debby put her books in her school b_____g and went to the library.

_____ 5. The leaves（葉子）turn red and fall down in a_____n.

III. 字彙選擇

( ) 1. Don't make friends with that _____ girl. She always tells lies.

(A) bag   (B) bad   (C) band   (D) bank

( ) 2. The little boy is playing with a(n) _____.

(A) answer   (B) autumn   (C) ball   (D) back

( ) 3. Daisy has a part-time job in that _____, and her work is to make delicious bread.

(A) ball   (B) band   (C) bag   (D) bakery

( ) 4. The _____ is heavy because it is full of books.

(A) bag   (B) band   (C) bakery   (D) banana

( ) 5. I walk to school every day. My home is not very far _____ from the school.

(A) autumn   (B) away   (C) angry   (D) always

B

11. **bank**
[bæŋk]

n. [C] 銀行
- Do you want to save your money in this **bank**?
  你想要在這家銀行裡存錢嗎?

n. [C] 堤;岸
- Danny likes to fish on the river **bank** on weekends.
  週末的時候,丹尼喜歡到河堤上釣魚。

12. **baseball**
[`bes,bɔl]

n. [C][U] 棒球
- There are many students playing **baseball** at the playground.
  有許多學生在操場上打棒球。

- Which **baseball** team do you like best?
  你最喜歡哪一支棒球隊?

球類運動最常用的動詞是 play,比方說打棒球用 play baseball,打籃球用 play basketball,踢足球用 play soccer 等等。

補充

MLB = Major League Baseball　美國職棒大聯盟

13. **basket**
[`bæskɪt]

n. [C] 籃子;簍子;筐
- Mother put the fruit she bought in the **basket**.
  媽媽把她買的水果放在籃子裡。

- Don't put all your eggs in one **basket**.
  [諺語] 別把所有的雞蛋放在同一個籃子裡。
  (引申為「不要孤注一擲。」)

14. **basketball**
[`bæskɪt,bɔl]

n. [C][U] 籃球
- Joe is a **basketball** player, and he dreams to join the NBA.
  喬是個籃球員,他夢想能加入 NBA。

- I will join the 3 on 3 **basketball** game today.
  我今天會參加三對三籃球賽。

NBA = National Basketball Association　全美籃球協會

B

15. **bath**
[bæθ]

n. [C] 沐浴；洗澡

- My dad likes to take a hot **bath** after he takes exercise.
  我爸爸運動後喜歡洗個熱水澡。

注意

洗澡是 <u>take/have</u> a bath，淋浴則是 <u>take/have</u> a shower。

16. **bathroom**
[ˋbæθ͵rum]

n. [C] 浴室

- Don't let the kids play in the **bathroom**. It's dangerous.
  不要讓小孩在浴室裡玩耍。這樣挺危險的。

17. **beach**
[bitʃ]

n. [C] 海灘；海濱

- We spent our holidays at the **beach**.
  我們在海濱度假。
- My boyfriend and I like to take a walk along the **beach**.
  我男朋友和我喜歡沿著海灘散步。

18. **bear**
[bɛr]

n. [C] 熊

- Teddy **bears** are loved by many children around the world.
  泰迪熊受到全世界許多小孩的喜愛。

v.t. 生（小孩）

過去式	過去分詞	現在進行式
bore [bor]	born [bɔrn]	bearing [ˋbɛrɪŋ]

- Maria just **bore** a little baby, so she is a mother now.
  瑪麗亞剛生了個小嬰兒，所以她現在已經是個媽媽了。

v.t. 忍受；經得起

- Turn the radio off. I can't **bear** the noise any more.
  把收音機關掉。我再也忍受不了這個噪音了。

B

19. **beautiful**

[ˋbjutəfəl]

adj. 美麗的，漂亮的

· Rebecca wore a **beautiful** dress to the party last night.
　蕾蓓卡昨晚穿了一件漂亮的洋裝去參加舞會。

20. **because**

[bɪˋkɔz]

because of + N/Ving
因為（由於）～

conj. 因為

· I can't talk to you now **because** I am busy with my work.
　我現在不能跟你說話，因為我忙於工作。

· ***Because*** *of* your help, I could finish my work in time.
　由於你的幫忙，我才能及時完成我的工作。

休息一下喔！

Exercise 2

I. 字彙翻譯

1. 浴室 _____
2. 籃球 _____
3. 沐浴 _____
4. 籃子 _____
5. 熊 _____

II. 字彙填充

_____ 1. Are there many people playing volleyball at the b_____h?

_____ 2. Salzburg is said to be one of the most b_____l city in the world.

_____ 3. Is there a b_____k nearby? I need to withdraw（提領）some money.

_____ 4. I gave a b_____l glove to my son on his birthday.

_____ 5. Mrs. Tang was very happy b_____e her husband gave her a present.

III. 字彙選擇

(   ) 1. A _____ is catching a fish to eat in the river.

     (A) bank   (B) bear   (C) bath   (D) beach

(   ) 2. I bought a _____ of eggs in the market. I want to make a cake.

     (A) baseball   (B) bank   (C) beach   (D) basket

(   ) 3. Can you tell me when and where you were _____?

     (A) bear   (B) bore   (C) borne   (D) born

(   ) 4. It feels so good to take a hot _____ after a day's hard work.

     (A) beach   (B) bath   (C) bank   (D) band

(   ) 5. The typhoon is coming. You should not fish on the _____ today.

     (A) band   (B) bathroom   (C) bear   (D) bank

B

Unit 04

B

1. **become**
[bɪ`kʌm]

過去式	過去分詞	現在進行式
became [bɪ`kem]	become [bɪ`kʌm]	becoming [bɪ`kʌmɪŋ]

v.t. 變成；成為

- Michelle has **become** a famous movie star in Hong Kong.
  蜜雪兒在香港已成為一個有名的電影明星。

2. **bed**
[bɛd]

go to bed
上床睡覺

n. [C] 床

- There are two **beds** and one desk in my room.
  在我的房裡有兩張床和一張書桌。
- She *went to bed* before 10 o'clock every night.
  她每天晚上十點以前上床睡覺。

3. **bedroom**
[`bɛd͵rum]

n. [C] 臥室；寢室

- When I was a kid, I shared a **bedroom** with my sister.
  在我小的時候，我和我姊姊共用一間臥室。

4. **bee**
[bi]

as busy as a bee
非常忙碌的

n. [C] 蜜蜂

- There are many **bees** and flowers in the garden.
  在花園裡有許多的蜜蜂和花。
- Thomas is *as busy as a bee* and he doesn't
  have time to rest.
  湯瑪士非常忙碌，沒有時間可以休息。

5. **beef**
[bif]

n. [U] 牛肉

- The American loves the **beef** noodles in Taiwan.
  那個美國人很喜歡臺灣的牛肉麵。

6. **before**
[bɪ`fɔr]

prep. 在～以前（後面接 N/Ving）↔ after [`æftɚ] 在～之後

- Ella had finished her homework **before** sleeping.
  艾拉在睡覺之前，已經做完了家庭作業。

B

conj. 在～以前（後面接子句）

· Hebe always has a glass of milk **before** she goes to school.

希碧在上學前總會喝杯牛奶。

adv. 較早；以前；之前

· Stella has never heard such a beautiful song **before**.

史黛拉以前從來沒聽過這麼美妙的歌曲。

---

7. **begin**

[bɪ`gɪn]

過去式	過去分詞	現在進行式
began [bɪ`gæn]	begun [bɪ`gʌn]	beginning [bɪ`gɪnɪŋ]

v.t. v.i. 開始 = start [start]

begin + to V/Ving
開始～

· At twelve o'clock, the ship **began** to move.

= At twelve o'clock, the ship **began** moving.

十二點整，船開始動了。

---

8. **believe**

[bə`liv]

v.t. v.i. 相信

· If you keep telling lies, nobody will **believe** you.

如果你一直說謊，就沒人會相信你了。

believe in
信仰，信任

· We **believe** in God.

我們信仰上帝。

---

9. **bell**

[bɛl]

n. [C] 鐘；鈴；門鈴；鐘聲；鈴聲

· Somebody is ringing the **bell**. Go and see who it is!

有人在按門鈴。去看看是誰!

· The **bell** is ringing. It's time to take a break!

鐘聲響了。是休息一下的時候囉!

---

10. **belong**

[bə`lɔŋ]

belong to + N
屬於～

v.i. 屬於

· That bicycle **belongs** to me.

那輛腳踏車是屬於我的。

· These new toys **belong** to the little boy.

這些新玩具是屬於這個小男孩的。

Exercise 1

I. 字彙翻譯

1. 相信 ＿＿＿＿＿＿＿＿　　2. 屬於 ＿＿＿＿＿＿＿＿　　3. 在～之前 ＿＿＿＿＿＿＿＿

4. 變成 ＿＿＿＿＿＿＿＿　　5. 鈴 ＿＿＿＿＿＿＿＿

II. 字彙填充

＿＿＿＿＿＿＿＿ 1. You should brush your teeth before you go to b ＿＿＿＿ d.

＿＿＿＿＿＿＿＿ 2. The b ＿＿＿＿ es are busy collecting honey in the flowers.

＿＿＿＿＿＿＿＿ 3. It is wonderful to see a little baby b ＿＿＿＿ g to walk.

＿＿＿＿＿＿＿＿ 4. I don't like b ＿＿＿＿ f steak.

＿＿＿＿＿＿＿＿ 5. Keep quiet. Janet is sleeping in her b ＿＿＿＿ m.

III. 字彙選擇

(　) 1. That new skirt doesn't ＿＿＿＿ you. It's mine.

      (A) belong　　　(B) belong with　　　(C) belong for　　　(D) belong to

(　) 2. No matter what I said, they just didn't ＿＿＿＿ me.

      (A) belong　　　(B) because　　　(C) believe　　　(D) before

(　) 3. ＿＿＿＿ leaving the office, you have to turn off the lights and computers.

      (A) Before　　　(B) Begin　　　(C) Belong　　　(D) Behind

(　) 4. When the ＿＿＿＿ rings, all students should get into the classroom.

      (A) bird　　　(B) bell　　　(C) bear　　　(D) belt

(　) 5. She ＿＿＿＿ a doctor after ten years.

      (A) became　　　(B) bore　　　(C) belonged　　　(D) believed

11. belt
[bɛlt]
seat belt
安全帶

n. [C] 腰帶；帶狀物
· Before you drive a car, remember to fasten your *seat **belt***.
在你開車之前，記得繫上安全帶。

12. bicycle
[ˋbaɪsɪkḷ]

n. [C] 單車；腳踏車 = bike [baɪk]
· Do you like to ride a **bicycle** along the country road?
你喜不喜歡沿著鄉村小路騎腳踏車?

13. big
[bɪg]

adj. 大的；巨大的 ↔ small [smɔl] 小的
· Mother made a **big** cake. It is **big** enough for ten people to eat.
媽媽做了一個大蛋糕，大的足夠讓十個人吃了。

14. bird
[bɝd]

n. [C] 鳥；禽
· I wish I could fly like a **bird**.
我希望我可以像鳥一樣飛翔。
· The early **bird** catches the worm.
[諺語] 早起的鳥兒有蟲吃。

15. birthday
[ˋbɝθ‚de]

n. [C] 生日；誕生的日子
· Happy **birthday** to you!
祝你生日快樂!

16. bite
[baɪt]

過去式	過去分詞	現在進行式
bit [bɪt]	bitten [ˋbɪtṇ]	biting [ˋbaɪtɪŋ]

v.t. 咬；啃；叮咬
· Jane was **bitten** by a dog yesterday.
珍昨天被狗咬了。
· A mosquito **bit** me just now.
剛才有一隻蚊子叮我。

bite off + N
咬下～
· He ***bit** off* a large piece of apple.
他咬下一大塊蘋果。

17. **black**
[blæk]
black coffee
黑咖啡
blackmail
黑函；恐嚇信

adj. 黑的；黑色的；黑暗的

· Please give me a cup of **black** *coffee*.
請給我一杯黑咖啡。

· All things about me in that **blackmail** are not true.
那封黑函上關於我的所有事全不是真的。

n. [U] 黑色；黑衣服

· The kids are dressed in **black** for their dead mother.
那些孩子為了他們死去的母親，穿著黑色的衣服。

18. **blackboard**
[ˋblæk͵bɔrd]

n. [C] 黑板

· The teacher wrote the answers on the **blackboard**.
老師把答案寫在黑板上。

注意

blackboard 屬複合字，為 black（黑色的）與 board（板；木板）的結合，此類的複合字中間不需要加連字號，類似的字還有 colorblind（色盲的）、seabird（海鳥）、bikeway（自行車專用道）等等。

19. **blind**
[blaɪnd]

adj. 瞎的；失明的

· Guide dogs help **blind** people a lot.
導盲犬對於盲人的幫助很大。

adj. 盲目的

· Love is **blind**.
愛情是盲目的。

20. **block**
[blɑk]

n. [C] 街區；阻礙物

· The store is just two **blocks** away. You can walk there.
那家店距離這兒只有兩個街區遠，你可以走路過去。

v.t. 阻礙

· After the earthquake, the road was **blocked** by rocks.
地震之後，這條路被岩石給擋住了。

Exercise 2

I. 字彙翻譯

1. 鳥 _____
2. 腳踏車 _____
3. 瞎的；盲目的 _____
4. 腰帶 _____
5. 咬（三態）_____ _____ _____

II. 字彙填充

_____ 1. I am a Chinese and my hair is b_____k.

_____ 2. Don't worry. My dog will not b_____e you. It just likes to bark (吠；叫).

_____ 3. I am the b_____g brother in my family and I have two little sisters.

_____ 4. After the typhoon, the big tree fell down and b_____ked the road.

_____ 5. The teacher wrote the class rules on the b_____d and asked the students to follow them.

III. 字彙選擇

( ) 1. You should help him if you see a _____ man crossing the street.
    (A) big   (B) blind   (C) boat   (D) bite

( ) 2. Years ago people could only see _____ and white movies, but now we have color ones.
    (A) black   (B) blue   (C) brown   (D) bright

( ) 3. James is an early _____. He gets up at six o'clock every morning.
    (A) baby   (B) bee   (C) bear   (D) bird

( ) 4. The _____ looks great with your pants. Where did you buy it?
    (A) bed   (B) bee   (C) beef   (D) belt

( ) 5. My mom gave me a baseball glove on my _____.
    (A) birthday   (B) block   (C) bicycle   (D) body

B

Unit 05

B

1. blow

[blo]

過去式	過去分詞	現在進行式
blew [blu]	blown [blon]	blowing [`bloɪŋ]

v.t. v.i. 吹；吹氣

- The strong wind **blew** my hat away.
  這大風吹走了我的帽子。
- Tina **blows** *her nose* all day. She must catch a cold.
  蒂娜一整天都在擤鼻涕。她一定是感冒了。
- The typhoon **blew** *down* several trees on the road.
  颱風刮倒了路上的好幾棵樹。

blow one's nose
擤鼻涕
blow down
吹倒，刮倒

2. blue

[blu]

adj. 藍色的

- The weather is great with the warm sun and **blue** sky.
  天氣很棒，有溫暖的太陽以及藍藍的天空。

n. [U] 藍色

- **Blue** is the color of the clean river and the clear sky.
  藍色是乾淨河水和晴朗天空的顏色。

adj. 憂鬱的

- Whenever I feel **blue**, I would go outside and take a walk.
  每當我覺得憂鬱的時候，我就會到戶外散散步。

3. boat

[bot]

n. [C] 小船；輪船

- We have to cross the river by **boat**.
  我們必須搭小船過河。
- You are poor and I have no money; we are *in the same **boat***.
  你很窮，而我沒有錢，我們處境相同。

in the same boat
處境相同

比較

單字	詞性	中譯
boat	*n.* [C]	小船；輪船
ship [ʃɪp]	*n.* [C]	大船；船艦；太空梭；飛艇

30

B

4. **body**
[`bɑdɪ]

a body language
肢體語言

n. [C] 身體；軀幹

· You had better wash your **body** before you go to bed.
上床睡覺前，你最好洗一下身體。

· Smiling is *a **body** language*. Everyone knows what it means.
微笑是一種肢體語言。每個人都知道它的意義。

5. **book**
[bʊk]

a phone book
電話簿

n. [C] 書，書本，書籍，本子

· When you read a **book**, do you like to listen to some music?
當你看書時，你喜歡聽些音樂嗎?

· I must check the *phone **book*** to get Mike's phone number.
我必須查過電話簿才能知道邁克的電話號碼。

v.t. v.i. 預訂，預約（餐廳、旅館房間、機票等）

· Do you know how to **book** a room online?
你知道怎麼在線上訂房嗎?

6. **bookstore**
[`bʊkˌstor]

n. [C] 書店

· On weekends, I like to go to the **bookstore** to read some books.
週末時，我喜歡去書店看看書。

7. **bored**
[bɔrd]

be bored with + N
對～感到厭煩

adj. 感到厭煩的；感到無聊的

· Jerry felt so **bored** because no one could play with him.
傑瑞覺得非常無聊，因為沒人可以陪他玩。

· George *is **bored** with* the same game.
喬治對於同樣的遊戲感到厭煩。

注意
有關情緒動詞的詳細用法請參閱附錄。

8. **boring**
[`bɔrɪŋ]

adj. 令人生厭的；令人感到無聊的

· Don't you think it **boring** to watch TV all day long?
你不認為整天看電視很無聊嗎?

B

- I don't want to watch the **boring** program.
  我不想看那個無聊的節目。

9. **born**
   [bɔrn]

   adj. 出生的；誕生的
   - My best friend was **born** on Christmas Eve.
     我最好的朋友在聖誕夜出生。

   adj. 天生的；出生就有的
   - Elizabeth Taylor is a **born** movie star.
     依莉莎白・泰勒是個天生的電影明星。

10. **borrow**
    [`baro]

    borrow + sth + from
    + N
    向～借～

    v.t. v.i. 借；借入
    - James wanted to **borrow** a sports car to pick up his girlfriend.
      詹姆士想借一台跑車來接他女朋友。
    - I usually *borrow* books *from* the library.
      我常向圖書館借書。

    比較

borrow [`baro]	*v.t.* 借入 / 來～；向（某人）借（某物）
	◎用 borrow 時，後面接的受詞表示借入的東西。
	• **I borrowed** some books to read last weekend. 上個週末我借了一些書來讀。
lend [lɛnd]	*v.t.* 借出～；借（某物）給（某人）
	◎用 lend 時，後面接的受詞表示借出的東西。
	• Peter lent his bicycle to me. 彼得把他的腳踏車借給我。

Exercise 1

I. 字彙翻譯

1. 書店 _____

2. 書本 _____

3. 藍色的 _____

4. 吹；吹氣 _____

5. 令人生厭的 _____

II. 字彙填充

_____ 1. She didn't say a word, but everyone understood her b_____y language.

_____ 2. Little Anna was very b_____d because no one could play with her.

_____ 3. There is no bridge. We could only cross the river by b_____t.

_____ 4. I forgot to bring my money with me. May I b_____w some from you?

_____ 5. I was b_____n and grew up in Taiwan.

III. 字彙選擇

( ) 1. This is a good _____. You should read it, too.

(A) boat　　　(B) block　　　(C) belt　　　(D) book

( ) 2. When we speak to others, _____ language is also important.

(A) ball　　　(B) body　　　(C) boat　　　(D) bell

( ) 3. It is such a _____ show that many people feel bored.

(A) boring　　　(B) bored　　　(C) born　　　(D) borne

( ) 4. Daniel is a _____ actor. Whenever he stands on the stage, there is laughter all around.

(A) bear　　　(B) bore　　　(C) born　　　(D) borne

( ) 5. Frank lost the game. He looked _____ all day long.

(A) blue　　　(B) black　　　(C) blind　　　(D) big

B

11. **boss**
[bɔs]

n. [C] 老闆；主人
- Who is the **boss** in this bookstore?
  誰是這家書店的老闆?

12. **both**
[boθ]

both A and B
A 和 B 都～

pron. 兩個～都～
- **Both** of his arms were hurt in the car accident.
  在車禍中,他的兩隻手臂都受傷了。

adv. 兩者皆～
- I like apples and oranges **both**.
  = I like **both** apples and oranges.
  蘋果和柳橙,我兩個都喜歡。
- *Both* Tim *and* Joy were late for school.
  提姆和裘依兩個人上學都遲到了。

13. **bottle**
[`bɑtḷ]

a bottle of + N
一瓶～(的量)

n. [C] 瓶子；酒瓶
- Annie found a letter in the **bottle**.
  安妮發現一封瓶中信。
- Give me *a bottle of* water.
  給我一瓶水。

14. **bottom**
[`bɑtəm]

n. [C] 底；底部；底層 ↔ top [tɑp] 頂部
- The **bottom** of the bottle is broken.
  這個瓶子的底部破了。
- It is so dark at the **bottom** of the sea.
  在海的底部是非常暗的。

15. **bowl**
[bol]

a bowl of + N
一碗～

n. [C] 碗
- Be careful. Don't break the **bowls** on the table.
  小心一點。不要把桌上的碗打破了。
- My mom cooked *a bowl of* hot chicken soup for me.
  我媽媽為我煮了一碗熱雞湯。

B

16. box
[bɑks]

a box of + N
一盒～；一箱～

n. [C] 盒子；箱子（複數：boxes [`bɑksɪz]）
- These **boxes** are all full of books and are very heavy.
  這些箱子裡全裝滿了書，很重。
- The boy was so happy to get *a **box** of* new toys on Christmas.
  這男孩很高興在聖誕節收到一箱子的新玩具。

17. boy
[bɔɪ]

n. [C] 男孩；少年 ↔ girl [gɝl] 女孩；少女
- There are twenty **boys** and twenty girls in our class.
  我們班上有二十個男生和二十個女生。

n. [C] 兒子 = son [sʌn] ↔ girl [gɝl] = daughter [`dɔtɚ] 女兒
- Mr. and Mrs. Chang have two **boys** and one girl.
  張先生和張太太有兩個兒子和一個女兒。

18. bread
[brɛd]

n. [U] 麵包
- Tina always has **bread** and milk for breakfast.
  蒂娜早餐總是吃麵包和牛奶。

19. break
[brek]

過去式	過去分詞	現在進行式
broke [brok]	broken [`brokən]	breaking [`brekɪŋ]

v.t. 打破；弄壞；毀壞
- My glasses were **broken** when I played basketball.
  我的眼鏡在打籃球時被打破了。

n. [C] 短暫的休息
- Give me a **break**.
  讓我休息一下吧!
  （可引申為「饒了我吧!」）

take a break/rest
休息一下

- We have been walking for three hours. Let's *take a **break**/rest*.
  我們已經走三個小時了。我們休息一下吧。

20. breakfast
[`brɛkfəst]

n. [C][U] 早餐；早點
- You should eat **breakfast** every morning.
  你應該每天早上吃早餐。

Exercise 2

I. 字彙翻譯

1. 麵包 _____
2. 碗 _____
3. 兩者皆～ _____
4. 早餐 _____
5. 毀壞（三態） _____ _____ _____

II. 字彙填充

_____ 1. There are a few b_____ys playing basketball in the park.

_____ 2. I put all my letters in a little b_____x.

_____ 3. Bill said he didn't mean to b_____k the window. It was an accident.

_____ 4. It is so hot. I want to drink a b_____e of cold coke.

_____ 5. There is no light at the b_____m of the sea. It is very dark.

III. 字彙選擇

( ) 1. Mr. Li owns several factories. He is the _____ of hundreds of people.

    (A) boats   (B) bowls   (C) boss   (D) books

( ) 2. You should eat your _____ before you go to school.

    (A) belt   (B) bookstore   (C) bottom   (D) breakfast

( ) 3. The bell is ringing, so let's take a _____.

    (A) break   (B) body   (C) book   (D) bowl

( ) 4. There are some juice left at the _____ of the bottle.

    (A) bread   (B) bottom   (C) boat   (D) bird

( ) 5. _____ May and Tera like to go to the movies. They have the same hobby.

    (A) Both   (B) Boss   (C) Box   (D) Boy

Unit 06

B

1. bridge
[brɪdʒ]

cross the bridge
過橋

n. [C] 橋；橋樑

- I stand on the **bridge** to see the fish in the clear river.
  我站在橋上，看著清澈河流中的魚兒。
- After we *cross the **bridge***, we will arrive at the next town.
  在我們過橋後，我們就會抵達下一個城鎮。

2. bright
[braɪt]

adj. 明亮的

- The **bright** sun made all of us even more lively.
  明亮的太陽使我們更有活力。

adj. 光明的

- Always look on the **bright** side of life.
  多看看人生的光明面。（可引申為「人生總是美好的。」）

3. bring
[brɪŋ]

過去式	過去分詞	現在進行式
brought [brɔt]	brought [brɔt]	bringing [ˋbrɪŋɪŋ]

v.t. 拿來；帶來

- Studying hard will **bring** you good grades.
  努力唸書會為你帶來好成績。

bring + sth + for + sb = bring + sb + sth
把某物帶給某人

- When you come back, please ***bring*** a cup of coffee *for* me.
  = When you come back, please ***bring*** me a cup of coffee.
  當你回來時，請帶杯咖啡給我。

4. brother
[ˋbrʌðɚ]

big brother
老大

n. [C] 兄弟

- How many **brothers** and sisters do you have?
  你有多少個兄弟姊妹?
- *Big **brother*** is watching you.
  老大哥正在看著你。　（～喬治·歐威爾「一九八四」）

B

5. **brown** [braʊn]

adj. 棕色的；褐色的
- I like to take sunbath, which makes me have **brown** skin.
  我喜歡做日光浴，這讓我有了褐色的肌膚。

n. [U] 棕色；褐色；棕色顏料；棕色衣服
- **Brown** is the color of coffee and chocolate.
  棕色是咖啡和巧克力的顏色。

6. **brush** [brʌʃ]

n. [C] 刷子；畫筆（複數：brushes）
- The art teacher taught us how to paint with a **brush** correctly.
  美術老師教我們如何正確地用畫筆畫畫。

v.t. 刷～
- Be sure to **brush** your teeth before going to bed.
  睡前務必刷牙。

7. **build** [bɪld]

過去式	過去分詞	現在進行式
built [bɪlt]	built [bɪlt]	building [ˋbɪldɪŋ]

v.t. 建造～（建築物）
- The workers are **building** a bridge at the small town.
  工人正在小鎮裡造一座橋。

8. **burn** [bɝn]

burn down
完全燒毀

v.t. v.i. 燃燒；燒毀
- The museum built in 1920 was **burned** *down* last night.
  這棟建於西元一九二〇年的博物館昨晚被燒毀了。

9. **bus** [bʌs]

take a bus = by bus
搭公車

miss the bus
錯過公車

n. [C] 公車（複數：buses）
- Lily *takes a* **bus** to school every day.
  = Lily goes to school *by* **bus** every day.
  莉莉每天搭公車上學。
- Peter was late for school because he *missed the* **bus**.
  彼得因為錯過公車所以上學遲到。

- a school bus　校車　　　• a tour bus　觀光巴士

B

10. business

[`bɪznɪs]

n. [C][U] 職業；日常生活；生意

- How is your **business** these days?
  這幾天生意如何啊？
- **Business** is **business**.
  [諺語] 公事公辦。
- The ***business** hours* of that shop are from ten a.m. to ten p.m.
  那家店的營業時間是從早上十點到晚上十點。
- You should *mind your* own **business** before you help others.
  在你幫別人忙之前，應該先管好自己的事。
- Go away. It's *none of your* **business**.
  走開。這不關你的事。

business hours
營業時間
mind one's business
管好某人的事
none of one's
business
不關某人的事

休息一下喔！

Exercise 1

B

I. 字彙翻譯

1. 刷子 ＿＿＿＿＿＿＿

2. 公車 ＿＿＿＿＿＿＿

3. 生意 ＿＿＿＿＿＿＿

4. 棕色的 ＿＿＿＿＿＿＿

5. 帶來 (三態) ＿＿＿＿＿＿＿ ＿＿＿＿＿＿＿ ＿＿＿＿＿＿＿

II. 字彙填充

＿＿＿＿＿＿＿ 1. The workers are b＿＿＿ding a new library for the school.

＿＿＿＿＿＿＿ 2. They are walking on the b＿＿＿e above the river.

＿＿＿＿＿＿＿ 3. The old house was b＿＿＿ned to the ground in a fire.

＿＿＿＿＿＿＿ 4. I like b＿＿＿t colors like yellow; I don't like dark colors like black.

＿＿＿＿＿＿＿ 5. James is my best friend. We are just like b＿＿＿rs.

III. 字彙選擇

( ) 1. It is raining now. Do you ＿＿＿ your umbrella with you?

(A) bring (B) buy (C) brush (D) borrow

( ) 2. He is my ＿＿＿. Of course I must help him if he has troubles.

(A) brush (B) brother (C) birthday (D) bottle

( ) 3. Ivy ＿＿＿ all the letters Gary sent to her after they broke up.

(A) brought (B) burned (C) bored (D) broke

( ) 4. I ＿＿＿ my teeth every morning.

(A) bridge (B) brush (C) buy (D) break

( ) 5. The bridge was ＿＿＿ over the big river.

(A) brushed (B) bought (C) built (D) brought

B

11. businessman

[`bɪznɪsˌmæn]

n. [C] 商人

- A good **businessman** should know how the market works.
  一個好的商人應該知道市場如何運作。

12. busy

[`bɪzɪ]

be busy (in) + Ving
忙於～

be busy with + N
忙於～

adj. 忙碌的

- He looks very **busy**; he has not taken a rest from 8:00 a.m.
  他看起來非常忙碌；他從早上八點起就沒休息過。
- Mom *is busy doing* dishes.
  媽媽正忙著洗碗盤。
- Students in the third grade *are busy with* their studies.
  三年級的學生正忙著他們的課業。

13. but

[bʌt]

not only...but
(also)...
不僅～而且～

conj. 但是；而是；可是；然而

- I really want to help you, **but** I have no money, either.
  我真的想幫你，可是我自己也沒錢。

- It was not me **but** him who won the game.
  不是我而是他贏得了比賽。
- The boy was *not only* handsome **but** (*also*) smart.
  那男孩不僅英俊而且還很聰明。

14. butter

[`bʌtɚ]

n. [U] 奶油

- Benny boy likes to spread some **butter** on the bread.
  班尼男孩喜歡在麵包上塗些奶油。

15. buy

[baɪ]

過去式	過去分詞	現在進行式
bought [bɔt]	bought [bɔt]	buying [`baɪɪŋ]

v.t. 購買；買 ↔ sell [sɛl] 賣

- Alan **bought** nothing at the shop.
  艾倫在這家商店什麼都沒買。

C

| buy + sb + sth = buy + sth + for + sb
買某物給某人 | · It's kind of you to **buy** me a Christmas present.
= It's kind of you to **buy** a Christmas present *for* me.
你很體貼買了個聖誕禮物給我。 |

16. cake
[kek]

n. [C] 蛋糕

· My girlfriend made a birthday **cake** for me.
我女朋友做了一個生日蛋糕給我。

a piece of cake
非常簡單的事

· Of course I can answer these questions. It's *a piece of cake*.
當然我可以回答這些問題。這是非常簡單的事。

17. call
[kɔl]

v.t. v.i. 打電話（給～）

· **Call** me when you get home, no matter how late it is.
不管多晚，當你到家時，打電話給我。

call + sb + back
回電（給～）

· Please **call** me *back* as soon as you get this message.
當你一聽到留言就請馬上回電給我。

v.t. 取名；叫～（名稱）

· Muhammad Ali was **called** the greatest boxer in the world.
穆罕默德‧阿里被稱為世界上最優秀的拳擊手。

call A after B
以 B 的名字為 A
命名

· The baby is **called** *after* her grandmother by her parents.
這小嬰兒被她父母以其祖母的名字命名。

v.i. v.t. 喊叫

call out
大聲喊叫

· On seeing the snake, Vivian **called** *out* "Help!"
一看到蛇，薇薇安就大喊「救命!」

n. [C] （一通）電話

· Give me a **call** if you need any help.
如果你需要任何的幫助，打一通電話給我。

18. camera
[ˈkæmərə]

n. [C] 相機

· Digital **cameras** are very popular today.
現今數位相機很受歡迎。

a camera face
很上相的臉

· Ivy has *a **camera** face*; she looks much prettier in the picture.
艾維的臉很上相。她在照片上看起來比較漂亮。

19. camp
[kæmp]

n. [C][U] 營地；營隊
- We walked back to the **camp**, and made a fire to cook.
  我們走回營地，並生火煮飯。
- We plan to join the basketball **camp** this summer vacation.
  我們今年暑假計劃參加籃球營。

v.i. 露營
- David went **camping** in the mountain and had a good time.
  大衛去山上露營並玩得很愉快。

20. can
[kæn]

aux. 能；可以；可能（過去式：could [kʊd]）
- He **can** speak very good English.
  他會說很流利的英語。
- I had no money with me so I **could** not buy that book.
  我身上沒帶錢，所以不能買那本書。

a can of + N
一罐～

garbage/trash can
垃圾桶

n. [C] （食物）罐頭；容器
- Mother bought *two cans of* peas to cook with.
  媽媽買了兩罐豆子用來做菜。
- Please put the banana peel into the *garbage/trash* **can**.
  請把香蕉皮放進垃圾桶裡。

Exercise 2

I. 字彙翻譯

1. 照相機 ＿＿＿＿＿＿＿＿
2. 露營 ＿＿＿＿＿＿＿＿
3. 但是 ＿＿＿＿＿＿＿＿
4. 蛋糕 ＿＿＿＿＿＿＿＿
5. 忙碌的 ＿＿＿＿＿＿＿＿

II. 字彙填充

＿＿＿＿＿＿＿ 1. I b＿＿＿＿t a new coat when I was shopping today.

＿＿＿＿＿＿＿ 2. I like to eat bread with some b＿＿＿＿r.

＿＿＿＿＿＿＿ 3. How c＿＿＿＿n you work for so long without any break?

＿＿＿＿＿＿＿ 4. I c＿＿＿＿led you several times, but you were not home.

＿＿＿＿＿＿＿ 5. The b＿＿＿＿n is good at selling computers.

III. 字彙選擇

(　　) 1. Dina likes apples ＿＿＿＿ I don't.
    (A) but   (B) and   (C) or   (D) so

(　　) 2. Remember to give me a ＿＿＿＿ tonight; I have something to tell you.
    (A) cake   (B) call   (C) brush   (D) bus

(　　) 3. Tom took a picture of me with his new ＿＿＿＿.
    (A) camera   (B) call   (C) cake   (D) camp

(　　) 4. Fruit ＿＿＿＿ are my favorite.
    (A) cars   (B) cares   (C) cakes   (D) cameras

(　　) 5. Do you want to ＿＿＿＿ some fruit. The apples and oranges are on sale now.
    (A) camp   (B) call   (C) burn   (D) buy

C

Unit 07

1. **candy**
[`kændɪ]

n. [C][U] 糖果

· Every kid loves sweet **candies**.
每個小孩都喜歡甜甜的糖果。

· Remember to brush your teeth after you eat **candy**.
吃完糖果後記得要刷牙。

2. **cap**
[kæp]

n. [C] 無邊帽，鴨舌帽

· Jack likes to wear a **cap** when he goes out.
傑克出門時，喜歡戴頂帽子。

比較

單字	詞性	意義
cap	*n.* [C]	無邊的便帽或制服帽（廚師帽、警察帽等）
hat	*n.* [C]	泛指所有有邊的帽子

3. **car**
[kɑr]

n. [C] 汽車；小型車

· There are over two million **cars** in Taiwan.
台灣有超過兩百萬輛的汽車。

· a sports car　跑車　　· a racing car　賽車

n. [C] 火車（有軌電車）車廂

· Lisa is eating lunch in the dining **car** of the train.
麗莎正在火車的餐車車廂裡吃午餐。

· a dining car　餐車車廂　　· a sleeping car　臥鋪車廂
· a smoking car　可抽煙的車廂

4. card

[kɑrd]

a business card
名片
a credit card
信用卡

n. [C] 卡片

· Christmas is coming, and everybody starts to send **cards**.
聖誕節即將來臨，所以大家都開始寄送卡片。

· This is my *business card*. Call me if you need help.
這是我的名片。如果你需要任何幫助，打電話給我。

· Most people buy things with their *credit cards* today.
現今大多數人都用信用卡購物。

5. care

[kɛr]

care about + N
關心～；在乎～
care for + N
照料～

take care of + N
照顧～

v.i. 在乎；關心

· I don't **care** which team won the game at all.
我一點都不在乎哪一隊贏了這場比賽。

· We should **care** *about* people around us.
我們應該關心我們週遭的人。

· Since everybody is busy, who could **care** *for* the garden?
既然每個人都在忙，誰能照料花園？

n. [C][U] 看護；保護

· You should *take* good **care** *of* yourself, and stop smoking.
你應該好好照顧自己，別再抽煙了。

6. careful

[`kɛrfəl]

adj. 小心的

· Be **careful** when you walk on the street at night, especially when you are alone.
晚上走在街上時要小心，特別是當你獨自一人的時候。

· You should be more **careful** about what you do.
你做事應該小心一點。

7. carry

[`kærɪ]

過去式	過去分詞	現在進行式
carried [`kærɪd]	carried [`kærɪd]	carrying [`kærɪɪŋ]

v.t. 攜帶

carry sth with sb
某人隨身攜帶某物

· Jack always **carries** his camera *with* him wherever he goes.
無論傑克到哪兒去，他總是隨身帶著他的相機。

8. case

[kes]

n. [C] 案子

- This is a murder **case**; we should call the police right now.
  這是件謀殺案，我們應該馬上通知警方。

n. [C] 情況

in that case
在那樣的情況下

- Ted is sick. *In that case*, he can't go to school.
  泰德生病了。在那樣的情況下，他不能去上學。

n. [C] 箱子；盒子；手提箱

- Carol put her clothes in the **case** and brought it out.
  卡蘿把她的衣服塞進手提箱，然後帶著它出門。

9. cat

[kæt]

n. [C] 貓

- Most people keep dogs or **cats** as their pets.
  大多數的人養狗或貓當寵物。

- It rains **cats** and dogs.
  [諺語] 下起傾盆大雨。

let the cat out of the
bag　洩漏秘密

- Keep your mouth closed. Don't *let the **cat** out of the bag*.
  閉上你的嘴巴，別洩漏了秘密。

10. catch

[kætʃ]

過去式	過去分詞	現在進行式
caught [kɔt]	caught [kɔt]	catching [`kætʃɪŋ]

v.t. 接住；抓住

- My dog can **catch** a baseball and a Frisbee.
  我的狗會接棒球和飛盤。

- **Catch** me if you can.
  抓得到我你就試試看啊!

v.t. 捕獲

- The hunter **caught** two rabbits and a fat pig today.
  那個獵人今天捕獲了兩隻兔子和一隻大肥豬。

v.t. 趕上

- John didn't **catch** the bus, so he was late for school.
  約翰並沒有趕上公車，所以他上學遲到了。

C

catch

C

比較

	片語		意義
catch	the bus, train, ship...	趕上	公車；火車；船…
miss		錯過	

◎此片語常用於趕上或錯過有預定時間出發的交通工具，比方說每隔幾分會有一班的公車，固定時間出發的火車、飛機、船等等。使用此片語時，千萬別忘了要在交通工具前加定冠詞 the。

v.t. 感染（疾病）

catch a cold
感冒

・I **catch** *a cold*, so Mother doesn't want me to play outside.
我感冒了，所以媽媽不准我出去玩。

休息一下喔！

Exercise 1

I. 字彙翻譯

1. 關心 ＿＿＿＿＿＿＿＿＿   2. 小心的 ＿＿＿＿＿＿＿＿＿   3. 案子 ＿＿＿＿＿＿＿＿＿

4. 糖果 ＿＿＿＿＿＿＿＿＿   5. 貓 ＿＿＿＿＿＿＿＿＿

II. 字彙填充

＿＿＿＿＿＿＿＿＿ 1. It is cold outside. You should wear a c＿＿＿＿p to keep your head warm.

＿＿＿＿＿＿＿＿＿ 2. I don't drive a c＿＿＿＿r. Most time I go to work by bus.

＿＿＿＿＿＿＿＿＿ 3. Kay c＿＿＿＿ies an umbrella with her when she goes out.

＿＿＿＿＿＿＿＿＿ 4. Benny sent me a Christmas c＿＿＿＿d from America. It was really a surprise.

＿＿＿＿＿＿＿＿＿ 5. It's time for bed. We have to c＿＿＿＿h the early bus tomorrow morning.

III. 字彙選擇

(   ) 1. Be ＿＿＿＿＿＿ when you cross the road.

       (A) care   (B) careful   (C) catch   (D) camp

(   ) 2. I forgot to ＿＿＿＿＿＿ my cell phone with me when I went out.

       (A) call   (B) carry   (C) case   (D) careful

(   ) 3. Put on your jacket, or you will ＿＿＿＿＿＿ a cold.

       (A) can   (B) care   (C) carry   (D) catch

(   ) 4. Nobody but you ＿＿＿＿＿＿ about me. Thank you so much.

       (A) care   (B) car   (C) card   (D) call

(   ) 5. Benny put all his pens in the pencil ＿＿＿＿＿＿.

       (A) candy   (B) cake   (C) case   (D) cat

11. **celebrate**
[`sɛlə,bret]

v.t. v.i. 慶祝

- We went to a great restaurant to **celebrate** Mom's birthday.
  我們去一家好棒的餐廳慶祝媽媽的生日。
- The tests are finally over; it's time to **celebrate**.
  考試終於結束；現在該是慶祝的時候了。

12. **cell phone**
[`sɛlfon]

n. [C][U] 手機；行動電話 = mobile phone [mobaɪl`fon]

- In Taiwan, almost everyone has a **cell phone**.
  在臺灣，幾乎每個人都有一支手機。
- I called Peter by **cell phone** in the car.
  我在車上用手機打電話給彼得。

注意

　　cell phone 當一般名詞使用時是可數的，如一支手機 (one cell phone)、兩支手機 (two cell phones)，但當它做為聯絡工具時，則為不可數名詞，前面不可加冠詞。

13. **cent**
[sɛnt]

n. [C] （一）分錢

- It cost me fifty **cents** to buy the ice cream.
  買冰淇淋花了我五十分錢。

比較

單位	美國、加拿大一元以下硬幣單位中譯與比較	
dollar [`dɑlɚ]	一元	= 4 quarters = 100 cents
quarter [`kwɔrtɚ]	二十五分	= 1/4 dollar = 25 cents
cent [sɛnt]	一分	= 1/100 dollar

14. **center**
[`sɛntɚ]

n. [C] 中心；中央；核心

- People believed that the earth is in the **center** of the space.
  以前人們相信地球位於宇宙的中心。
- The big city is the business **center** of that country.
  那個大城市是該國的商業中心。

15. chair

[tʃɛr]

a rocking chair
安樂椅；搖椅

n. [C] （通常指單人用的）椅子

- There are fifty desks and fifty **chairs** in the classroom.
  教室裡有五十張桌子和五十張椅子。
- My grandpa sits in the *rocking **chair*** and watches us playing.
  我爺爺坐在安樂椅裡，看著我們玩樂。

16. chalk

[tʃɔk]

n. [C][U] 粉筆

- I need a **chalk** to write on the blackboard.
  我需要一支粉筆來寫黑板。

17. chance

[tʃæns]

the chance of a
lifetime
一生中難得的機會

n. [C][U] 機會

- You should get the **chance** to make your dream come true.
  你應該抓住機會讓你的夢想成真。
- We should give children more **chances** to learn.
  我們應該給小孩更多學習的機會。
- Space trip is *the **chance** of a lifetime*.
  上太空旅遊是一生中難得的機會。

18. change

[tʃendʒ]

change one's mind
改變某人的想法

v.t. v.i. 改變，變化

- Nothing has **changed** in the small town since I was ten.
  自我十歲起，這小鎮一直沒有任何變化。
- After thinking carefully, Jason decided to *change his mind*.
  在仔細地思考之後，傑森決定改變他的想法。

n. [C][U] 改變，變化

- My life is boring now. I think I need some **changes**.
  我現在的生活很無聊，我想我需要一些變化。

19. cheap

[tʃip]

adj. 便宜的 ↔ expensive [ɪkˋspɛnsɪv] 昂貴的

- Almost everything is **cheap** in the flea market.
  在跳蚤市場裡，幾乎每樣東西都便宜。
- Nothing **cheap** is good.
  便宜沒好貨。

20. **cheat**
[tʃit]

cheat sb (out) of sth
向某人騙取～

v.i. 作弊
- You shouldn't have **cheated** on the test.
  你考試不該作弊。

v.t. 欺騙
- You cannot **cheat** me. You are not smart enough.
  你騙不了我的。你還不夠聰明呢。
- The young woman *cheated* the rich man (*out*) *of* a lot of money.
  那名年輕女郎騙了那個有錢人一大筆錢。

n. [C] 欺騙；作弊（事件）
- There are more and more **cheats** in these years.
  近幾年有愈來愈多的詐騙事件發生。

Exercise 2

I. 字彙翻譯

1. 粉筆 _____

2. 慶祝 _____

3. 機會 _____

4. 改變 _____

5. 便宜的 _____

II. 字彙填充

_____ 1. I have to sit on the c_____r; I'm too tired.

_____ 2. The book cost me fifty dollars and twenty c_____ts.

_____ 3. It is convenient to go everywhere if you live in the c_____r of the city.

_____ 4. Our teacher was sad because Ray c_____ted on the exam.

_____ 5. I can't find Peter because he doesn't bring his c_____l p_____e.

III. 字彙選擇

( ) 1. We _____ Ben's good grades on the exam by eating at the restaurant.

    (A) carried   (B) caught   (C) cheated   (D) celebrated

( ) 2. Things have _____ a lot since you left here.

    (A) changed   (B) cheated   (C) caught   (D) camped

( ) 3. Digital cameras now are even _____ than before.

    (A) catcher   (B) cheaper   (C) carrier   (D) cheater

( ) 4. The playground is in the _____ of the school.

    (A) case   (B) card   (C) center   (D) cent

( ) 5. Tony doesn't have any _____ to talk to the girl he likes.

    (A) can   (B) chance   (C) change   (D) chalk

Unit 08

1. **check**
[tʃɛk]

check in/out
登記／結帳

v.t. 檢查
- **Check** your answers again before you hand in the paper.
  在你交考卷前，再檢查一次你的答案。
- Kim *checked in* at the hotel on Wednesday night.
  金在週三晚上登記入住旅館。

n. [C] 檢查
- Remember to give the car a **check** once a year.
  記得每年幫車子做一次檢查。

2. **cheer**
[tʃɪr]

cheer for + sb
為某人加油
Cheer up!
振作點!

v.t. v.i. 歡呼；喝采
- Jenny **cheered** crazily when she won two million dollars.
  珍妮在贏得兩百萬時瘋狂地歡呼。
- Tom's family *cheered for* him during the game.
  湯姆的家人在那場比賽中為他加油。
- *Cheer up*! It's not the end of the world.
  振作點! 這又不是世界末日。

v.t. 鼓舞～
- The hope to win **cheered** me (up) and brought me success.
  想要獲勝的希望鼓舞了我，並為我帶來成功。

3. **cheese**
[tʃiz]

cheesecake
酪餅；起司蛋糕

n. [C][U] 乳酪；起司
- Some people don't like the smell of **cheese**.
  有些人不喜歡乳酪的味道。
- Say **cheese.**
  說起司。(拍照常用語。)
- **Cheesecake** is my favorite snack.
  起司蛋糕是我最愛的點心。

4. **chicken**
[`tʃɪkən]

n. [U] 雞肉
- I like **chicken** most but not beef, pork or fish.
  我最喜歡雞肉而非牛肉、豬肉或魚肉。

fried chicken 炸雞	• KFC is famous for its *fried **chicken***. 肯德基以其炸雞聞名。 *adj.* 雞肉的
chicken soup 雞湯	• I like to have the delicious ***chicken*** soup made by my mother. 我喜歡喝我媽媽做的美味雞湯。 • I ordered a **chicken** steak in the restaurant. 我在餐廳點了一客雞排。 *n.* [C] 雞；小鳥 • My uncle keeps **chickens** and pigs on his farm. 我叔叔在他的農場飼養雞和豬。 *n.* [C] 懦夫；膽小鬼 • Jack was called a **chicken** because he was afraid of darkness. 傑克被叫成膽小鬼，因為他怕黑。 *adj.* 膽怯的 • The shy boy was too **chicken** to ask the girl he liked for a date. 那害羞的男孩太膽怯而不敢約他喜歡的女孩出去約會。

5. **child**
[tʃaɪld]

n. [C] 小孩（複數：children [`tʃɪldrən]）= kid [kɪd]
• Don't be so hard on him. He's a **child** after all.
別如此苛責他。畢竟他只是個孩子。

6. **China**
[`tʃaɪnə]

n. 中國（首字母 C 大寫）
• I have been to Beijing, **China**, once one year ago.
我一年前去過一次中國的北京。
china *n.* [U] 瓷器（首字母 c 小寫）
• Please be careful with the **china**, or you'll break them.
請小心處理這些瓷器，不然你可能會打破它們。

7. **Chinese**
[tʃaɪ`niz]

n. [C] 中國人
• I'm a **Chinese**, not an American.
我是中國人，不是美國人。
• There are more and more **Chinese** studying in the U.S.A.
有愈來愈多的中國人去美國唸書。

C

Chinese 當「中國人」時，是可數名詞，但單複數同形，複數時並不需要加 s。

n. [U] 中文

· Grace is an American. She is learning **Chinese** in Taiwan.
葛蕾絲是美國人。她正在台灣學習中文。

adj. 中國的

· **Chinese** Kung Fu is usually shown in Hollywood movies.
中國功夫時常出現在好萊塢電影中。

8. **chocolate**
[`tʃɔklət]

n. [U] 巧克力

· It might make you fat if you eat too much **chocolate**.
吃太多巧克力可能會讓你發胖。

n. [C] 巧克力糖

· Jessie bought a box of **chocolates** for John on Valentine's Day.
潔西在情人節為約翰買了一盒巧克力糖。

n. [C][U] 巧克力飲料（牛奶）

· It is so cold. Could you give me a hot **chocolate**?
好冷。可以給我一杯熱巧克力嗎?

9. **chopsticks**
[`tʃɑp,stɪks]

n. [C] 筷子

· Some foreigners have trouble using **chopsticks** when they eat Chinese food.
有些外國人在吃中國食物時，在使用筷子上發生困難。

chopsticks 通常用複數，因為用一支筷子是無法吃飯的。

10. **Christmas**
[`krɪsməs]

n. [U] 聖誕節 = Xmas

· **Christmas** falls on December 25th every year.
聖誕節在每年的十二月二十五號。

· Merry **Christmas**.
聖誕快樂。

聖誕節的相關詞語有裝禮物 (present) 的襪子 (socks)、聖誕樹 (Christmas tree)、聖誕老人 (Santa Claus)、星星 (star)、麋鹿 (reindeer) 等等。

C

休息一下喔！

Exercise 1

I. 字彙翻譯

1. 中國人 _____
2. 檢查 _____
3. 雞 _____
4. 乳酪 _____
5. 瓷器 _____

II. 字彙填充

_____ 1. We c_____red on hearing that our team won the game.

_____ 2. We wish you a Merry C_____s and Happy New Year.

_____ 3. On such a cold day, a cup of hot c_____e is just what I need.

_____ 4. Mrs. Smith has three c_____n, two boys and one girl.

_____ 5. We eat Chinese food with c_____ks.

III. 字彙選擇

( ) 1. When I lived in America, I used to visit the _____ Town.

    (A) Chinese   (B) China   (C) Chicken   (D) Cheese

( ) 2. When I _____ my e-mail box, I found many junk mails（垃圾郵件）.

    (A) cheered   (B) changed   (C) checked   (D) cared

( ) 3. I like fish and _____, but I don't eat beef.

    (A) chicken   (B) child   (C) cell phone   (D) card

( ) 4. After staying in Taiwan for five years, the American can speak good _____.

    (A) chocolate   (B) China   (C) Chinese   (D) cheese

( ) 5. Jimmy is the only _____ in his family. His parents love him very much.

    (A) child   (B) chopstick   (C) cheese   (D) check

11. church

[tʃɝtʃ]

n. [C] 教堂

- The Father lives in the **church** near the town.
  那位神父就住在城鎮旁的教堂裡。

n. [U] 禮拜儀式

go to church
上教堂（做禮拜）

- Matthew believes in God. He *goes to church* every Sunday.
  馬修相信上帝，他每個禮拜天都上教堂做禮拜。

12. circle

[ˋsɝk!]

n. [C] 圓圈

- To play the game, we sit in a **circle** on the floor.
  為了要玩遊戲，我們圍成圓圈坐在地板上。

v.t. 圈出；圍著

- Listen to the questions and **circle** the correct answers, class.
  同學們，仔細聽問題並圈選出正確的答案。

13. city

[ˋsɪtɪ]

n. [C] 城市（複數：cities）

- Living in the **city** is more convenient than living in the country.
  住在都市比住在鄉下方便。

adj. 城市的；都會的

- **City** people are always in a hurry.
  都市人總是匆匆忙忙的。

14. class

[klæs]

n. [C][U] 班級；（一節）課；上課（複數：classes [ˋklæsɪz]）

- Polly is the most beautiful girl in my **class**.
  波莉是我班上最漂亮的女孩。

- I have an English **class** today.
  我今天有一堂英文課。

in/during class
上課中

- The teacher tells us not to talk *in/during class*.
  老師叫我們上課中不要講話。

n. [C] 等級；級別；種類

high-class
高級的

- Paul and Mary ate at a *high-class* restaurant on Christmas Eve.
  保羅和瑪莉聖誕夜在一家高級餐廳用餐。

15. classmate
[`klæs,met]

n. [C] 同班同學

· Stewart is my **classmate**. We study in the same class.
史都華是我的同班同學。我們在同一班上課。

16. classroom
[`klæs,rum]

n. [C] 教室

· The **classroom** is too small for forty students.
這間教室太小，容不下四十個學生。

17. clean
[klin]

adj. 乾淨的 ↔ dirty [`dɝtɪ] 髒的

· The park is a public place; you should keep it **clean**.
公園是公共場所，你應該讓它保持乾淨。

v.t. 打掃

· It won't take you much time to **clean** the room.
打掃房間不會花掉你太多時間。

clean up
徹底清理

· Don't be lazy! It's time for you to *clean up* your bedroom.
別懶惰了！該是你把寢室徹底打掃乾淨的時候了。

18. clear
[klɪr]

adj. 清楚的

· Am I making myself **clear**?
我講得夠清楚嗎?

adj. 清澈的；透明的；潔淨的（流水）

· We could see the fish swimming in the **clear** river.
我們可以看見魚兒在清澈的河水中游著。

adj. 晴朗的（天氣）

· On a **clear** day, you can see the mountains easily from here.
在晴天時，你可以輕易地從這裡看到山。

v.t. 清除

· The garbage must be **cleared** away at once.
垃圾必須馬上清除。

clear the air
化解誤會

· You should talk to each other to *clear the air*.
你們應該互相談一談以化解誤會。

19. climb

[klaɪm]

go mountain
climbing 去爬山

v.t. 攀登～；爬～

- The kids are **climbing** a tree.
  孩子們正在爬樹。
- We *went mountain **climbing*** last Friday.
  我們上星期五去爬山。

v.i. 攀登～；爬～

- The bad man **climbed** into the house through a window.
  壞人經由窗戶爬進房子。

20. clock

[klɑk]

an alarm clock
鬧鐘

n. [C] 時鐘

- The **clock** on the wall tells us what time it is.
  牆上的時鐘告訴我們現在是幾點。
- I set my *alarm **clock*** at 7:00 a.m. before I go to bed.
  要去睡覺前，我把鬧鐘調到早上七點。

C

練習題 (二)

Exercise 2

I. 字彙翻譯

1. 教室 _____
2. 教堂 _____
3. 城市 _____
4. 攀登 _____
5. 清澈的 _____

II. 字彙填充

_____ 1. Jammy is not my c_____e. I knew him in the club.

_____ 2. They sing and dance in a big c_____e to celebrate the festival.

_____ 3. This is a high-c_____s restaurant, so please keep your voice down.

_____ 4. Be sure to c_____n your room up before you go out.

_____ 5. My alarm c_____k doesn't work anymore. It stopped running this morning.

III. 字彙選擇

( ) 1. There are fewer people in a country than in a big _____.
(A) city   (B) class   (C) church   (D) cheese

( ) 2. My bedroom is very _____; you couldn't even find any dust in it.
(A) clean   (B) clear   (C) climb   (D) cheap

( ) 3. We can swim in the _____ water.
(A) cheese   (B) clear   (C) cheap   (D) class

( ) 4. Are you ready to _____ the hill?
(A) climb   (B) circle   (C) clean   (D) clock

( ) 5. I didn't know my watch was ten minutes slow until I saw the _____ on the wall.
(A) circle   (B) chopsticks   (C) classmate   (D) clock

Unit 09

1. close
[kloz]

v.t. 關；（商店）打烊 ↔ open [`opən] 打開

- Dolly **closes** all the windows to make the room warmer.
  桃莉把所有的窗戶關起來，想讓房間暖和些。
- The bookstore opens at 10:00 a.m. and **closes** at 10:00 p.m.
  那家書店早上十點開始營業，晚上十點打烊。

adj. 接近的

- The convenience store is **close** to the train station.
  那家便利商店的位置接近火車站。
- Betty was almost hit by a truck. *That was* (really) *close*!
  貝蒂差一點點就被卡車撞了。（真是）好險哪！

adj. 親密的

- Mary and Anne are **close** friends; they always play together.
  瑪莉和安是親密的朋友，她們總是一起玩。

That was close!
好險哪！

2. clothes
[kloz]

n. [C] 衣服

- Stop buying **clothes**. There is no more space for them.
  別再買衣服了。再也沒有多餘的空間可以放它們了。
- Pual put on his sports **clothes** to go jogging.
  保羅穿上運動服去慢跑。

注意

clothes 指衣服的各部分，所以只能用複數形式，但為可數名詞，所以前面可接 many 或 a few 等形容數量的數量詞。cloth 為單數形式，意思為「布」，是不可數名詞。

3. cloudy
[`klaʊdɪ]

adj. 多雲的；陰天的

- The weather report says it will be **cloudy** with rain today.
  氣象報告指出，今天多雲且有雨。

63

4. club
[klʌb]

n. [C] 社團
- Danny is the best player in the tennis **club** of school.
  丹尼是學校網球社裡的最佳球員。

n. [C] 俱樂部
- Mother joined the swimming **club** last year and went swimming twice a week from then on.
  媽媽去年加入了游泳俱樂部，從那時起她每週去游泳兩次。

5. coat
[kot]

raincoat　雨衣

n. [C] 外套；大衣
- Take off your winter **coat**. It's not cold at all in the house.
  脫掉你的冬季外套。屋子裡一點都不冷。
- John put on his **raincoat** and rode his motorcycle away.
  約翰穿上雨衣並騎摩托車走了。

比較

單字	詞性	意義
coat	*n.* [C]	外套；外衣（前面扣合且有袖）；西裝上衣
jacket	*n.* [C]	（有袖的）短上衣；夾克；外套

6. coffee
[ˋkɔfɪ]

n. [U] 咖啡
- I have made it a habit to drink a cup of **coffee** every morning.
  我已經養成每天早上喝一杯咖啡的習慣。

n. [C] （一杯）咖啡
- I want two **coffees** without sugar, thanks.
  我想要兩杯咖啡不加糖，謝謝。

7. Coke
[kok]

n. [U] 可樂 = coke = Coca-Cola
- Drinking too much **Coke** isn't good for you.
  喝太多的可樂對你不好。

n. [C] （一杯）可樂
- Please give me two small **Cokes**.
  請給我兩杯小杯可樂。

8. cold

[kold]

catch a (heavy) cold
得了（重）感冒

adj. 冷的 ↔ hot [hɑt] 熱的

· It's really **cold** outside.

外面真的很冷。

n. [C][U] 感冒；傷風

· Willy *caught a **cold*** for he got wet in the rain yesterday.

威利昨天被雨淋濕，所以感冒了。

9. collect

[kə`lɛkt]

make a collect call
打對方付費的電話

v.t. 收集

· **Collecting** baseball cards was my hobby when I was still a kid.

當我還是個小朋友時，收集棒球卡是我的興趣。

adj. 由對方付費的（電話）

· I *made **collect** calls* to my parents when I studied in America.

我在美國唸書的時候，打過由對方付費的電話給我父母。

10. color

[`kʌlɚ]

a color book
著色本
color-blind
色盲的

n. [C] 顏色；色彩

· You can see seven different **colors** in a rainbow.

你可以看到彩虹有七種不同的顏色。

· You could **color** all the pictures in the *color* book.

你可以為著色本裡的所有圖畫上色。

· Dogs are born *color-blind*.

狗兒天生就色盲。

v.t. 給～上色

· I **colored** the sky blue and then finished the picture.

我把天空塗成藍色，然後就完成這幅畫了。

C

Exercise 1

I. 字彙翻譯

1. 衣服 _____ 2. 咖啡 _____ 3. 親密的 _____

4. 顏色 _____ 5. 多雲的 _____

C

II. 字彙填充

_____ 1. I join a card c _____b; I go there to play cards every Saturday.

_____ 2. Drinking more water and less C _____e would be better for you.

_____ 3. The weather may change, so you should bring your c _____t with you.

_____ 4. We'll have a very c _____d winter this year.

_____ 5. My little sister c _____ted dolls as a hobby.

III. 字彙選擇

(　　) 1. Dad bought a new _____ TV last night.

    (A) clean　　　(B) clear　　　(C) color　　　(D) cold

(　　) 2. It is very hot today, so you should not wear too many _____.

    (A) Cokes　　　(B) classes　　　(C) clubs　　　(D) clothes

(　　) 3. The _____ doesn't taste good, so I put some sugar and milk in it.

    (A) Coke　　　(B) coffee　　　(C) cookie　　　(D) cook

(　　) 4. If you want to buy something, you must be quick; the shop is going to _____.

    (A) close　　　(B) class　　　(C) color　　　(D) clean

(　　) 5. When it is so _____ outside, I hope I could stay in my bed for more time.

    (A) cold　　　(B) cloudy　　　(C) clean　　　(D) clear

11. come
[kʌm]

過去式	過去分詞	現在進行式
came [kem]	come [kʌm]	coming [ˈkʌmɪŋ]

v.i. 來；過來；來到 ↔ go [go] 走；去

· **Come** here. I will give you candies to eat.
　過來這兒，我會給你糖果吃。

· Tell Jack I want to meet him when he **comes** tomorrow.
　傑克明天過來的時候，告訴他我想見他。

· Whenever I **come** home, my mother will cook for me.
　每當我回家的時候，我媽媽都會為我煮飯。

come from + N
來自於～

· The boy told us that he *came* *from* California, United States.
　那男孩告訴我們他來自美國加州（加利福尼亞州）。

12. comfortable
[ˈkʌmfɚtəbḷ]

adj. 舒適的

· Taking a hot bath after work always makes me **comfortable**.
　工作完洗個熱水澡總是讓我感到舒適。

adj. 使人舒適的

· I like to take a walk in the **comfortable** weather.
　我喜歡在使人舒適的天氣中散步。

13. comic
[ˈkamɪk]

adj. 喜劇的；使人發笑的

· I can't help laughing when I watch the **comic** show on TV.
　在我看電視上那齣喜劇的時候，我忍不住笑。

comic book(s)
漫畫書

· I love reading *comic* books in my free time.
　在我空閒的時間，我喜歡看漫畫書。

14. common
[ˈkamən]

adj. 普通的，常見的，一般的

· Cell phones are very **common**. You can see them everywhere.
　手機非常常見，你到處都可以看到它們。

adj. 共同的，共有的

· Love of money is **common** to all people.
　愛好金錢是人人相同的。

C

| have something/ nothing in common 有／沒有共同點 | · My sister *has nothing in common* with me except for the looks.
我妹妹除了外表以外跟我沒有任何共同點。
adj. 公共的，公眾的
· For **common** interests, we must keep the law.
為了公眾的利益，我們必須遵守法律。 |

15. **computer**
[kəm`pjutɚ]

n. [C] 電腦
· Many teenagers often use **computers** to play online games.
許多青少年常用電腦玩線上遊戲。

16. **convenient**
[kən`vinjənt]

adj. 方便的
· It's **convenient** for students to go to school by MRT.
對學生而言，搭捷運上學很方便。

17. **cook**
[kʊk]

v.t. 烹煮～
· When I got home, Mom was **cooking** dinner.
當我到家時，媽媽正在煮晚餐。
· I **cooked** some noodles for dinner.
我煮了一些麵當晚餐。
v.i. 煮飯；做菜
· Mother is **cooking**, and she wants us to set the table first.
媽媽正在煮飯，她要我們先擺設好飯桌。
n. [C] 廚師
· The **cook** prepared several delicious dishes for us.
那位廚師為我們準備了許多道美味的菜餚。

注意
　　常有人會誤認 cooker 的意思是廚師，但實際上 cook 才是廚師，而 cooker 是「炊具；烹調器具」的意思喔！

18. **cookie**
[`kʊkɪ]

n. [C] 餅乾
· The **cookie** tastes delicious. Give me one more, please.
這餅乾嚐起來真美味，請再給我一塊。

C

19. **cool**

[kul]

as cool as a
cucumber
鎮定自若

cool + N + down
使～冷靜（卻）下來

adj. 涼的 ↔ warm [wɔrm] 溫暖的

- It's a nice and **cool** day, isn't it?
  今天是個涼爽的好天氣，不是嗎?
- He was *as **cool** as a cucumber* when his home was on fire.
  在他家著火的時候，他鎮定自若。

adj. 很棒的，酷的

- It is really **cool** to take an airplane.
  搭飛機的感覺真的很酷。

v.t. 使～變涼

- Ron tries to **cool** the soup quickly by blowing it.
  朗吹吹湯，試著藉此讓它快些變涼。
- Jenny is so angry that I can't *cool* her *down* no matter how hard I try.
  珍妮實在太生氣了，以致於不管我多努力都無法讓她冷靜下來。

20. **copy**

[`kɑpɪ]

copyright
版權；著作權

n. [C][U] 副本；影本；（相同書、報、雜誌等的）一本，一份

- I will send you a **copy** of this book as soon as possible.
  我會儘快寄一本相同的書給你。
- The writer holds the **copyright** on that book.
  該名作者擁有那本書的著作權。

 補充

- a copy machine　影印機

v.t. v.i. 抄寫；臨摹；複製

過去式	過去分詞	現在進行式
copied [`kɑpɪd]	copied [`kɑpɪd]	copying [`kɑpɪɪŋ]

- Please **copy** these papers for me as fast as you can.
  請儘快幫我抄寫一份這些文件。

copy

· Bill did not do homework by himself. He **copied** from mine.
比爾沒有自己做功課。他是抄我的。

注意

　　copy 當動詞用是抄寫或複製的意思，並不等於影印。影印的正式說法應該是 photocopy。用印表機列印則叫 print。

C

休息一下喔！

Exercise 2

I. 字彙翻譯

1. 餅乾 _____   2. 舒服的 _____   3. 電腦 _____

4. 過來 _____   5. 常見的 _____

II. 字彙填充

_____ 1. As a c_____c star, you have to know how to make people laugh.

_____ 2. Tonight Mother will c_____k delicious dishes to celebrate my birthday.

_____ 3. Thousands of c_____ies of the book have been sold out.

_____ 4. It is c_____l and comfortable today, so let's go out for a picnic.

_____ 5. If it's c_____t for you, please pick me up at 7:00 p.m.

III. 字彙選擇

(   ) 1. Jackie is the head _____ of the restaurant.

   (A) cook   (B) cookie   (C) copy   (D) color

(   ) 2. Autumn is a _____ season.

   (A) comic   (B) cook   (C) cool   (D) color

(   ) 3. I think we could be good friends because we have many interests in _____.

   (A) copy   (B) common   (C) computer   (D) coffee

(   ) 4. Try this _____. It tastes good.

   (A) cook   (B) club   (C) coat   (D) cookie

(   ) 5. We will have a picnic tomorrow. Would you like to _____ with us?

   (A) copy   (B) collect   (C) come   (D) close

Unit 10

1. **correct**
[kə`rɛkt]

adj. 正確的 = right [raɪt]

· The answer you just told me is not **correct**. Try it again.

你剛剛告訴我的答案不是正確的。再試一次。

v.t. 糾正

· Would you please **correct** my mistakes?

能請你幫我糾正錯誤嗎？

2. **cost**
[kɔst]

過去式	過去分詞	現在進行式
cost [kɔst]	cost [kɔst]	costing [`kɔstɪŋ]

v.t. 花費～（金錢）

· It **cost** me five hundred dollars to buy the dress.

買這件洋裝花了我 500 元。

· The new pair of shoes **cost** me 3,000 NT dollars.

這雙新鞋花了我新臺幣 3,000 元。

cost an arm and a leg 非常昂貴

· The present I gave to my girlfriend *cost an arm and a leg.*

我送女友的禮物非常昂貴。

比較

	v.t. 花費（精力；金錢）；使付出
cost [kɔst]	◎cost 的用法是以事物或 it 為主詞，動詞 cost 後接花費者（通常是人），然後才是花費的東西（通常是金錢）。 ◎使用 cost 時，花費者可省略，省略時的句意通常指某事物值多少錢。 · This book **cost** Peter three hundred dollars. 　這本書花了彼得三百元。 · This book **cost** three hundred dollars. 　這本書價值三百元。

spend [spɛnd]	*v.t.* 花費（時間；金錢）
	◎spend 的用法是以花費者（通常是人）為主詞，動詞 spend 後接花費的東西（通常是時間或金錢），其後再接動名詞，或者是介系詞 on 加名詞。
	· Peter spent three hundred dollars buying this book. = Peter spent three hundred dollars on this book. 彼得花了三百元買這本書。

C

---

3. **couch**
[kautʃ]

a couch potato
電視迷

n. [C] 長沙發
· I like to lie on the **couch** and watch TV in the living room.
我喜歡躺在客廳的長沙發上看電視。
· ***Couch Potatoes*** spend hours watching TV every day.
「電視迷」每天都花好幾個小時看電視。

---

4. **count**
[kaunt]

count in + N
把～算進去
count on + sb
依靠～；倚賴～

v.i. v.t. 數，計算
· The little boy is learning to **count** from one to one hundred.
這小男孩正在學習從一數到一百。
· The number is wrong because you didn't ***count*** yourself *in*.
人數錯了是因為你沒把自己算進去。
· You can always ***count*** *on* me no matter what happens.
無論發生什麼事，你總是可以倚賴我的。

---

5. **country**
[ˋkʌntrɪ]

in the country
在鄉下

n. [C] 國家
· America and England are both big **countries**.
美國和英國都是大國家。
n. [C] 鄉下 ↔ city [ˋsɪtɪ] 城市
· I enjoyed my life *in the **country*** during the summer vacation.
我很享受我在暑假期間的那一段鄉間生活。

---

6. **cousin**
[ˋkʌzṇ]

n. [C] 表兄弟姊妹；堂兄弟姊妹
· My **cousins** and my aunt came to visit us last weekend.
上週末我表兄弟和我阿姨一起來拜訪我們。

7. cover
[`kʌvɚ]

v.t. 遮蓋；覆蓋
· The girl felt shy and **covered** her face with her hands.
這女孩覺得害羞，所以用她的手遮蓋住她的臉。
· The roof *is covered with* snow in winter.
在冬天，這屋頂被雪所覆蓋。

be covered with + N
被～所覆蓋

n. [C]（書的）封面
· The **cover** of this book is very interesting.
這本書的封面很有趣。

8. cow
[kaʊ]

n. [C] 母牛，乳牛
· There are many **cows** and sheep on the farm.
農場裡有許多乳牛和綿羊。

9. crazy
[`krezɪ]

adj. 發瘋的；瘋狂的
· You must be **crazy** if you eat ice cream in the cold winter.
如果這麼冷的冬天你還吃冰淇淋，那你一定是發瘋了。
· I think Hitler is a **crazy** man because he killed so many people.
我覺得希特勒是個狂人，因為他殺了那麼多人。
adj. 著迷的

be crazy about
著迷於～
be crazy for
為～瘋狂

· Many young people *are crazy about* online games.
許多年輕人著迷於線上遊戲。
· My sister loves Bruce Lee very much; she *is crazy for* him.
我姊姊超愛李小龍；她為他而瘋狂。

10. cross
[krɔs]

v.t. 越過；穿過
· You must be careful when you **cross** the street.
穿越馬路時，你一定要小心。

Exercise 1

I. 字彙翻譯

1. 表（堂）兄弟姊妹 _____
2. 長沙發 _____
3. 乳牛 _____
4. 正確的 _____
5. 花費（三態）_____ _____ _____

II. 字彙填充

_____ 1. England is a beautiful c _____y. You should go there some day.

_____ 2. Gill has collected lots of watches. She is so c _____y about them.

_____ 3. Be careful when you c _____s the bridge; don't fall into the river.

_____ 4. John c _____ted how much money he had before buying his dinner.

_____ 5. The ground is c _____red with garbage after the show.

III. 字彙選擇

( ) 1. The bridge is broken. Now we have to _____ the river by boat.

(A) cut   (B) cup   (C) cover   (D) cross

( ) 2. Don't sleep on the _____; go to your bed if you want to sleep.

(A) cousin   (B) couch   (C) cow   (D) cookie

( ) 3. In winter, the ground of this place is always _____ snow.

(A) covering with   (B) covered of   (C) covered with   (D) covering for

( ) 4. My _____, Karen, is the daughter of my uncle and aunt.

(A) color   (B) cousin   (C) cow   (D) couch

( ) 5. It is a _____ dog. Don't get close to it.

(A) crazy   (B) hot   (C) copy   (D) cold

11. cry
[kraɪ]

過去式	過去分詞	現在進行式
cried [`kraɪd]	cried [`kraɪd]	crying [`kraɪɪŋ]

v.i. 哭；哭泣 ↔ laugh [læf] 笑

- When you **cry**, you **cry** alone; when you laugh, the world laughs with you.
  當你哭的時候，你獨自哭泣；但當你微笑，全世界會跟你一起笑。
- Don't **cry**. I will try my best to help you.
  不要哭。我會盡力幫你的。

cry for + N
因～而哭泣

- Peter is ***crying** for* his poor grades.
  彼得為了他的成績不好而哭泣。

cry over + N
為～而悲慟

- The mother is ***crying** over* her dead son.
  那母親為了死去的兒子悲慟不已。

v.i. （大聲）叫喊

cry for + N
為～而大叫

- The girl ***cried** for* help when she saw the fire.
  那女孩在看到火災時大聲呼救。

12. cup
[kʌp]

n. [C] 杯子

- Sue filled my **cup** with tea.
  蘇在我的杯子裡倒滿了茶。

a cup of + N
一杯～

- I am used to having *a **cup** of* coffee in the morning.
  我早上習慣喝杯咖啡。

n. [C] 獎盃

- Emily won the gold **cup** of swimming this year.
  艾蜜莉贏得今年游泳的金盃（第一名）。

13. cut
[kʌt]

過去式	過去分詞	現在進行式
cut [kʌt]	cut [kʌt]	cutting [`kʌtɪŋ]

v.t. 切；割；削；剪；砍

- Would you please **cut** the birthday cake into twelve pieces?
  請你把這個生日蛋糕切成十二塊好嗎？

have one's hair cut 某人剪頭髮 cut classes 蹺課	• Jean will *have her hair cut* this afternoon. 珍今天下午要去剪頭髮。 • You shouldn't *cut classes* to play video games. 你不該蹺課去打電動。 *v.t.* 切斷（電路、電源等） • The police **cut** the power of the house to catch the bad man. 警方切斷那棟房子的電源，希望藉此抓住那個壞人。 *v.i.*（電影）停拍 • When the director said "**cut**," all people stopped moving. 當導演說「停拍（卡）」的時候，所有人都停下動作。

D

14. **cute**
[kjut]

adj. 可愛的；漂亮的
• The **cute** Teddy Bear is loved by children.
這個可愛的泰迪熊很受小朋友的喜愛。

15. **dance**
[dæns]

donce with + sb
與～一起跳舞

v.t. v.i. 跳舞
• Shall we **dance**?
可以請妳跳支舞嗎？
• Do you want to **dance** with me?
你想不想和我一起跳舞？
n. [C] 跳舞；舞蹈
• Street **dance** is now very popular.
街舞現在很受歡迎。
n. [C] 舞會
• Ivy went to a **dance** with her boyfriend and had a good time.
艾維跟她男友參加一個舞會，玩得很愉快。

比較

單字	詞性	意義
prom	*n.* [C]	美國高中生、大學生所舉辦的舞會
party	*n.* [C]	一般的集會、聚會、宴會
dance	*n.* [C]	較正式的舞會
ball	*n.* [C]	比 dance 更正式且盛大的舞會

16. dangerous

[`dɛndʒərəs]

adj. 危險的；不安全的 ↔ safe [sef] 安全的

- It is very **dangerous** for a girl to go out late at night.
  對一個女生來說，深夜出去是很危險的。

17. dark

[dɑrk]

adj. 黑暗的 ↔ bright [braɪt] 明亮的

- It is **dark** after 6:00 p.m.; you shouldn't go out then.
  下午六點過後天色就很黑了，那時候你就不該出門。

adj. 深（暗）色的

- Brian likes to wear **dark** clothes like black or brown.
  布萊恩喜歡穿黑色或棕色等深暗色的衣服。

n. [C][U] 黑暗；暗處

in the dark
在黑暗中

- I cannot see anything *in the* **dark**.
  在黑暗中我什麼東西都看不到。

n. [U] 黃昏；黑夜 = night [naɪt]

from dawn to dark
從清晨到黃昏

- In old times, farmers worked *from dawn to* **dark**.
  古時候，農夫們從清晨工作到黃昏。

18. date

[det]

n. [C] 日子；日期

- Laura and her boyfriend have decided the **date** to get married.
  蘿拉和她的男友已經決定好結婚的日子了。

比較

day [de]	*n.*[C] 日；一天；白晝；特定日子（大寫：如 Valentine's Day）
	• What day is today? (It's) Wednesday. 今天星期幾？星期三。
date [det]	*n.*[C] 日期；日子
	• What **date** is today? October 10th. = What is the **date** today? October 10th. 今天幾月幾日？十月十日。

◎what day 以及 what date 都是常見的問法，前者問的是星期，後者問的則是月日，兩者之間的分別務必要清楚，不可搞混。

78

n. [C] 約會

- Never be late for a **date** with your girlfriend.
  跟你女朋友約會，絕對不要遲到。

19. **daughter**
['dɔtɚ]

n. [C] 女兒

- Mr. and Mrs. Smith have three pretty and smart **daughters**.
  史密斯夫婦有三個漂亮又聰明的女兒。

20. **day**
[de]

n. [C] 日；一天

- There are seven **days** in a week.
  一個星期有七天。

n. [C] 白天（的時間）↔ night [naɪt] 夜晚

- The workers work during the **day** and rest at night.
  這些工人白天工作，晚上休息。

day and night
日日夜夜

- Ellen studied ***day and night*** to catch up with his classmates.
  艾倫日日夜夜的唸書以趕上他的同班同學。

練習題 (二)

Exercise 2

I. 字彙翻譯

1. 女兒 ＿＿＿＿＿＿＿＿＿

2. 杯子 ＿＿＿＿＿＿＿＿＿

3. 哭泣 ＿＿＿＿＿＿＿＿＿

4. 跳舞 ＿＿＿＿＿＿＿＿＿

5. 切；割 ＿＿＿＿＿＿＿＿＿

II. 字彙填充

D

＿＿＿＿＿＿＿＿＿ 1. It is getting d＿＿＿k; the sun is going down.

＿＿＿＿＿＿＿＿＿ 2. Jeff is so excited because he is going to have a d＿＿＿e with the girl he likes.

＿＿＿＿＿＿＿＿＿ 3. Don't drive after drinking, because it is quite d＿＿＿s.

＿＿＿＿＿＿＿＿＿ 4. The writer worked d＿＿＿y and night to finish his book.

＿＿＿＿＿＿＿＿＿ 5. My cat is so c＿＿＿e, and everybody loves it.

III. 字彙選擇

( ) 1. Mr. and Mrs. Wang have three sons, but they have no ＿＿＿＿.

(A) cup   (B) date   (C) cousin   (D) daughter

( ) 2. "Would you like to have a ＿＿＿＿ of tea?" "Yes, please."

(A) cut   (B) cup   (C) cow   (D) couch

( ) 3. The little baby ＿＿＿＿ out loudly when he felt hungry.

(A) cried   (B) cut   (C) covered   (D) copied

( ) 4. It is so ＿＿＿＿ in your bedroom; you should turn on the light.

(A) cute   (B) crazy   (C) dark   (D) dangerous

( ) 5. I had my hair ＿＿＿＿ short yesterday.

(A) covered   (B) cute   (C) cut   (D) crossed

D

Unit 11

1. dead
[dɛd]

adj. 死的；枯的；無生命的

· Because Ice forgot to water the flowers, they were all **dead**.
因為艾斯忘了澆花，那些花都枯死了。
· The little girl was afraid when she saw the **dead** mouse.
小女孩看到那隻死老鼠的時候，感到非常害怕。
· The story is about *the dead* who come back to the world.
這故事是有關死去的人回到這個世界的事。

the dead
死去的人；死者

注意
the + Adj 可代表同一類的人或事物全體（此時為複數名詞），如 the dead 代表「死者」，the blind 泛指所有的「盲人」，the poor 代表「窮人」等。

2. dear
[dɪr]

adj. 親愛的；可愛的

· Our **dear** daughter is ten now, and we love her very much.
我們可愛的女兒現在十歲，我們非常愛她。

注意
dear 是常用於信件開頭的稱謂語，如 My dear daughter（我親愛的女兒）、My dear friend（我親愛的朋友），Dear Mr. Brown（親愛的布朗先生）等等。

adj. 珍貴的

be dear to + sb
對～而言是珍貴的

· The ring my parents gave me *is* very *dear to* me.
我父母給我的戒指對我而言非常珍貴。

3. decide
[dɪ`saɪd]
decide to + V
= make up one's
  mind to + V
決定～

v.t. v.i. 決定；決意

· I *decide to* study at home tonight.
= I *make up my mind to* study at home tonight.
我決定今天晚上在家裡唸書。
· I haven't **decided** what to do tonight yet.
我尚未決定今天晚上要做什麼。

D

4. **delicious**
[dɪ`lɪʃəs]

adj. 美味的，可口的，好吃的

· Ice cream is very **delicious**, but you will get fat if you eat too much of it.
  冰淇淋很好吃，可是如果你吃太多，
  你就會變胖。

5. **department store**
[dɪ`pɑrtmənt ˏstor]

n. [C] 百貨公司

· There is a big sale on shoes in the **department store**.
  這間百貨公司有個鞋子的大拍賣。

補充

department　*n.* [C]（百貨公司的）某部門；（大學的）某科系

· The Women's **Department** is holding an end-of-season sale.
  女裝部正舉行換季大拍賣。

· Matt studied in the English **department** of NCCU.
  馬特就讀於政大英語系。

6. **desk**
[dɛsk]

at the desk
在書桌前

n. [C] 書桌；辦公桌

· The **desks** in our school are made of wood.
  我們學校的書桌是木製的。

· Stefanie was writing a letter *at the desk*.
  史蒂芬妮正在書桌前寫信。

比較

desk [dɛsk]	*n.* [C] 書桌；辦公桌；寫字台
	· George is studying English at his **desk**. 喬治正在他的書桌旁唸英文。
table [`tebl]	*n.* [C] 桌子；餐桌
	· I put the forks and knives on the table. 我把叉子跟刀子放在桌上。
◎一般會擺在餐廳、飯廳、客廳的桌子我們會叫做 table，而擺在教室、辦公室、寢室以及圖書館的桌子我們就叫做 desk。主要是以功能做為兩者的區別。	

the information
desk　諮詢櫃檯

n. [C] 櫃檯；服務台

· If you can't find the restroom, ask at *the information **desk***.
如果你找不到洗手間，就到諮詢櫃檯去詢問。

---

7. **dictionary**
[ˋdɪkʃənˏɛrɪ]

n. [C] 字典；辭典

· It is useful to have a **dictionary** when studying English.
學習英語時，有一本字典是很有用的。

· Charles looks up the words he doesn't know in a **dictionary**.
查爾斯用字典查他不認識的單字。

> **注意**
> 查閱字典的用法並不是 look up the dictionary，而是 look...up in the dictionary，切記不要弄錯囉！

---

8. **die**
[daɪ]

過去式	過去分詞	現在進行式
died [daɪd]	died [daɪd]	dying [ˋdaɪɪŋ]

v.i. 死，去世 ↔ live [lɪv] 活，活著

· When Diane's father **died**, she was very sad.
當黛安的父親去世的時候，她非常難過。

· The dog is **dying** because it is sick.
那隻狗快要死了，因為牠病的很重。

> **注意**
> die 為現在進行式時，其中文意義並不是「某人（物）正在死亡」，而是「某人（物）正瀕臨死亡」。

---

9. **different**
[ˋdɪfərənt]

be different in + N
在～方面不同
be different from
+ N/Ving 與～不同

adj. 不同的，不一樣的 ↔ the same 同樣的

· The foreigner speaks **different** language from us.
那個外國人說的是和我們不一樣的語言。

· The two brothers *are **different** in* many ways.
這兩兄弟在很多方面都不一樣。

· My answer *is **different** from* yours; I think mine is correct.
我的答案與你的不同，我覺得我的才對。

10. **difficult**
[ˋdɪfəˌkʌlt]

adj. 難的；困難的 = hard [hɑrd] ↔ easy [ˋizɪ] 簡單的，容易的

· It is **difficult** for a child to move the heavy box.
  對一個孩子來說，要移動那個沈重的箱子是困難的。

· I can't answer that **difficult** question.
  我無法回答那個困難的問題。

D

Exercise 1

I. 字彙翻譯

1. 決定 ＿＿＿＿＿＿＿＿＿　2. 不同的 ＿＿＿＿＿＿＿＿＿　3. 美味的 ＿＿＿＿＿＿＿＿＿

4. 死的 ＿＿＿＿＿＿＿＿＿　5. 百貨公司 ＿＿＿＿＿＿＿＿＿ ＿＿＿＿＿＿＿＿＿

D

II. 字彙填充

＿＿＿＿＿＿＿＿＿ 1. I kissed my d＿＿＿＿r daughter good-night and turned off the light.

＿＿＿＿＿＿＿＿＿ 2. If Mark were here, he would be able to solve the d＿＿＿＿t math problem.

＿＿＿＿＿＿＿＿＿ 3. You can understand a new word by looking it up in the d＿＿＿＿y.

＿＿＿＿＿＿＿＿＿ 4. Many people d＿＿＿＿ed in the serious earthquake (地震) on September 21, 1999.

＿＿＿＿＿＿＿＿＿ 5. You should do your homework at your d＿＿＿＿k, not on the bed.

III. 字彙選擇

( ) 1. I have ＿＿＿＿＿ to go shopping this afternoon; nobody can change my mind.

(A) difficult　　(B) danced　　(C) died　　(D) decided

( ) 2. When my dog ＿＿＿＿＿, I cried for several days.

(A) decided　　(B) danced　　(C) died　　(D) dead

( ) 3. Though Tina and Betty come from ＿＿＿＿＿ countries, they are good friends.

(A) different　　(B) difficult　　(C) dangerous　　(D) delicious

( ) 4. How can you study well if there is no enough light on your ＿＿＿＿＿?

(A) desk　　(B) date　　(C) dear　　(D) department

( ) 5. My mother cooks a ＿＿＿＿＿ meal for me when I come home every evening.

(A) difficult　　(B) delicious　　(C) different　　(D) dangerous

D

11. **dig**
[dɪg]

過去式	過去分詞	現在進行式
dug [dʌg]	dug [dʌg]	digging [`dɪgɪŋ]

v.t. v.i. 挖掘～（洞）

- Peter **dug** a hole in the garden and hid some things in it.
  彼得在花園裡挖了一個洞，把某些東西藏在裡面。

dig out
挖掘出～

- The dog is *digging* out a small bell in the earth.
  那隻狗兒正在把土裡的小鈴鐺挖出來。

- Everyone tells lies, so it is not easy to *dig* out the fact.
  每個人都在說謊，所以想挖掘出事實的真相並不容易。

12. **dining room**
[`daɪnɪŋ͵rum]

n. [C] 飯廳

- My family usually eat dinner at the **dining room**.
  我家人通常在飯廳用晚餐。

13. **dinner**
[`dɪnɚ]

n. [C][U] 晚餐

- Do you want to eat/have **dinner** at a French restaurant tonight?
  你今天晚上想不想在法國餐廳吃晚餐？

14. **dirty**
[`dɝtɪ]

adj. 骯髒的；污穢的
   ↔ clean [klin] 乾淨的

- The river is so **dirty** that there is almost no fish living in it.
  這條河太髒了，以致於河裡幾乎沒有魚還活著。

15. **dish**
[dɪʃ]

wash/do the dishes
洗碗盤

n. [C] 盤子；餐盤

- You two brothers should *wash/do the* **dishes** by turns.
  你們兄弟兩人應該輪流洗碗盤。

n. [C] 菜餚

- Sweet and sour chicken is my favorite **dish**.
  糖醋雞是我最喜愛的菜餚。

16. do
[du]

aux. 助動詞（可構成疑問、否定、強調、倒裝句，或代替出現過的動詞）

- "**Do** you like playing basketball?" "Yes, I **do**."
  「你喜歡打籃球嗎?」「是的，我喜歡打籃球。」
  （第一個 do 構成疑問句）
  （第二個 do 代替前面的動詞片語 like playing basketball）

- I **do** not/**do**n't know the boy standing over there.
  我不認識站在那裡的男孩。
  （do 之後加 not 構成否定句）

- I **do** know how to use the computer.
  我真的知道怎麼用電腦。
  （do 之後加原形動詞表強調，可翻成「真的」）

- "I like that doll." "So **do** I."
  「我喜歡那個洋娃娃。」「我也是。」
  （do 構成倒裝句，等於動詞片語 like that doll）

注意
　　do 當「助動詞」使用時，如果主詞是「第三人稱單數」，則應變化為 does，而如果時態是「過去式」，則應該用 did。
v.t. 做～；進行～；處理～

過去式	過去分詞	現在進行式
did [dɪd]	done [dʌn]	doing [`duɪŋ]

- I have finished **doing** my homework.
  我已經做完我的家庭作業了。

17. doctor (Dr.)
[`dɑktɚ]

go to/see a doctor
看醫生

n. [C] 醫生

- My dream is to become a **doctor** and save people's lives.
  我的夢想是當個醫生，拯救人類的性命。

- You had better *go to/see a doctor* if you don't feel well.
  如果你覺得不舒服，你最好去看醫生。

Dr. [`dɑktɚ] *abbr.*
醫生；博士

n. [C] 博士

· Bill is a **Doctor** of Laws.
比爾是個法學博士。

· **Dr.** Lin told Mary to take the medicine on time.
林醫生／博士叫瑪莉要準時服藥。

注意

　稱呼某某醫生或某某博士可用 Dr. 表示，用法與 Mr. 和 Ms. 相同，後面必定要和姓或名連用，不可單獨出現。例如 Dr. Wang is... 是正確的；而 The Dr. is... 則是錯誤的用法。

18. **dog**
[dɔg]

n. [C] 狗

· **Dogs** have been the best friends of people since old times.
自古以來，狗兒就是人們最好的朋友。

19. **doll**
[dɑl]

n. [C] 洋娃娃；玩偶

· Little girls always love to play with **dolls** like Barbie.
小女孩總喜歡玩像是芭比之類的洋娃娃。

20. **dollar**
[`dɑlɚ]

n. [C] 元；一元紙幣；一元硬幣

· Cathy bought an expensive dress for 2,000 **dollars** yesterday.
凱西昨天買了一件價值兩千元的昂貴洋裝。

Exercise 2

I. 字彙翻譯

1. 挖掘 _____
2. 玩偶 _____
3. 晚餐 _____
4. 做～ _____
5. 飯廳 _____ _____

II. 字彙填充

_____ 1. I cooked for you, so you should do the d_____hes for me.

_____ 2. Many people believe that d_____gs are men's best friends.

_____ 3. You should go to see a d_____r if you catch a cold.

_____ 4. Put your d_____y clothes in the basket, and I will wash them later.

_____ 5. It cost me thousands of d_____rs to buy the PlayStation II.

III. 字彙選擇

(　　) 1. "_____ you like cats?" "Yes, I love them. I have a pet cat myself."
　　　　(A) Does　　　　(B) Do　　　　(C) Did　　　　(D) Done

(　　) 2. Mark's parents hope him to be a _____ someday, but he wants to be a teacher.
　　　　(A) doctor　　　(B) dog　　　　(C) dress　　　(D) daughter

(　　) 3. Could you lend me one _____? I have to make a phone call.
　　　　(A) dog　　　　(B) doll　　　　(C) dollar　　　(D) dish

(　　) 4. Irene liked to play toy cars rather than _____ when she was a little girl.
　　　　(A) dreams　　　(B) dishes　　　(C) dinners　　　(D) dolls

(　　) 5. After we finished our dinner in the _____, we went to the living room to watch TV.
　　　　(A) dining room　　(B) bathroom　　(C) classroom　　(D) rest room

Unit 12

1. door

[dɔr]

n. [C] 門

· Hello! Is anybody home? Please open the **door**.

哈囉！有人在家嗎？請開門。

D

2. down

[daʊn]

adv. 向下；往下；在下面 ↔ up [ʌp] 向上；往上

· Walk **down** the road, and you will see the park.

沿這條路往下走，你就會看到公園了。

· Nancy felt sick, so she sat **down** for a rest.

南西覺得噁心，所以她坐下休息。

adj. (情緒) 低落的

· Kenny has been feeling **down** since he broke up with Barbie.

肯尼自從和芭比分手之後，就一直覺得情緒低落。

---

3. dozen

[`dʌzn̩]

a dozen of + N
一打～

dozens of + N
幾十個～

n. [C] 一打；十二個

· These pencils are sixty dollars a **dozen**.

這些鉛筆一打值六十元。

· Please buy *a **dozen** of* eggs for me on your way home.

在你回家途中，請幫我買一打雞蛋回來。

· ***Dozens** of* foreigners drink beers at the pub every night.

每天晚上，幾十個老外在這家酒吧裡喝啤酒。

---

4. draw

[drɔ]

過去式	過去分詞	現在進行式
drew [dru]	drawn [drɔn]	drawing [`drɔɪŋ]

v.t. v.i. 畫畫；繪製

· The kid is **drawing** a picture with his color pens.

那小孩正在用他的彩色筆畫圖。

v.t. v.i. 拖；拉

· The drunken man was **drawn** to his home by the policeman.

這個酒醉的男子被警察拖回家。

5. dream

[drim]

dream of/about
夢見～

n. [C] 夢

- Last night I had a **dream** about Mickey Mouse.
  昨天晚上我做了一個有關米老鼠的夢。

v.i. 做夢；夢見

- I *dreamed of/about* my family again. I miss them so much.
  我又夢到了我的家人；我非常的想念他們。

n. [C] 夢想

- Jessie's greatest **dream** is to travel around the world.
  潔西最大的夢想就是去環遊世界。

v.i. 夢想；嚮往

- I **dream** to become a bird, flying high in the sky.
  我嚮往成為一隻小鳥，在高空中飛翔。

6. dress

[drɛs]

n. [C] 洋裝；連身裙

- Do you like to wear **dresses** or pants to work?
  你喜歡穿洋裝還是長褲去上班?

v.t. 為～穿衣打扮

- Daisy's mother is **dressing** her for the party tonight.
  黛西的媽媽為了今晚的宴會，正在為黛西打扮。

7. drink

[drɪŋk]

過去式	過去分詞	現在進行式
drank [dræŋk]	drunk [drʌŋk]	drinking [`drɪŋkɪŋ]

v.t. 飲；喝（酒；飲料）

- I am thirsty to death. Please give me a cold Coke to **drink**.
  我渴死了。請給我一杯冰可樂喝。

v.i. 喝酒（或其他飲料）；酗酒

- Don't **drink** too much. You have to drive home later.
  別喝太多（酒），你待會兒還得開車回家呢!

注意

drink 當不及物動詞時，雖然可以泛指喝任何飲料，但在大部分情況下還是指「喝酒」。

n. [C] 飲料（包含酒及無酒精飲料）

· Let's go for a **drink**.

　咱們去喝一杯（酒）吧!

· Do you have any cold **drinks** in the kitchen?

　你廚房裡有任何冷飲嗎?

soft drink(s)
不含酒精的飲料

· I am still under 18 years old, so I can only have *soft **drinks***.

　我還未滿十八歲，所以我只能喝無酒精飲料。

D

---

8. **drive**

[draɪv]

過去式	過去分詞	現在進行式
drove [drov]	driven [`drɪvən]	driving [`draɪvɪŋ]

v.t. v.i. 開（車）；駕駛（車輛）

· Don't **drive** a car when you are tired.

　當你疲勞的時候，不要開車。

drunken driving
酒醉駕車

· *Drunken **driving*** is very dangerous.

　酒醉駕車是非常危險的。

比較

drive [draɪv]	*v.t.* 駕駛～（四輪的交通工具，如汽車、卡車）
	· You can't **drive** a car until you are eighteen. 　你要到十八歲才可以開車。
ride [raɪd]	*v.t.* 騎乘～（兩輪的交通工具或動物、如機車、馬）
	· I like to ride a horse on the farm. 　我喜歡在農場上騎馬。

---

9. **driver**

[`draɪvɚ]

n. [C] 駕駛；司機

· He is a careful **driver** for he always drives slowly and safely.

　他是個很謹慎的司機，因為他總是慢慢地安全地開車。

補充

· a bus driver　公車司機　　· a taxi driver　計程車司機

10. **drop**
[drap]

v.t. 丟下；扔下

- Tina **dropped** the letter into the garbage can and went away.
  蒂娜把這封信扔到垃圾桶裡便走掉了。

v.i. 滴下；落下；掉下

- James was so sad that tears **dropped** from his eyes.
  詹姆士很難過，淚水從眼中一滴滴落下。

n. [C]（一）滴

- I like to feel little **drops** of rain falling on my face.
  我喜歡小雨滴滴落在我臉上的感覺。

D

休息一下喔！

Exercise 1

I. 字彙翻譯

1. 往下 _____

2. 畫畫 _____

3. 洋裝 _____

4. 司機 _____

5. 丟下 _____

D

II. 字彙填充

_____ 1. Never d_____e a car if you are tired. It is very dangerous.

_____ 2. It is so hot. I have to d_____k some ice water.

_____ 3. Please open the d_____r. I have to talk with you.

_____ 4. I bought two d_____ns of eggs. That means I bought twenty four eggs.

_____ 5. My d_____m is to become a doctor in the future.

III. 字彙選擇

( ) 1. You look tired. You had better sit _____ to take a rest.

(A) dozen　　　(B) down　　　(C) doll　　　(D) dream

( ) 2. Windy bought a _____ yesterday. She looked great when she put it on.

(A) dress　　　(B) door　　　(C) dream　　　(D) driver

( ) 3. Don't _____ the book from the upper floor; you may hurt the people below.

(A) drop　　　(B) draw　　　(C) drive　　　(D) dry

( ) 4. Jean's father is a bus _____ and he always drives slowly and carefully.

(A) dinner　　　(B) dictionary　　　(C) dozen　　　(D) driver

( ) 5. I was so thirsty that I _____ three glasses of juice in two minutes.

(A) drank　　　(B) drove　　　(C) dreamed　　　(D) danced

11. dry
[draɪ]

adj. 乾的；乾燥的 ↔ wet [wɛt] 濕的；潮濕的
- The paint is not **dry** yet, so don't sit on that chair.
  油漆還沒乾，所以別坐在那張椅子上。

v.t. 把～弄乾；使乾燥
- Remember to **dry** your hair after you take a bath.
  洗完澡以後，記得把你的頭髮弄乾。

12. each
[itʃ]

adj. 各自的；每一 = every [ˋɛvrɪ]
- **Each** student should turn in his/her homework before noon.
  每一個學生中午以前都必須交上作業。

pron. 每一個
- **Each** of you will get an apple after dinner.
  你們每一個在晚餐之後都會拿到一顆蘋果。

13. ear [ɪr]

believe one's ears
相信聽到的話
turn a deaf ear to
對～充耳不聞
earring(s) 耳環

n. [C] 耳朵
- You said the tickets are free? I can't *believe my ears*.
  你說這些票是免費的？我簡直不敢相信。
- The proud girl *turned a deaf ear to* others.
  那個傲慢的女孩不願聽別人的話。
- The young girl put on her **earrings** before going out.
  那年輕的女孩在出門前戴上她的耳環。

14. early
[ˋɝlɪ]

原級	比較級	最高級
early [ˋɝlɪ]	earlier [ˋɝlɪr]	earliest [ˋɝlɪst]

adv. 早地
- I'll go jogging **early** tomorrow morning.
  我明天一大早要去慢跑。
- Get up **early**, or you will be late again.
  早點起床，否則你又要遲到了。

adj. 早的；早先的；早起的；先前的 ↔ late [let] 遲的
- The **early** birds catch the worms.
  [諺語] 早起的鳥兒有蟲吃。

E

E

15. **earth**
[ɝθ]

on earth
在世界上

on earth
到底；究竟（放在疑問詞之後）

n. 地球 (the Earth)

· Thousands of years ago, people thought the **Earth** was flat.
數千年前，人們以為地球是平的。

· There are many poor people *on **earth***.
世界上有很多窮人。

· I can't understand what *on **earth*** you want.
我不能了解你到底想要什麼。

n. [U] 陸地；地面；地上 = ground [graʊnd]

· The glass fell from the table to **earth**, breaking into pieces.
那玻璃杯從桌上掉到了地上，摔成碎片。

16. **east**
[ist]

n. 東方；東邊

· The sun rises in the **east** and sets in the west.
太陽從東邊升起，從西邊落下。

adj. 東方的；東邊的

· The **east** side of the house is painted yellow.
這棟房子的東面被漆成黃色。

17. **easy**
[`izɪ]

as easy as pie
非常簡單

take it easy
別緊張；放輕鬆

adj. 簡單的，容易的 ↔ difficult [`dɪfəˌkʌlt] 困難的

· It is **easy** for Michael Jordan to play basketball.
對麥可·喬丹而言，打籃球是容易的。

· The question is *as **easy** as pie*. I can answer it soon.
這問題非常簡單，我很快就能回答出來。

· *Take it **easy***. You will pass the test.
別緊張，你會通過考試的。

18. **eat**
[it]

過去式	過去分詞	現在進行式
ate [et]	eaten [`itn̩]	eating [`itɪŋ]

v.t. 吃～

· Max was so hungry that he **ate** a cake in one minute.
馬克斯餓到在一分鐘之內吃了一個蛋糕。

v.i. 吃飯；進食

· I want to **eat** in the Italian restaurant; I hear it is great.

我想去那家義大利餐廳吃飯，聽說那裡很棒。

19. **egg**

[ɛg]

n. [C] 蛋；雞蛋

· Mary usually has an **egg** and a glass of milk for breakfast.

瑪莉早餐通常都吃一個蛋、喝一杯牛奶。

20. **either**

[ˋiðɚ]

adv. 也（不）

· Bill can't ride a bike, and Frank can't, **either**.

比爾不會騎腳踏車，法蘭克也不會。

E

注意

either 當「也」時，只用於「否定句」。

· My grandparents will come here ***either*** tonight *or* tomorrow.

我的祖父母不是今晚，就是明天會來這裡。

either A or B

不是 A 就是 B

ᓬExercise 2

I. 字彙翻譯

1. 東方 _____
2. 雞蛋 _____
3. 耳朵 _____
4. 乾的 _____
5. 吃（三態） _____ _____ _____

II. 字彙填充

_____ 1. E_____h student should go to school on time.

_____ 2. It is not e_____y for me to answer this question. It is too difficult.

_____ 3. You should go to bed e_____y, or you would not have enough sleep.

_____ 4. What on e_____h do you want to say?

_____ 5. "That was really a bad movie." "Yes. I don't like it, e_____r."

III. 字彙選擇

( ) 1. Take it _____. We still have a lot of time.

    (A) early   (B) earth   (C) easy   (D) either

( ) 2. I want to _____ steak tonight. How about you?

    (A) eat   (B) east   (C) ate   (D) each

( ) 3. _____ you _____ I have to do this difficult work.

    (A) Either / nor   (B) Neither / but   (C) Or / either   (D) Either / or

( ) 4. There is no water around that place. It is a _____ land.

    (A) dry   (B) down   (C) drop   (D) dream

( ) 5. We have only one _____ so we should not make it dirty.

    (A) ear   (B) earth   (C) each   (D) either

Unit 13

1. elementary school

[ˌɛləˈmɛntərɪ skul]

n. [U] 小學（指教育階段）
- Kids study in **elementary school** when they are six to twelve.
  小孩在六到十二歲時在小學學習。

n. [C] 小學（指硬體設施、建築）
- There are about 150 **elementary schools** in Taipei City.
  台北市總共有約一百五十所小學。

2. elephant

[ˈɛləfənt]

n. [C] 大象
- **Elephants** are the biggest animals on earth.
  大象是陸地上最大的動物。

3. else

[ɛls]

adv. 其他；另外
- Besides a hamburger and a coke, what **else** do you want?
  除了漢堡和可樂之外，你還想要什麼其他的?
- I don't think there is anything **else** we can do now.
  我不認為我們現在還有什麼其他的事可做。

注意
else 用於「疑問詞」或「不定代名詞」之後。

4. e-mail

[iˈmel]

n. [C] 電子郵件 = email = electronic mail
- You've got an **e-mail**.
  你有一封電子郵件。

n. [U] 電子郵件 = email = electronic mail
- Now, it is very convenient to use **e-mail**.
  現在，使用電子郵件是非常方便的。

e-mail address
電子郵件地址
- Give me your *e-mail* address and I will send you **e-mails**.
  把你的電子郵件地址給我，我會寄電子郵件給你。

注意
電子郵件地址的唸法，例：sanmin@yahoo.com.usa

E

@ 英文要唸成 at。小點唸做 dot [dɑt]，意思是「點；小圓點」。com 指 company [`kʌmpənɪ]（公司）。usa 指美國；如果是台灣，會用 tw。所以這個電子郵件地址應該唸成 sanmin at yahoo dot com dot usa。

v.t. 寄送電子郵件給〜 = email...

- Remember to **e-mail** me when you get on the Internet.
  你上網的時候，記得寄封電子郵件給我。

5. **end** [ɛnd]

at the end of...
在〜結束時
come to an end
結束
in the end
最後；終於

n. [C] 結束；盡頭

- At the **end** of the story, the family lived happily ever after.
  在故事的結尾，這一家人從此過著幸福快樂的日子。
- No matter how great the story is, it has to *come to an end*.
  無論這個故事有多美好，最後終究要結束。
- In children's stories, good people always win *in the end*.
  在兒童故事裡，好人最後總是會獲勝。

v.t. v.i. 結束；終止 ↔ begin [bɪ`gɪn] 開始

- When will the boring movie **end**?
  這部無聊的電影什麼時候會結束？
- The speaker **ended** his speech with an interesting story.
  演說者最後以一個有趣的故事結束他的演講。

6. **English** [`ɪŋglɪʃ]

the English
英國人（總稱）

n. [U] 英語；英文

- America and England are both **English**-speaking countries.
  美國和英國都是說英語的國家。
- She speaks Chinese but does not speak **English**.
  她會說中文，但不會說英文。
- Peter does not like Americans but he does love the **English**.
  彼得不喜歡美國人，卻很喜歡英國人。

注意

the English 代表英國人全體，而當要說某人是英國人時，則說 an Eglishman/Eglishwoman。

adj. 英國的；英國人的；英語的
- Do you have any **English**-Chinese dictionary?
  你有任何英漢字典嗎?

7. **enjoy**
[ɪn`dʒɔɪ]
enjoy + N/Ving
享受～；喜歡～

v.t. 享受；喜愛
- My brother lay down on the grass to *enjoy the winter sun*.
  我弟弟躺在草地上，享受冬天的太陽。
- I *enjoy taking* a walk along the beach in the early morning.
  我喜歡在清晨沿著海灘散步。

E

8. **enough**
[ə`nʌf]
(not) + *Adj / Adv* +
enough to + V
（不）足夠～以致於
（不）可以～

adv. 足夠地；充份地
- My little sister is not *tall enough to* get the candy can on the shelf.
  我的小妹妹還不夠高以致於拿不到架子上的糖果罐。
- Sheri sings *well enough to* be a singer.
  雪莉歌唱得好到可以當歌手了。

adj. 足夠的；充足的
- I am afraid that we don't have **enough** food for everyone.
  我恐怕我們沒有足夠的食物給所有的人。

9. **enter**
[`ɛntɚ]

v.t. v.i. 進入（房間、網路、網頁等）
- Do we have to take off our shoes before we **enter** the room?
  在我們進房間之前，必須脫掉鞋子嗎?

v.t. 參加；加入（組織、社團、戰事等）= join [dʒɔɪn]
- My brother **entered** the tennis club in senior high school.
  我弟弟高中時加入網球社。

10. **eraser**
[ɪ`resɚ]

n. [C] 橡皮擦
- All you need for the test are a pencil and an **eraser**.
  參加那場測驗，你所需要的只是一枝鉛筆和一個橡皮擦。

- blackboard eraser　板擦

Exercise 1

I. 字彙翻譯

1. 大象 ＿＿＿＿＿＿　　2. 進入 ＿＿＿＿＿＿　　3. 結束 ＿＿＿＿＿＿

4. 橡皮擦 ＿＿＿＿＿＿　5. 電子郵件 ＿＿＿＿＿＿

II. 字彙填充

E

＿＿＿＿＿＿＿ 1. Students in e＿＿＿＿y school are still kids; they couldn't take care of themselves yet.

＿＿＿＿＿＿＿ 2. You said you need a notebook, a pencil, and what e＿＿＿＿e?

＿＿＿＿＿＿＿ 3. One cake would be e＿＿＿＿h; I don't want another.

＿＿＿＿＿＿＿ 4. I e＿＿＿＿y listening to music, especially popular music.

＿＿＿＿＿＿＿ 5. I don't know you can speak E＿＿＿＿h so well. Where did you learn it?

III. 字彙選擇

( ) 1. Our teacher asked us to take a pencil and an ＿＿＿＿ to school tomorrow.

　　　(A) everybody　　(B) evening　　(C) enter　　(D) eraser

( ) 2. When you ＿＿＿＿ the room, you had better take your hat off.

　　　(A) enter　　(B) eraser　　(C) eat　　(D) enjoy

( ) 3. I have a friend on Internet. We send ＿＿＿＿ to each other.

　　　(A) elephants　　(B) e-mails　　(C) English　　(D) earth

( ) 4. I don't have ＿＿＿＿ money to buy the bike, but I want it so much.

　　　(A) else　　(B) enough　　(C) end　　(D) early

( ) 5. This is really an interesting book. I ＿＿＿＿ reading it.

　　　(A) entered　　(B) enough　　(C) enjoyed　　(D) ended

11. eve
[iv]

n. [U]（節日的）前夕（此時必須大寫）

· My friends and I give gifts to each other on Christmas **Eve**.
我朋友和我在聖誕夜互相交換禮物。

12. even
[`ivən]

even though
即使

adv. 甚至～；還～

· This dress is **even** more expensive than that one.
這件洋裝甚至比那一件還要貴。

· *Even though* I am full, I can still eat one more cake.
即使我已經飽了，我還是可以再多吃一塊蛋糕。

13. evening
[`ivnɪŋ]

in the evening
在傍晚；在晚上

Good evening.
晚安

n. [C][U] 傍晚；晚上

· My family usually eat dinner at about 7:30 p.m. every **evening**.
我家人通常在每天傍晚七點半左右吃晚餐。

· The MRT stations are always full of people from five to seven p.m. *in the evening*.
捷運站在傍晚五點到七點的時段總是擠滿了人。

· *Good evening*. How have you been today?
晚安！今天過的如何呢？

注意

Good evening. 是晚上見面時所用的招呼語，晚上道別時則用 Good night.，兩者的分別請不要搞混。

14. ever
[`ɛvɚ]

adv. 曾經；從來；至今 ↔ never [`nɛvɚ] 從未

· Have you **ever** seen the popular movie *Harry Potter*?
你曾經看過這部受歡迎的電影——「哈利波特」嗎？

· No one in my family has **ever** been to America.
我家沒有人去過美國。

· Lisa is the most beautiful girl I have **ever** seen.
麗莎是我至今為止見過最美麗的女孩。

注意

ever 常用於「疑問句」和「否定句」；或者用來「強調」。

E

15. every
[ˈɛvrɪ]

adj. 每一；每個 = each [itʃ]
- **Every** student has to get to school on time every day.
  每個學生每天都必須準時到校。

16. everyone
[ˈɛvrɪˌwʌn]

pron. 每個人 = everybody [ˈɛvrɪˌbɑdɪ]
- **Everyone** in the room is talking and laughing.
  在房裡的每個人都在談天說笑。
- Not **everyone** likes to eat steak.
  不是每個人都喜歡吃牛排。

17. everything
[ˈɛvrɪˌθɪŋ]

pron. 每件事；每個東西
- You can take a rest when **everything** is done.
  當每件事都做好時，你就可以休息了。

18. example
[ɪgˈzæmpl̩]

for example
舉例來說

n. [C] 例子；範例
- I don't understand your idea. Could you give me an **example**?
  我不明白你的想法，可以給我一個例子嗎？
- Amy is a kind girl. *For example*, she always helps others.
  艾咪是個善良的女孩。舉例來說，她總是幫助他人。

n. [C] 模範；楷模；榜樣（介系詞用 to）
- Eddie is both smart and kind. He is a good **example** to us.
  艾迪既聰明又仁慈，他是我們的好榜樣。

19. excellent
[ˈɛksl̩ənt]

adj. 出色的；傑出的；優秀的
- The steak is **excellent**. It is the best one I have ever tasted.
  這牛排很出色。它是我所嚐過最好的牛排。

20. excited
[ɪkˈsaɪtɪd]

adj. 感到興奮的（介系詞用 about）
- Ken is very **excited** about the trip to America.
  肯對於美國之旅感到非常興奮。

注意

有關情緒動詞的詳細用法請參閱附錄。

E

 休息一下喔！

Exercise 2

I. 字彙翻譯

1. 前夕 _____
2. 每個 _____
3. 每個人 _____
4. 甚至 _____
5. 曾經 _____

II. 字彙填充

_____ 1. The show is e_____t. I haven't seen such a wonderful show for a long time.

_____ 2. Linda felt so e_____d when she saw the popular singer face to face.

_____ 3. Steve is a good e_____e to all of you. You should learn from him.

_____ 4. E_____g in this park belongs to the public, so you could not take it home.

_____ 5. In the e_____g, most people finish their work and are ready to go home.

III. 字彙選擇

( ) 1. "Have you _____ been to America?" "No, I have never been there."

    (A) ever   (B) eve   (C) even   (D) every

( ) 2. _____ student should turn in his homework on time.

    (A) Ever   (B) Every   (C) Even   (D) Eve

( ) 3. You have to be a good _____ to your little brother.

    (A) eye   (B) example   (C) fact   (D) excuse

( ) 4. Adam and his wife had a great meal on Christmas _____.

    (A) Every   (B) Ever   (B) Even   (D) Eve

( ) 5. Ian did an _____ job, so his boss gave him a raise（加薪）.

    (A) elephant   (B) everything   (C) excited   (D) excellent

Unit 14

1. exciting
[ɪk`saɪtɪŋ]

adj. 令人興奮的；刺激的

- It is so **exciting** that the movie star is coming to Taiwan.
  那個電影明星即將來到台灣，真是太令人興奮了。
- Let's go to see the **exciting** movie.
  我們去看那部刺激的電影吧!

注意
有關情緒動詞的詳細用法請參閱附錄。

2. excuse
[ɪk`skjuz]
excuse me
不好意思；借過

v.t. 讓～離開；原諒

- *Excuse* me. Do you know where the bank is?
  不好意思。你知不知道銀行在哪裡?

n. [C] 藉口

- You should try to do your job well but not make any **excuse**.
  你應該試著把工作做好，而不是製造任何的藉口。

3. exercise
[`ɛksɚ͵saɪz]

n. [C][U] 運動；鍛鍊

- The doctor said that Ron needed more **exercise**.
  醫生說，朗需要做更多的運動。

take exercise
做運動

- Do you have the habit of *taking* some *exercise* every morning?
  你有沒有每天早上做些運動的習慣呢?

v.i. 做運動；做練習

- You should **exercise** more to have a healthier body.
  你應該多做點運動，才能有更健康的身體。

n. [C] 練習，習題

- Today's homework is to finish the **exercise** of Lesson Five.
  今天的家庭作業是做完第五課的練習題。

4. expensive
[ɪk`spɛnsɪv]

adj. 貴的；昂貴的 ↔ cheap [tʃip] 便宜的

- The cell phone is nice but too **expensive**.
  這手機很好，不過太貴了。

E

5. **experience**

[ɪk`spɪrɪəns]

n. [C][U] 經驗

· Do you have the **experience** of being bitten by a dog?

你有被狗咬的經驗嗎?

v.t. 經歷

· Tom has **experienced** the most difficult time on a small island.

湯姆在小島上已經歷過他最困苦的時候了。

F

6. **eye**

[aɪ]

n. [C] 眼睛

· Sue comes from the west and has blue **eyes**.

蘇來自西方,有藍色的眼睛。

注意

眼睛出現時通常是複數,因為一般人都是兩個眼睛。

7. **face**

[fes]

in the face of + N
面對～

face the music
面對困難／懲罰

n. [C] 臉;面孔;表情

· Nancy is a girl with a beautiful **face** and a cold heart.

Nancy 是個有漂亮臉孔和冷酷心腸的女生。

· Many children begin to cry *in the **face** of* doctors.

許多小孩在面對醫生的時候,都開始哭了。

v.t. 面對

· Ben couldn't say a word when he **faced** the girl he liked.

當班面對他喜歡的女孩時,他一個字都說不出來。

· Since the wrong has been done, you should *face the music*.

既然錯誤已經造成,你就應該接受應得的懲罰。

8. **fact**

[fækt]

the fact + that 子句
～的事實

n. [C][U] 事實;實情;真相 ↔ lie [laɪ] 謊言

· You can't change the **fact** no matter what you do.

無論你做什麼,都改變不了事實。

· *The **fact** that* we had lost made everyone sad.

我們失敗的事實讓每個人都感到難過。

| in fact
實際上；事實上 | • He is not a boss at all; *in fact*, he is a worker.
他根本就不是老闆；事實上，他是個工人。 |

9. factory
[`fæktrɪ]

n. [C] 工廠；製造廠

• Debby's dad is the boss of this **factory**.
黛比的爸爸是這家工廠的老闆。

10. fall
[fɔl]

過去式	過去分詞	現在進行式
fell [fɛl]	fallen [`fɔlən]	falling [`fɔlɪŋ]

v.i. 落下 = drop [drɑp]

• An apple **fell** from the tree and hit the young man.
一顆蘋果從樹上掉下來，打到這個年輕人。

n. 秋天

• The weather is cool in **fall**.
秋天的天氣很涼爽。

F

Exercise 1

I. 字彙翻譯

1. 眼睛 ＿＿＿＿＿＿＿＿＿
2. 臉孔 ＿＿＿＿＿＿＿＿＿
3. 事實 ＿＿＿＿＿＿＿＿＿
4. 經驗 ＿＿＿＿＿＿＿＿＿
5. 落下（三態）＿＿＿＿＿＿ ＿＿＿＿＿＿ ＿＿＿＿＿＿

II. 字彙填充

＿＿＿＿＿＿＿＿ 1. I don't have enough money to buy that watch. It is too e＿＿＿＿e.

＿＿＿＿＿＿＿＿ 2. Taking more e＿＿＿＿e would make you thin and healthy.

＿＿＿＿＿＿＿＿ 3. E＿＿＿＿e me. I have to leave for a while.

＿＿＿＿＿＿＿＿ 4. I think the roller coaster（雲霄飛車）is too e＿＿＿＿g for me.

＿＿＿＿＿＿＿＿ 5. Ben is a worker. He works in a f＿＿＿＿y near his home.

III. 字彙選擇

(　　) 1. Tom's ＿＿＿＿ for being late today is that his mother didn't wake him up.

(A) exercise　　　(B) excuse　　　(C) experience　　　(D) example

(　　) 2. When I saw the little boy, he had ＿＿＿＿ from the chair.

(A) fallen　　　(B) fell　　　(C) faced　　　(D) fact

(　　) 3. Remember why you lose this time. It would be a good ＿＿＿＿ for you.

(A) experience　　　(B) exercise　　　(C) eye　　　(D) evening

(　　) 4. When I opened my ＿＿＿＿, I saw my mother smiling at me.

(A) ears　　　(B) ends　　　(C) eves　　　(D) eyes

(　　) 5. I am so sorry to tell you this, but in ＿＿＿＿, I don't want to go out with you.

(A) Fall　　　(B) factory　　　(C) fact　　　(D) face

11. family

[`fæməlɪ]

n. [C] 家庭

- The tsunami made many **families** broken.
  那場海嘯使許多家庭破碎。

n. 家人（集合名詞）

- I love my **family**. They are the dearest in the world to me.
  我愛我的家人。對我而言，他們是世上最珍貴的。

12. famous

[`feməs]

be famous for
+ N/Ving 以～著名

adj. 有名的，著名的，出名的

- Michael is a **famous** man; everyone knows him.
  麥克是個有名的人，每個人都認識他。

- The singer *is **famous** for* her sweet smile.
  那位歌手以她甜美的笑容聞名。

13. fan

[fæn]

electric fans
電風扇

n. [C] 扇子；風扇

- In the hot summer, we can not do without the *electric **fans***.
  在炎熱的夏天，我們不能沒有電風扇。

n. [C] ～迷（影迷；歌迷；球迷）

- Gary is a **fan** of that movie star; he sees every movie of his.
  蓋瑞是那個電影明星的影迷；他的每部電影他都會看。

14. farm

[fɑrm]

on the farm
在農場

n. [C] 農場；畜牧場

- Old MacDonald had a **farm**.
  老麥當勞先生有個農場。

- There are many cows and sheep on the **farm**.
  這個牧場裡有許多乳牛和綿羊。

15. farmer

[`fɑrmɚ]

n. [C] 農夫；農場經營者

- The **farmer** is working on the farm under the sun.
  這個農夫在大太陽下的農場裡工作。

16. fast

[fæst]

adv. 快速地

- Run **fast**, or you won't catch the bus!
  跑快一點，不然你就趕不上公車了。

adj. 快的，迅速的 ↔ slow [slo] 慢的

- I'll teach you a **fast** and easy way to be thin.
  我教你一個快速又簡單的方法變瘦。
- I like ***fast*** *food* like hamburgers and fries.
  我喜歡像漢堡和薯條之類的速食。

fast food
速食

---

17. **fat**
[fæt]

adj. 胖的，肥胖的 ↔ thin [θɪn] 瘦的

- Irene was a **fat** girl before, but now she is thin and pretty.
  艾琳以前是個胖胖的女孩，但她現在又苗條又漂亮。

---

18. **father**
[ˋfɑðɚ]

n. [C] 父親，爸爸 = dad [dæd] 爹 = daddy [ˋdædɪ] 爹地

- My **father** takes good care of my family all the time.
  我爸爸總是好好地照顧我的家人。

---

19. **favorite**
[ˋfevərɪt]

adj. 最喜愛的

- Jackie Chan is her **favorite** movie star.
  成龍是她最喜愛的電影明星。

n. [C] 最喜愛的人、事、物

- Chocolate is Sara's **favorite**.
  巧克力是莎拉的最愛。

---

20. **feel**
[fil]

過去式	過去分詞	現在進行式
felt [fɛlt]	felt [fɛlt]	feeling [ˋfilɪŋ]

v.t. 感覺；覺得

- When Betty knew that her grandfather died, she **felt** very sad.
  當貝蒂知道她的祖父去世時，她覺得很難過。
- I don't ***feel*** *like* going out today. I want to stay at home.
  我今天不想出去。我想待在家裡。

feel like + N/Ving
想要～

F

Exercise 2

I. 字彙翻譯

1. 風扇 _____

2. 農場 _____

3. 著名的 _____

4. 父親 _____

5. 感覺（三態）_____ _____ _____

II. 字彙填充

_____ 1. My parents love me very much. I have a happy f_____y.

_____ 2. Jack is a f_____r; he grows rice and a few kinds of vegetables.

_____ 3. The butter cake is my f_____e snack; I hope I can eat it every day.

_____ 4. Don't eat too much sweet food, or you will get f_____t easily.

_____ 5. Don't walk so f_____t. I can't follow you!

III. 字彙選擇

( ) 1. Tim is a _____ of PC games; he plays it every day.

　　(A) farm 　　(B) fan 　　(C) face 　　(D) factory

( ) 2. It won't take you too much time if you go home by the _____ train.

　　(A) famous 　　(B) farm 　　(C) fast 　　(D) fat

( ) 3. After writing *Harry Potter*, J. K. Rowling became the most _____ writer in the world.

　　(A) fast 　　(B) family 　　(C) fat 　　(D) famous

( ) 4. All my brothers will come home tonight because we are going to have a _____ meeting.

　　(A) famous 　　(B) farmer 　　(C) family 　　(D) fan

( ) 5. Frank's father _____ angry when he knew that Frank didn't pass the exam (考試).

　　(A) felt 　　(B) fell 　　(C) fast 　　(D) farm

F

Unit 15

1. festival
['fɛstəvl̩]

n. [C] 節日

· The Chinese eat moon cakes on the Moon **Festival**.
中國人在中秋節吃月餅。

n. [C] 慶祝活動；慶祝會

· We had lots of **festivals** during the Chinese New Year.
在農曆過年期間我們舉辦了許多的慶祝活動。

節日	中譯	日期（農曆）
Chinese New Year	中國新年	一月一日
Lantern Festival	元宵節	一月十五日
Dragon Boat Festival	端午節	五月五日
Chinese Valentine's Day	七夕	七月七日
Ghost Festival	中元節（鬼節）	七月十五日
Moon Festival	中秋節	八月十五日

2. few
[fju]

adj. 很少的；幾乎沒有的（後面只能接可數名詞）

· **Few** people want to see that movie again. It was too boring.
幾乎沒有人想要再看一次那部電影。它太無趣了。

pron. 少數；幾乎沒有（只能代替可數名詞）

· **Few** of the students could answer this question, but John could.
很少學生能夠回答出這個問題，但約翰可以。

注意

few, a few, little, a little 的比較參閱 Unit 1 的 a few。

3. fill [fɪl]
fill A with B
用 B 填滿 A

v.t. 填滿；裝滿；使充滿

· The waiter ***filled*** my glass *with* orange juice.
侍者用柳橙汁裝滿了我的杯子。

F

| be filled with + N 充滿～；擠滿～ | · The department store *is **filled** with* people on weekends. 百貨公司週末時擠滿了人潮。 |

4. finally
[ˋfaɪnəlɪ]

adv. 最後；終於 ↔ first [fɜst] 首先

· **Finally**, the long meeting ended and we could take a break.
最後，冗長的會議總算結束，我們也才能休息。

· After working hard for days, May **finally** finished the paper.
在辛苦工作數天之後，梅終於完成了這份報告。

5. find
[faɪnd]

過去式	過去分詞	現在進行式
found [faʊnd]	found [faʊnd]	finding [ˋfaɪndɪŋ]

v.t. 找到

· The man will give five thousand dollars to anyone who **finds** his missing dog.
這個人會把五千元給任何找到他失蹤的狗的人。

v.t. 發現；發覺

· I **found** that the train had left when I arrived at the station.
當我到達車站的時候，我發現火車已經離開了。

· I **found** the book interesting.
我發覺這本書挺有趣的。

比較

find	*v.t.* 尋找；發現；找到
	◎find 通常用於偶然發現（某物），或者經過重重尋找過程，最後終於找到目標物的時候。
	· I **found** the lost book finally after several days. 好幾天後，我終於找到了那本弄丟了的書。
look for	*phr.* 尋找
	◎look for 指正在尋找某物，但還沒有找到的時候。
	· I am looking for my watch. Did you see it? 我正在找我的手錶，你有看到嗎？

F

F

search [sɝtʃ]	*v.t. v.i.* 搜尋；調查
	◎search 較常用於仔細、深入或利用精密儀器的搜查。當不及物動詞時較常搭配的介系詞為 for（尋找）或 into（調查）。
	・Jeffrey lost his job; he is searching for a new one. 傑佛瑞失業了，他正在找新的工作。
	◎找工作用 search for a job 或 look for a job 都可以，找到的時候當然就是說 find a job 囉！

6. **fine**
[faɪn]

adj. 健康的；舒適的

・"How are you?" "I'm **fine**, thank you."
「你好嗎?」「我很好，謝謝。」

adj. （天氣）晴朗的

・The weather is **fine** today and we can go out for a picnic.
今天天氣晴朗，我們可以出外野餐。

n. [C] 罰金；罰款

・You have to pay a **fine** of five hundred dollars for losing the book of the library.
因為你遺失了圖書館的藏書，所以必須繳五百元的罰金。

v.t. 處以～罰金

・Peter was **fined** lots of money for he broke the traffic rules.
彼得因為違反交通規則，所以被罰了許多錢。

7. **finger**
[ˈfɪŋgɚ]

n. [C] 手指；大拇指以外的其他所有手指

・Alice wears a ring on her little **finger**.
愛麗斯在小指上戴了一枚戒指。

比較

中文	英文	意義
大拇指	thumb [θʌm]	
食指	index **finger**	表明、指示用的手指
中指	middle **finger**	中間的手指
無名指	ring **finger**	戴戒指的手指

小指	little **finger**	小手指
腳趾頭	toe [to]	

F

8. finish
[ˋfɪnɪʃ]
finish + N/Ving
完成～

v.t. 完成；做完；吃完
- Have you **finished** your homework?
  你做完你的回家功課了嗎？
- When I **finished** (eating) my lunch, I slept for minutes.
  在吃完午餐之後，我睡了幾分鐘。

9. fire
[faɪr]

n. [U] 火
- You must be very careful when you use **fire**.
  用火時你一定要非常小心。

n. [C][U] 火災
- Five people died in the **fire**.
  五個人死於這場火災。
- The *fire fighters* put out the fire soon.
  消防隊員們很快就撲滅了火災。

fire fighter
消防隊員

v.t. 開除；解雇
- Larry was **fired** by his boss because he was too lazy.
  賴瑞因為太懶惰而被老闆開除。

10. first
[fɝst]

adj. 首先的；第一的；最早的 ↔ last [læst] 最後的
- Who was the **first** student to get to school this morning?
  誰是今天早上最早到校的學生？

adv. 首先；第一；最初 ↔ finally [ˋfaɪnḷɪ] 最後，終於
- Before you play, you must finish your homework **first**.
  在你去玩之前，你必須先做完你的家庭作業。

Exercise 1

I. 字彙翻譯

1. 很少的 _____
2. 裝滿 _____
3. 首先 _____
4. 舒適的 _____
5. 火災 _____

II. 字彙填充

_____ 1. Since you have f_____hed reading the book, tell me how you feel about it.

_____ 2. John practiced for several months, and f_____y he won the game.

_____ 3. I cannot f_____d my key. I don't remember where I put it.

_____ 4. It is said that all ghosts (鬼) will come out on the Ghost F_____l.

_____ 5. Everyone should have ten f_____rs.

III. 字彙選擇

( ) 1. When I saw the house on _____, I called 119 right away.

    (A) face   (B) farm   (C) fire   (D) finger

( ) 2. I was so angry with Joe when I _____ he lied to me,.

    (A) found   (B) filled   (C) finished   (D) fell

( ) 3. There are _____ students in the library; most of them go outside to play basketball.

    (A) fast   (B) first   (C) fine   (D) few

( ) 4. Please _____ my glass with water. Thank you.

    (A) fill   (B) find   (C) finish   (D) feel

( ) 5. _____, you have to do your homework, and then you can play your video games.

    (A) Fine   (B) First   (C) Finally   (D) Few

F

11. **fish**
[fɪʃ]

n. [C][U] 魚

- There are many kinds of **fishes** living under the sea.
  海裡住著許多種類的魚。
- Many **fish** swim in the clear water.
  許多魚在清澈的水裡游著。

注意

　　fish 的複數型態仍然是 fish，所以「很多條魚」的英文是 many fish；唯有在指不同「種類」的魚時，才會說 fishes。

n. [U] 魚肉

- I like **fish** but I don't like beef.
  我喜歡吃魚肉，但我不喜歡吃牛肉。

v.i. 釣魚；捕魚

go fishing
去釣魚

- If you feel bored, you can *go **fishing*** at the lake with us.
  如果你覺得無聊的話，你可以和我們去湖邊釣魚。

12. **fisherman**
[ˋfɪʃɚmən]

n. [C] 漁夫；捕魚的人（複數：fishermen）

- The **fishermen** caught a lot of fish.
  這些漁民們捕了很多魚。

13. **fix**
[fɪks]

v.t. 修理

- The computer can't work; you have to call someone to **fix** it.
  電腦無法運作，你必須打電話找個人來修理。

have + sth + fixed
把～修好

- I need to *have* the car ***fixed*** or I can't go out.
  我必須把車修好，不然我無法出門。

14. **floor**
[flor]

n. [C] 地板；地面

- Don't sleep on the **floor**, or you will catch a cold.
  不要在地板上睡覺，不然你會感冒。

n. [C] （樓房的）層、樓

- Mr. White lives on the second **floor** of the apartment.
  懷特先生住在這棟公寓的二樓。

15. flower
[`flauɚ]

n. [C] 花；花朵

· Some **flowers** in the garden are red, and others are white.
花園裡的花有些是紅的，其它則是白的。

16. fly
[flaɪ]

過去式	過去分詞	現在進行式
flew [flu]	flown [flon]	flying [`flaɪɪŋ]

v.i. 飛；飛翔；飛行

· When I was a child, I often dreamed about **flying** in the sky.
當我還是孩子的時候，我常常夢想在天空中飛翔。

v.i. 搭飛機

· I am so excited because I am going to **fly** to Tokyo tomorrow.
我好興奮，因為我明天就要搭飛機到東京去。

n. [C] 蒼蠅（複數：flies）

· I cover the food to keep it away from the **flies**.
我把食物蓋起來以隔離蒼蠅。

17. follow
[`falo]

v.t. v.i. 跟隨；接在～之後

· Wherever the mother went, her children **followed** her.
不論媽媽走到哪裡，她的孩子都跟著她。

v.t. 聽從；採用

· If you don't **follow** my words, you will lose the game.
如果你不聽從我的話，你就會輸掉比賽。

v.t. 追趕；追求

· Jay has been **following** Grace after he met her in the party.
自從傑在宴會上遇到葛蕾絲之後，他就一直在追求她。

18. food
[fud]

n. [C][U] 食物；食品

· Do you have any **food** to eat? I am so hungry!
你有任何食物可以吃嗎？我好餓。

fast food 速食 sweet food(s) 甜食	• There are *fast **food*** restaurants like McDonald's in Taiwan. 在台灣有像是麥當勞之類的速食店。 • Don't eat too many *sweet **foods***; they will make you fat. 別吃太多甜食，它們會讓你變胖。

19. foot
[fʊt]

at the foot of + N
在～的腳下
on foot
步行

n. [C] 腳；足部（複數：feet [fit]）

• I wear socks to keep my **feet** warm.
我穿襪子讓我的腳保持溫暖。

• There is a beautiful lake *at the **foot** of* the mountain.
山腳下有個美麗的湖泊。

• Sometimes I go to school *on **foot***, and sometimes by bus.
有時候我步行到學校，有時候則搭公車。

注意

leg 指的是從大腿 (thigh) 到腳踝 (ankle) 的部分，foot 指的則是腳踝以下的部分（主要是腳掌）。

n. [C] 英尺（複數：feet [fit]）

• The basketball player is seven feet tall.
那個籃球員有七呎高。（213.36 公分）

20. foreign
[`fɔrɪn]

adj. 外國的

• Tim is not a Taiwanese; he is from a **foreign** country.
提姆不是台灣人，他來自外國。

F

Exercise 2

I. 字彙翻譯

1. 漁夫 _____

2. 食物 _____

3. 魚 _____

4. 修理 _____

5. 飛行 (三態) _____ _____ _____

II. 字彙填充

_____ 1. There are many trees and f_____rs in the park.

_____ 2. You have to f_____w what I say, so please listen carefully.

_____ 3. You can take a rest in my bedroom; it's on the third f_____r.

_____ 4. How long would it take to go to the park on f_____t?

_____ 5. It is always exciting to visit a f_____n country.

III. 字彙選擇

( ) 1. My father likes to go _____ at the lake every weekend.

    (A) finding   (B) fixing   (C) flying   (D) fishing

( ) 2. Before my car is _____, I have to go to work by bus.

    (A) fished   (B) fixed   (C) followed   (D) flown

( ) 3. Time _____, so we have to use it well.

    (A) flies   (B) fixes   (C) fishes   (D) follows

( ) 4. I have not eaten for a day. Please give me some _____.

    (A) flowers   (B) food   (C) floors   (D) fire

( ) 5. _____ me. I will show you where the school is.

    (A) Flower   (B) Follow   (C) Fly   (D) Finish

F

Unit 16

1. foreigner
[`fɔrɪnɚ]

n. [C] 外國人；老外

- You can practice English by talking with **foreigners**.
  你可以藉著和外國人交談來練習英文。

2. forget
[fɚ`gɛt]

過去式	過去分詞	現在進行式
forgot [fɚ`gat]	forgot/forgotten [fɚ`gatn̩]	forgetting [fɚ`gɛtɪŋ]

v.t. v.i. 忘記；忘記帶

- I **forgot** everything I had read after the test.
  考試過後，我就把讀過的東西全忘光了。

- I **forgot** my umbrella and now it is raining.
  我忘了帶雨傘，而現在下雨了。

forget to + V
忘記去做～（未做）

- I *forgot to bring* my keys so I couldn't open the door.
  我忘了帶鑰匙所以我開不了門。

forget + Ving
忘記做過～（已做）

- John *forgot sending* the mail for Betty, but he did.
  約翰忘了他已經幫貝蒂寄了信，但他的確寄了。

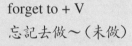

3. fork
[fɔrk]

n. [C] 叉子

- When you eat steak, you have to use a knife and a **fork**.
  當你吃牛排的時候，你必須使用刀叉。

4. free
[fri]

adj. 免費的

- In some restaurants, tea and coffee are **free**.
  在某一些餐廳，茶和咖啡是免費的。

adj. 有空的；空閒的

- If you are **free** tomorrow, we can have a cup of coffee.
  如果你明天有空的話，我們可以一起喝杯咖啡。

F

adj. 自由的

- The exams are all finished. You are **free** now.
  考試全結束了。你現在自由啦!

5. **fresh**
[frɛʃ]

adj. 新鮮的；清爽的

- The air in the country is much **fresher** than that in the big city.
  鄉下的空氣比大城市的新鮮多了。

freshman　新鮮人

- Paul is a **freshman** and has no working experience.
  保羅是個新鮮人，還沒有任何工作經驗。

6. **friend**
[frɛnd]

n. [C] 朋友；友人

- Charlie helped me a lot; he was my best **friend**.
  查理幫過我很多忙，他是我最好的朋友。

make friends with
和～做朋友

- Nancy is proud, so few people want to *make* ***friends*** *with* her.
  南西很驕傲，所以沒什麼人想和她做朋友。

7. **friendly**
[`frɛndlɪ]

adj. 友善的；友好的

- Angela is a very **friendly** person, so she has lots of friends.
  安琪拉是個很友善的人，所以她有很多朋友。

8. **front**
[frʌnt]
in front of + N
在～前面
in the front of + N
在～的前面

n. [U] 前面；正面 ↔ back [bæk] 後面

- The boy becomes shy *in* ***front*** *of* the girl he likes.
  這個男孩在他喜歡的女生面前害羞了起來。
- The teacher stood *in the* ***front*** *of* the classroom and spoke to us.
  老師站在教室的前端，向我們講話。

adj. 前面的

- The old lady grows many flowers in her **front** garden.
  這位老太太在她的前院種了許多的花朵。

9. **fruit**
[frut]

n. [C] 水果（指稱不同水果種類時為可數名詞）

- My favorite **fruits** are apples, bananas and oranges.
  我最喜歡的水果有蘋果、香蕉和柳橙。

n. [U] 水果（泛指所有水果時為不可數名詞）

- Eating more **fruit** and vegetables would be good for you.

  多吃水果和蔬菜會對你有益。

10. **full**

[fʊl]

be full of + N

充滿～；擠滿～

adj. 滿的；充滿的

- The playground *is* always ***full*** *of* kids on weekends.

  這個遊樂場在週末時總是擠滿了小孩。

adj. 吃飽的 ↔ hungry [ˋhʌŋgrɪ] 肚子餓的

- I am **full**. I can't eat any more.

  我飽了。不能再吃了。

F

休息一下喔！

125

Exercise 1

I. 字彙翻譯

1. 滿的 _____

2. 水果 _____

3. 外國人 _____

4. 叉子 _____

5. 友善的 _____

II. 字彙填充

_____ 1. Tea and coffee in this restaurant are f_____e. You don't have to pay for them.

_____ 2. I have f_____t what the teacher told us to do. Do you remember it?

_____ 3. There is a river in f_____t of my house.

_____ 4. Jenny is a kind girl, so she has many f_____ds.

_____ 5. I enjoy the f_____h air in the country. It is different from the air in the city.

III. 字彙選擇

( ) 1. The Chinese-food restaurant in New York is _____ people every night.

(A) fill of   (B) fill with   (C) full with   (D) full of

( ) 2. There is a cat sleeping in _____ my house.

(A) front with   (B) front of   (C) fruit with   (D) fruit of

( ) 3. After the final exam, the students will be _____.

(A) free   (B) full   (C) front   (D) friend

( ) 4. If you can speak good English, you can talk to those _____ there.

(A) fruits   (B) foreigners   (C) fresh   (D) forks

( ) 5. I have to turn in the paper today, but I _____ to bring it.

(A) free   (B) forget   (C) foreign   (D) full

F

11. fun [fʌn]

it's a lot of fun to V
～是很有趣的
make fun of + N
取笑～
have fun
玩得開心

n. [U] 娛樂；樂趣

- *It's a lot of* ***fun*** *to* play volleyball at the beach.
  在沙灘上打排球是很有趣的。
- My friends *make* ***fun*** *of* my cat because it is too fat.
  我朋友取笑我的貓，因為牠太肥了。
- We *had* lots of ***fun*** in the playground yesterday.
  我們昨天在遊樂場玩得很開心。

adj. 有趣的；愉快的

- We had a **fun** holiday in Hualien last week.
  我們上禮拜在花蓮過了個愉快的假期。

12. funny

[`fʌnɪ]

adj. 好笑的；滑稽的

- This is the **funniest** joke I have ever heard.
  這是我聽過最好笑的笑話。

adj. 古怪的 = strange [strendʒ]

- There is a **funny** noise outside.
  外面有個古怪的聲音。

13. future

[`fjutʃɚ]
in the future
（在）未來

n. 未來；將來 ↔ past [pæst] 過去

- Nobody knows what will happen *in the* **future**.
  沒有人知道未來會發生什麼事。

n. [C] 前途

- He is smart and he works hard; he has a great **future**.
  他既聰明又勤勉，他的前途無量。

n. [U] 成功的可能性（較常用於否定及疑問句）

- The plan has no **future** because it is too stupid.
  這計畫太愚蠢，不可能成功的。

adj. 未來的；將來的

- Jim's **future** dream is to travel around the world.
  吉姆未來的夢想是環遊世界。

14. game

[gem]

video games

電動遊戲

n. [C] 遊戲
- I won't go out because I want to play *video games* at home.
  我不會出去，因為我想在家裡打電動遊戲。

n. [C] 比賽
- There will be a basketball **game** on the playground today.
  今天在操場將有一場籃球比賽。

15. garbage

[ˋɡɑrbɪdʒ]

garbage can

垃圾桶

n. [U] 垃圾；廢物
- You should not put the **garbage** on the ground.
  你不應該把垃圾放在地上。

- The tomatoes are bad so I put them into the *garbage* can.
  那些蕃茄壞掉了，所以我把它們放垃圾桶裡。

16. garden

[ˋɡɑrdn̩]

n. [C] 花園；庭院
- There are many different kinds of flowers in the **garden**.
  在花園裡有著很多不同種類的花。

17. gas

[ɡæs]

a gas station

加油站

n. [U] 瓦斯
- We are out of **gas** so that we could not cook anything now.
  我們的瓦斯用完了，所以現在沒辦法煮任何的東西。

n. [U] 氣體
- There are several different kinds of **gas** in the air.
  空氣中有好幾種不同的氣體。

n. [U] 汽油
- I am running out of **gas**; I must find *a gas station* soon.
  我的汽油快用完了，我得趕快找到一家加油站才行。

18. get

[ɡɛt]

過去式	過去分詞	現在進行式
got [ɡɑt]	gotten [ˋɡɑtn̩]/got	getting [ˋɡɛtɪŋ]

v.t. 贏得；獲得；得到；收到
- I **got** many presents on my birthday.
  我生日的時候得到很多禮物。

v.t. 抓住；捕獲

- The cat ran after the mouse and finally **got** it.

  那隻貓追在老鼠後面，並在最後抓住了牠。

v.t. v.i. （使）成為～（狀態）

- We **got** tired for we had worked for hours without any rest.

  因為一連工作幾個小時沒有休息，我們都累了。

v.i. 變成；成為

- I think you are **getting** fat these days.

  我認為你最近有變胖。

get up
起床

- I *get up* at seven thirty a.m. every morning.

  我每天早上都七點半起床。

v.i. 趕上；搭到（車、飛機等）

get on
登上～（交通工具）

- I must *get on* the train or I will be late for the meeting.

  我一定要趕上那班火車，不然我開會就遲到了。

19. **gift**
[gɪft]

n. [C] 禮物 = present [`prɛznt]

- This watch is a birthday **gift** from my father.

  這只手錶是我父親送我的生日禮物。

n. [C] 天賦；才能

a gift for + N/Ving
有～天賦

- Amy has *a gift for* playing the piano.

  艾咪有彈鋼琴的天分。

20. **girl**
[gɝl]

n. [C] 女孩 ⟷ boy [bɔɪ] 男孩

- Sophia's parents have decided to send her to a **girls'** school.

  蘇菲亞的父母已經決定要把她送到女校就讀。

n. [C] 女兒 = daughter [`dɔtɚ] ⟷ son [sʌn] 兒子

- Mr. and Mrs. Wang have two **girls**, but they have no boy.

  王氏夫婦有兩個女兒，但他們沒有兒子。

Exercise 2

I. 字彙翻譯

1. 娛樂 _____

2. 獲得 _____

3. 好笑的 _____

4. 瓦斯 _____

5. 女孩 _____

II. 字彙填充

_____ 1. What do you want to do in the f_____e?

_____ 2. Judy got a lot of g_____ts from her friends on her birthday.

_____ 3. Some people throw g_____e into the river and make the river dirty.

_____ 4. Ali played g_____es with his classmates after he finished his homework.

_____ 5. Mr. Wilson bought a house with a small g_____n.

III. 字彙選擇

( ) 1. Peter is good at telling _____ jokes and he always makes us laugh.

    (A) garbage   (B) full   (C) future   (D) funny

( ) 2. The police finally _____ the thief.

    (A) got   (B) gas   (C) gift   (D) gave

( ) 3. My classmates and I are going to watch the baseball _____ in the afternoon.

    (A) garden   (B) gift   (C) game   (D) gas

( ) 4. It is said that _____ like to eat chocolate more than boys.

    (A) girls   (B) gifts   (C) games   (D) gas

( ) 5. The little girl and her grandma are watering flowers in the _____.

    (A) garbage   (B) garden   (C) future   (D) fun

G

Unit 17

1. give
[gɪv]

過去式	過去分詞	現在進行式
gave [gev]	given [`gɪvən]	giving [`gɪvɪŋ]

v.t. 給；送給 ↔ take [tek] 拿走

give sb sth
給某人某物

give sth to sb
把某物給某人

- Mandy *gave* her mom a ring as a gift for Mothers' Day.
  曼蒂送給她媽媽一個戒指當作母親節禮物。
- The kind woman *gave* all her love *to* those kids.
  那仁慈的女人把她的愛全給了那些孩子。

v.i. 付出

- The more you *give*, the more you get.
  你付出的越多，你得到的就越多。

give up
放棄

give up + N/Ving
戒除～（癮）

- I will never *give* up no matter what happens.
  不論發生什麼事，我絕不會放棄。
- I *gave* up smoking several years ago.
  我好幾年前就戒煙了。

2. glad
[glæd]

adj. 高興的；快活的 = happy [`hæpɪ]

- I'm **glad** to meet you.
  很高興認識你。

3. glass
[glæs]

n. [U] 玻璃

- Be careful of the **glass** on the ground.
  小心地上的玻璃。

n. [C] 玻璃杯

a glass of + N
一杯～

- Rose likes to have *a glass of* orange juice every morning.
  蘿絲喜歡每天早上喝一杯柳橙汁。

n. 眼鏡（必須用複數）

a pair of glasses
一副眼鏡

- The man can't see clearly; maybe he needs *a new pair of glasses*.
  那男人看不清楚，也許他需要一副新的眼鏡。

G

4. glove

[glʌv]

a pair of gloves
一雙手套

n. [C] 手套

- When you play baseball, you need to wear a **glove**.
  當你打棒球時，你需要戴上一隻手套。

- Gina gave her boyfriend *a pair of* ***gloves*** in the winter.
  吉娜在冬天送給她男朋友一雙手套。

5. go

[go]

過去式	過去分詞	現在進行式
went [wɛnt]	gone [gɔn]	going [ˋgoɪŋ]

v.i. 去；離去 ↔ come [kʌm] 來；來到

- The girl asked her mom not to **go** away from her.
  這女孩要她媽媽不要走開。

go to + N
到～地方去

- We will ***go*** *to* the supermarket to do some shopping.
  我們要到超市去買些東西。

go + Ving
去～

- Mr. Hansen likes to ***go*** *mountain climbing* on holidays.
  韓森先生喜歡在假日去登山。

v.i. 進行

- If everything **goes** well, the work could be done in three days.
  如果一切進行順利的話，這件工作三天內就可以完成。

6. goat

[got]

n. [C] 山羊

- There are many **goats**, sheep and horses on my uncle's farm.
  在我叔叔的農場裡，有許多山羊、綿羊和馬兒。

7. good

[gʊd]

原級	比較級	最高級
good [gʊd]	better [ˋbɛtɚ]	best [bɛst]

adj. 好的；有益的

be good for + sb
對～有益

- You should read this **good** book. It *is* ***good*** *for* you.
  你應該讀這本好書。它對你有益。

- The weather is **good**. I want to play basketball outside.
  天氣很好，我想出去打籃球。

| have a good time 玩的很愉快 be good at + N/Ving 擅長於～ | · We *had a* very ***good*** *time* at the beautiful beach last weekend. 我們上週末在那漂亮的海灘上玩得非常愉快。
· Jay *is **good** at* math; he can answer a hard math question soon. 杰擅長於數學，他可以很快地就回答出一道數學難題。 |

8. grade
[gred]

n. [C] 成績
· Kelly was happy that she got a high **grade** in the English test.
凱莉很高興她的英文考試得了很高的成績。

n. [C] 等級；年級
· My younger sister will enter the sixth **grade** this fall.
我妹妹今年秋天要升上六年級了。

9. grandfather
[ˋgrænˏfɑðɚ]

n. [C] 祖父，爺爺；外公 = grandpa [ˋgrænpɑ]
· My **grandfather** is very old but healthy.
我爺爺非常老了，但很健康。

10. grandmother
[ˋgrænˏmʌðɚ]

n. [C] 祖母，奶奶；外婆 = grandma [ˋgrænmɑ]
· My **grandmother** is old; she is sick and lies in bed all day.
我祖母老了，她生病了整天躺在床上。

G

Exercise 1

I. 字彙翻譯

1. 離去 _____

2. 玻璃 _____

3. 山羊 _____

4. 手套 _____

5. 祖父 _____

II. 字彙填充

_____ 1. My g_____r is a kind old woman. She often gives us a lot of candies.

_____ 2. Peter speaks g_____d English. He had stayed in America for years.

_____ 3. I am so g_____d to see you. How have you been these years?

_____ 4. I g_____e Janet a cat as her birthday present, and she liked it very much.

_____ 5. I got a bad g_____e in math, but I did much better in English.

III. 字彙選擇

(　　) 1. I _____ to America last month and had a lot of fun there.

(A) gave　　　　(B) went　　　　(C) forgot　　　　(D) fixed

(　　) 2. There are _____ in the box. Be careful not to break them, please.

(A) glad　　　　(B) gloves　　　　(C) glasses　　　　(D) goats

(　　) 3. If you have a _____ chance to make it, why don't you give it a try?

(A) good　　　　(B) goat　　　　(C) glad　　　　(D) grade

(　　) 4. I wear _____ to keep my hands warm on cold days.

(A) goes　　　　(B) grades　　　　(C) goats　　　　(D) gloves

(　　) 5. I have to put on my _____, or I cannot read this book.

(A) glasses　　　　(B) grades　　　　(C) gloves　　　　(D) gives

11. grass
[græs]

n. [U] 草；草地；牧草

- Goats eat **grass**.
  山羊吃草。
- We will have a picnic on the **grass** tomorrow.
  我們明天將在草地上野餐。

12. gray
[gre]

adj. 灰色的 = grey [gre]

- Our hair will turn **gray** when we get old.
  當我們變老時，頭髮會轉成灰色的。

n. [U] 灰色 = grey [gre]

- I don't like dark colors like black or **gray**; I like bright colors.
  我不喜歡黑色或灰色等暗色；我喜歡亮麗的顏色。

13. great
[gret]

adj. 大的（指數量上或規模上）= big [bɪg]

- Mr. Li is rich and has a **great** house.
  李先生很有錢，而且有一棟大房子。

adj. 偉大的

- Dr. Sun Yat-sen is a **great** man in the Chinese history.
  孫中山先生在中國的歷史中，是個偉大的人物。

adj. 棒的

- This is the **greatest** movie I have ever seen.
  這是我看過最棒的電影。

14. green
[grin]

adj. 綠色的；青蔥的

- The traffic light has turned **green**. We may go now.
  交通號誌燈已經變綠，我們可以走了。

n. [U] 綠色

- **Green** is the color of grass and leaves.
  綠色是草地和樹葉的顏色。

15. ground
[graʊnd]

n. 地；地面 (the ground)

- The wet **ground** shows that it rained last night.
  潮溼的地面顯示昨晚下雨了。

G

n. [C] 場地

- His land is five times bigger than a baseball **ground**.
  他的地比棒球場還要大五倍。

16. group

[grup]

a group of + N
一群～

n. [C] 群體；團體

- Sue has joined a **group** which helps the poor.
  蘇已加入了一個幫助窮人的團體。
- *A **group*** of students are sitting under a big tree.
  一群學生正坐在一棵大樹下。

17. grow

[gro]

過去式	過去分詞	現在進行式
grew [gru]	grown [gron]	growing [ˋgroɪŋ]

v.t. 種植

- My parents like to **grow** flowers in the garden.
  我父母喜歡在花園裡種花。

v.i. 成長

grow up
長大；成長

- Susan said she wants to be a singer when she ***grows up***.
  蘇珊說她長大後想當個歌手。

18. guess

[gɛs]

v.t. 猜；猜測

- I **guess** that you are hiding something in your hand, right?
  我猜你手裡藏著東西，對不對？

v.t. 猜中；猜對

- Mothers can always **guess** what their children are thinking about.　媽媽們總是能猜中他們的小孩在想些什麼。

n. [C] 猜測

make a guess of + N/
Ving　猜猜看

- *Make a **guess*** of the price of this dress.
  你猜這件洋裝值多少錢。

19. habit

[ˋhæbɪt]

n. [C] 習慣

- Almost everyone has some bad **habits**.
  幾乎每個人都有些壞習慣。

H

have the habit of + <u>N/</u> <u>Ving</u> 有～的習慣 get into the habit of 養成～的習慣	• Do you *have the **habit** of* listening to music when reading? 你有沒有閱讀時聽音樂的習慣？ • Don't *get into the **habit** of* smoking; it is bad for you. 別養成抽煙的習慣；那對你有害。
20. **hair** [hɛr] make one's hair stand on end 讓～毛骨悚然	*n.* [C][U] 頭髮；毛髮（大部分時為不可數） • How often do you wash your **hair**? 你多久洗一次頭髮？ • The horrible movie *made my **hair** stand on end*. 那部恐怖電影讓我看的毛骨悚然。

H

休息一下喔！

Exercise 2

I. 字彙翻譯

1. 草地 _____

2. 頭髮 _____

3. 灰色的 _____

4. 成長 _____

5. 團體 _____

II. 字彙填充

_____ 1. You should eat more g_____n vegetables. They are good for you.

_____ 2. The g_____d is so hot because of the weather. It is not easy to walk on it without wearing shoes.

_____ 3. I am so bored now. It would be g_____t if you have time to talk with me.

_____ 4. I have the h_____t of drinking a glass of milk before sleeping every day.

_____ 5. "Can you g_____s what I am?" "A teacher. Am I right?"

III. 字彙選擇

( ) 1. You can only _____ if you don't know which answer is correct.

(A) give   (B) grow   (C) glass   (D) guess

( ) 2. A _____ of boys are running here. We had better step aside.

(A) group   (B) green   (C) ground   (D) grass

( ) 3. The _____ leaves turn red because of the cool weather.

(A) green   (B) gray   (C) grade   (D) ground

( ) 4. Phil wants to be a doctor when he _____ up.

(A) guesses   (B) grows   (C) goes   (D) gives

( ) 5. It is a good _____ to exercise every day.

(A) ground   (B) hair   (C) group   (D) habit

Unit 18

1. half
[hæf]

adj. 一半的，二分之一的
- Joan has been talking on the phone for **half** an hour.
  瓊安已經講了半個小時的電話了。

n. [C][U] 一半，二分之一
- Only **half** of the students passed the test.
  只有一半的學生通過了考試。

2. ham
[hæm]

n. [U] 火腿
- I had **ham**, cheese, and an egg in my sandwich.
  我的三明治裡有火腿、起司和一個蛋。

3. hamburger
[`hæmbɝgɚ]

n. [C] 漢堡
- We will have **hamburgers** at McDonald's this evening.
  我們今天晚上將在麥當勞吃漢堡。

4. hand
[hænd]

give + sb + a hand
= help + sb
幫～的忙

n. [C] 手
- Remember to wash your **hands** before eating.
  吃東西之前，記得洗手。
- I can't move the heavy box. Who can *give* me *a **hand***?
  我搬不動這個重箱子。誰可以幫我一下？

n. [C]（鐘錶的）指針
- The minute **hand** of the clock is broken.
  這個時鐘的分針壞掉了。

5. handsome
[`hænsəm]

adj. 帥氣的；英俊的；俊美的
- **Handsome** and rich men are more popular.
  帥氣又有錢的男人比較受歡迎。

6. happen
[`hæpən]

v.i. 發生
- An accident **happened** last week, but luckily no one got hurt.
  上禮拜發生了一場意外，但幸好沒有人受傷。

H

- What **happened** to you? = What's wrong with you?
  你怎麼了？（你發生什麼事了？）

7. **happy** [`hæpɪ]

adj. 快樂的，高興的 ↔ unhappy [ʌn`hæpɪ] 不快樂的

- When you help other people, you will feel **happy** yourself.
  當你幫助他人的時候，你自己也會覺得快樂。
- **Happy** birthday to you.
  祝你生日快樂。

8. **hard** [hɑrd]

adj. 困難的 = difficult [`dɪfə,kʌlt]

- This question is too **hard** for an elementary school student to answer.
  這問題要一個小學生回答,是太難了。

adj. 硬的；堅固的

- The steak is as **hard** as a rock.
  這牛排像石頭一樣硬。

adv. 努力地

- Vanessa works **hard** in order to make money to buy a car.
  凡妮莎努力地工作，為了要賺錢買一輛車。

9. **hard-working** [`hɑrd`wɝkɪŋ]

adj. 努力工作的；勤勉的 = hardworking

- All bosses like **hard-working** people.
  所有的老闆都喜歡努力工作的人。

10. **hat** [hæt]

n. [C] （有邊的）帽子

- The man wears a **hat** and a jacket.
  那個男子戴一頂帽子，穿一件夾克。

H

Exercise 1

I. 字彙翻譯

1. 帽子 _____

2. 火腿 _____

3. 快樂的 _____

4. 英俊的 _____

5. 努力工作的 _____

II. 字彙填充

_____ 1. You look very sad. What h_____ned to you?

_____ 2. My daughter likes to eat the h_____rs and French Fries in McDonald's.

_____ 3. Wash your h_____ds before you eat dinner.

_____ 4. It took me h_____f an hour to do my homework.

_____ 5. If you want to pass the exam, you have to study very h_____d.

III. 字彙選擇

( ) 1. I have some trouble now. Can you give me a _____.

(A) hair   (B) ham   (C) hamburger   (D) hand

( ) 2. I have only one piece of bread, but I can give you _____ of it.

(A) ham   (B) half   (C) hair   (D) hand

( ) 3. This question is too _____ for me. I cannot answer it.

(A) hard   (B) happy   (C) half   (D) ham

( ) 4. Nothing special _____ today. It is just another common day.

(A) hams   (B) happens   (C) hats   (D) hamburgers

( ) 5. The _____ boy is very popular with the girls in his class.

(A) ham   (B) handsome   (C) hamburger   (D) half

H

11. hate
[het]

v.t. 討厭；憎厭；恨 ↔ love [lʌv] 愛；喜愛

- Kathy **hates** tomatoes; she never eats them.
  凱西討厭蕃茄，她從不吃它們。

n. [U] 仇恨；厭惡

- The **hate** between the two countries is hard to erase.
  這兩個國家之間的仇恨很難消除。

12. have
[hæv]

過去式	過去分詞	現在進行式
had [hæd]	had [hæd]	having [`hævɪŋ]

v.t. 擁有

- I **have** many delicious cookies; do you want some?
  我有很多美味的餅乾，你想要吃一些嗎？

v.t. 吃（喝）

- May I **have** some ice cream after dinner?
  晚餐後我可以吃點冰淇淋嗎？

aux. 已經；曾經

- Mr. Jones **has** finished his dinner; he is watching TV now.
  瓊斯先生已經吃完晚餐，現在他正在看電視。

注意

　　have/has + p.p 為完成式（可謂為「已經」或「曾經」），have/has 為用於完成式之助動詞，後面加過去分詞。

13. head
[hɛd]

n. [C] 頭；頭顱；頭部

- Kevin fell off a tree, but luckily he wasn't hurt in the **head**.
  凱文從樹上摔下來，但幸好他的頭沒有受傷。

n. [C] 頭目；首腦 = leader [`lidɚ]

- The **head** of the group has been caught by the police.
  這個團體的首腦已經被警方捉到了。

n. [C] 頭腦；才智

- Ellen has a good **head** for math.
  艾倫很有數學頭腦。

H

14. **headache**
[`hɛd͵ek]

n. [C] 頭痛
- Tommy always has a **headache** before tests.
  湯米總是會在考試前頭痛。

15. **health**
[hɛlθ]

n. [U] 健康
- Taking some exercise every day is good for your **health**.
  每天做一些運動對你的健康有益。

16. **healthy**
[`hɛlθɪ]

adj. 健康的 ↔ sick [sɪk] 病的
- If you want to keep **healthy**, you have to eat more vegetables.
  如果你想要保持健康，你就要多吃一點蔬菜。

17. **hear**
[hɪr]

過去式	過去分詞	現在進行式
heard [hɝd]	heard [hɝd]	hearing [`hɪrɪŋ]

H

v.t. v.i. 聽；聽見
- Did you **hear** the strange sound just now?
  你剛才有沒有聽見那個怪聲音？

v.t. v.i. 聽說
- I have never **heard** *of* such a strange thing in my life.
  我一生中從沒聽說過這樣的怪事。

hear <u>about/of</u> + N
聽說～

比較

	v.t. v.i. 聽；聽取；聽見
hear [hɪr]	◎和 listen 比起來，hear 指「聽見；聽說（某事）」。
	• I **heard** that a typhoon is coming. Is that true? 我聽說有個颱風要來。是真的嗎？
listen [`lɪsn̩]	*v.i.* 聽；傾聽；留神聽
	◎和 hear 比較起來，listen 指比較「集中注意力、專心的去聽」。片語為 listen to~。

> · She is listening to the news on the radio.
> 她正在（專心）聽收音機上播放的新聞。
>
> ◎listen 和 hear 兩字以單詞使用時，如 Listen! Hear!，都可以表示「注意聽」。

H

18. **heart**
[hɑrt]

break one's heart
傷～的心

with all one's heart
真心誠意地

n. [C] 心；心臟
· Her coldness *broke my heart*.
她的冷酷傷了我的心。
· When I knew that Mary had got married, my **heart** was broken.
當我知道瑪麗已婚的時候，我的心碎了。
· I'm sorry *with all my heart*. Can you give me one more chance?
我真心誠意地感到抱歉。你能再給我一次機會嗎？

19. **heat**
[hit]

n. [U] 熱度；高溫
· The **heat** of the sun made us feel uncomfortable.
太陽的高溫讓我們覺得不舒服。

v.t. 加熱
· The moon cake will taste better if you **heat** it.
如果你把月餅加熱的話，它會更好吃。

20. **heavy**
[ˋhɛvɪ]

heavy rain
大雨；豪雨

adj. 重的；沈重的 ↔ light [laɪt] 輕的
· The box is too **heavy** for a girl to move.
這個箱子太重了，女孩子搬不動它。

adj. 大的；大量的，多的
· There will be *heavy rain* this afternoon.
今天下午將有大雨。

Exercise 2

I. 字彙翻譯

1. 健康的 _____
2. 重的 _____
3. 頭痛 _____
4. 熱度 _____
5. 擁有 _____

II. 字彙填充

_____ 1. Mr. Wang is the h_____d of the factory. Every worker there must listen to him.

_____ 2. Smoking and drinking are not good for your h_____h.

_____ 3. We are all happy to h_____r about the good news.

_____ 4. I h_____e to go outside in bad weather.

_____ 5. You really broke my h_____t when you said you didn't love me anymore.

H

III. 字彙選擇

(　　) 1. I can _____ the birds singing when I get up in the morning.

(A) hear　　　(B) hate　　　(C) head　　　(D) hand

(　　) 2. It is said that you should love people who _____ you.

(A) have　　　(B) hear　　　(C) hate　　　(D) happen

(　　) 3. If you want to have a happy life, you must have a _____ body.

(A) heavy　　　(B) hard　　　(C) half　　　(D) healthy

(　　) 4. This job is too _____ for me. I need someone else to help me.

(A) happy　　　(B) heavy　　　(C) half　　　(D) healthy

(　　) 5. I have a _____, and I can not sleep well. Do you have any medicine?

(A) head　　　(B) hand　　　(C) headache　　　(D) heart

Unit 19

H

1. **help** [hɛlp]

help + sb + with + N
在某事上幫助某人
help + sb + (to) + V
幫助某人做某事
cannot help but + V
不得不～

v.t. 幫忙；協助

· Jack often *helps* his brother *with* his homework.
傑克常常幫他弟弟做功課。

· Can you *help* me (*to*) carry the box to the third floor?
你能幫我把這個箱子提到三樓嗎?

· I *cannot* *help* *but* leave now because I still have to work.
我不得不現在離開，因為我還得工作。

n. [U] 幫忙，幫助

· Without your **help**, I couldn't make it.
沒有你的幫忙，我無法成功。

2. **helpful** [ˋhɛlpfəl]

adj. 有幫助的；有益的（介系詞 to）

· Vegetables and friut are very **helpful** to our health.
蔬菜和水果對我們的健康是很有益的。

· Reading more books is **helpful** to us.
多讀書對我們是有幫助的。

3. **here** [hɪr]

Here you are.
這是你要的東西

adv. 這裡；在這裡 ↔ there [ðɛr] 那裡；在那裡

· Can I put my school bag **here**?
我可不可以把我的書包放在這裡?

· "Could you give me a pack of candies?" "Sure. **Here** you are."
「可以給我一包糖果嗎?」「當然，這是您要的東西。」

n. [C] 這裡

· The hotel is fifty miles away from **here**.
那家旅館離這裡有五十哩遠。

4. **hide** [haɪd]

過去式	過去分詞	現在進行式
hid [hɪd]	hidden [ˋhɪdn̩]	hiding [ˋhaɪdɪŋ]

v.t. 把～藏起來

· Rose **hid** the love letters under her bed.
蘿絲把情書藏在床底下。

hide sth from sb 把～藏起來不讓～ 發現	• Mr. Chen **hides** his money *from* his wife. 陳先生把錢藏起來，不讓他老婆發現。 *v.i.* 隱藏，躲藏 ↔ show [ʃo] 顯示，露出 • I **hid** behind the door to give my mother a surprise. 我躲在門後，想給我媽一個驚喜。

5. **high** [haɪ]

adj. 高的（位置；地位）↔ low [lo] 低的
• It is said that cats like to stay in **high** places.
據說貓喜歡待在高的地方。
adj. 高的（價格；價值；評價）
• The price of the car is too **high** for me.
那輛車的價格對我來說太過昂貴。
adv. 向高處；在高處
• I wish that I could fly **high** like a bird.
我希望我可以像鳥一樣在高處飛翔。

H

6. **hill** [hɪl]

n. [C] 山丘；丘陵
• Can you see the old tree on the **hill**?
你能看見山丘上的老樹嗎?

比較

hill [hɪl]	*n.*[C] 小山；丘陵 • I walked up the **hill** to see the houses far away. 我爬上小山，觀看遠處的房子。
mountain [ˈmaʊntn̩]	*n.*[C] 山；山脈 • Clint likes to go mountain climbing. 克林喜歡登山。

7. **history** [ˈhɪstrɪ]

n. [C][U] 歷史
• China is a country with a long **history**.
中國是個擁有悠久歷史的國家。

make history
名垂青史
• Mother Teresa *made* **history** by helping the poor.
德蕾莎修女因幫助貧窮者而名垂青史。

n. [U] 來歷；沿革；由來

- How could you believe him without knowing his **history**?

  你還不知道他的來歷，怎麼可以相信他？

8. **hit** [hɪt]

過去式	過去分詞	現在進行式
hit [hɪt]	hit [hɪt]	hitting [ˋhɪtɪŋ]

v.t. 打；打擊；擊中

- Even if you hate him, you can't **hit** him.

  即使你討厭他，你也不可以打他。
- Danny **hit** the ball and started to run.

  丹尼擊中了球並開始跑了起來。

v.t. 碰撞

- The dog was **hit** by a car and was sent to the hospital.

  那隻狗被車撞了，並很快被送到醫院。

hit-and-run
肇事逃逸

- The *hit-and-run* driver was finally caught by the police.

  那名肇事逃逸的司機最後終於遭警方逮捕。

v.t. 襲擊；侵襲

- A strong typhoon **hit** Taiwan last month.

  上個月有個強烈颱風襲擊台灣。

9. **hobby** [ˋhɑbɪ]

n. [C] 嗜好（複數：hobbies [ˋhɑbɪz]）

- His favorite **hobby** is to listen to music.

  他最大的嗜好就是聽音樂。

10. **hold** [hold]

過去式	過去分詞	現在進行式
held [hɛld]	held [hɛld]	holding [ˋholdɪŋ]

v.t. 握住；抓住

- The little girl **held** her dad's hand when crossing the street.

  過馬路時，這個小女孩握住她爸爸的手。
- The baby **holds** a toy car in his hand.

  小寶寶手上拿著一個玩具車。

v.t. 舉行

- A basketball game is **held** in our school every October.
  我們學校每年十月都會舉行籃球比賽。

v.t. 抑制；約束

hold back
抑制

- The boy could not **hold** *back* his love for the game.
  那男孩無法抑制他對那款遊戲的熱愛。

hold on
不掛斷電話

- *Hold* on please. Mr. Wu is coming in one minute.
  請不要掛斷電話（請稍待），吳先生一
  分鐘之內就會來了。

hold one's breath
屏住氣息

- I can **hold** *my breath* under water for
  about three minutes.
  我可以在水裡閉氣達三分鐘之久。

H

休息一下喔！

Exercise 1

I. 字彙翻譯

1. 幫助 _____

2. 躲藏 _____

3. 丘陵 _____

4. 打擊 _____

5. 保持 _____

II. 字彙填充

_____ 1. It will be very h_____l if you can bring me the book tomorrow.

_____ 2. I don't know the h_____y of that country. What I know is that it is a good place to visit.

_____ 3. My h_____y is to buy books. I have bought hundreds of books already.

_____ 4. It is said that cats like h_____h places. I don't know whether it is true or not.

_____ 5. Come h_____e. I have something to show you.

H

III. 字彙選擇

(   ) 1. You can run, but you can't _____. We will find you sooner or later.

(A) hide　　　　(B) help　　　　(C) hold　　　　(D) hide

(   ) 2. The mother must put the glasses in a _____ place, or her kids might break them.

(A) heavy　　　　(B) high　　　　(C) here　　　　(D) healthy

(   ) 3. You look so busy. I can _____ you if you want me to.

(A) hide　　　　(B) hold　　　　(C) hear　　　　(D) help

(   ) 4. "A chocolate ice cream, please." "_____ you are."

(A) Heat　　　　(B) Here　　　　(C) Hear　　　　(D) Heart

(   ) 5. We will _____ a birthday party for Matt tonight. Do you want to join us?

(A) hold　　　　(B) help　　　　(C) heat　　　　(D) hide

11. holiday
[ˋhɑləˏde]

n. [C] 假日

- I will spend my **holidays** in Kenting next month.
  我下個月要在墾丁度假。

比較

holiday [ˋhɑləˏde]	*n.* [C] 假日 〈介系詞用 on〉
	◎holiday 通常指一兩天等較短的休息日子。
	• I like to go fishing on **holidays**. 我喜歡在假日的時候去釣魚。
vacation [veˋkeʃən]	*n.* [C] 假期 〈介系詞用 in〉
	◎vacation 則指寒暑假、春假等較長的休息時期。
	• I learned swimming in the summer vacation. 我在暑假期間學會了游泳。

12. home
[hom]

make oneself at
home　不要拘束

n. [C] 家；家庭 （介系詞：at）

- I have a sweet **home**. All my family love me.
  我有個甜蜜的家庭。所有的家人都愛我。

adv. 在家；回家

- After your dad comes **home**, we can have dinner.
  你爸爸回家之後，我們就可以吃晚餐了。
- Please make yourself *at* ***home*** in my place.
  在我的地方請不要拘束。

比較

home [hom]	*n.*[C] 家，家庭
	• Those who have no **home** are very poor. 那些沒有家的人很可憐。
house [haʊs]	*n.*[C] 房子，住宅
	• Mark made money by buying and selling houses. 馬克藉著買賣房屋賺錢。
◎home 在意義上，除了指居住的建築物之外，通常還包含了住在裡面的家人，所以會帶有溫暖、親切的感覺，而 house 通常就是指建築物，不帶任何感情。	

13. homework

[`hom,wɝk]

do one's homework
做功課

n. [U] 回家作業

- The students are happy that they don't have **homework** today.
  學生們很高興他們今天沒有回家作業。
- You should *do your **homework*** before watching TV.
  在看電視之前，你應該先做功課。

14. honest

[`ɑnɪst]

adj. 誠實的；老實的；正直的 ↔ dishonest [dɪs`ɑnɪst]

- Jack is an **honest** boy. He doesn't like to tell a lie.
  傑克是個誠實的男孩。他不喜歡說謊。
- You must be **honest** with your parents.
  對你的父母，你一定要老實。

15. hope

[hop]

hope to + V
希望～
hope that + 子句
希望～

v.t. v.i. 希望；盼望

- Amy *hopes* to enter a good school next year.
  艾咪希望明年進入一所好學校。
- Ginger *hopes that* she can become a star in the future.
  金潔希望她未來可以成為明星。

n. [C] 希望；盼望

- I have a **hope** that I can play video games every day.
  我有一個希望，就是可以每天打電動玩具。

比較

hope [hop]	*n. v.* 希望；期待 • I **hope** (that) you could come to my birthday party. 　我希望你能來參加我的生日宴會。
wish [wɪʃ]	*v. n.*[C] 希望；渴望 • I wish (that) I could fly like a bird. 　我希望我能夠像鳥一樣飛翔。 • I wish (that) I had never known him before. 　我希望我從來沒有認識過他。
◎hope 和 wish 兩個字都當動詞「希望」解釋時，前者後面所加的通常是將來有可能實現的理想、夢想；而後者通常加不可能實現的空想、幻想，或者過去已發生但不希望發生的事。	

16. **horse**
[hɔrs]

ride a horse
騎馬

n. [C] 馬；馬匹

- Don't get too close to those **horses**; they may kick you.
  不要太接近那些馬；牠們可能會踢你。
- Have you ever *ridden a **horse***?
  你可曾騎過馬?

17. **hospital**
[`hɑspɪtl̩]

n. [C] 醫院

- Those who got hurt in the fire were all sent to the **hospital**.
  那些在火災中受傷的人全都被送到醫院去了。

18. **hot**
[hɑt]

adj. 熱的；炎熱的 ↔ cold [kold] 冷的；寒冷的

- It is so **hot** outside; I want to eat some ice cream.
  外面天氣熱極了，我想吃些冰淇淋。

19. **hot dog**
[`hɑt͵dɔg]

n. [C][U] 熱狗

- Mother says I will be very fat if I eat too many **hot dogs**.
  媽媽說如果我吃太多熱狗的話，我就會變得很肥。

20. **hotel**
[ho`tɛl]

n. [C] 旅館；飯店

- We lived in the **hotel** because the house was burned down.
  因為房子被燒毀，所以我們都住飯店。

H

Exercise 2

I. 字彙翻譯

1. 家庭 _____

2. 馬 _____

3. 希望 _____

4. 炎熱的 _____

5. 熱狗 _____

II. 字彙填充

_____ 1. Many parents take their children to the zoo on h_____ys.

_____ 2. I have no h_____k today, so I can play outside all afternoon.

_____ 3. Joe has to stay in the h_____l for a few days because he got hurt when he played basketball yesterday.

_____ 4. You should be h_____t with your parents. You cannot tell lies to them.

_____ 5. We will play in Hualien this weekend, and we will stay in the h_____l on Saturday night.

III. 字彙選擇

( ) 1. I _____ you can feel like home here. If you need any help, just let me know.

(A) hope (B) help (C) hold (D) hide

( ) 2. It's too late, and I have to go _____ now.

(A) hospital (B) hotel (C) home (D) horse

( ) 3. Riding a _____ is not as easy as riding a bike; it takes experience to do it well.

(A) hotel (B) hobby (C) hot dog (D) horse

( ) 4. My sister is a nurse, and she works in a _____ nearby.

(A) home (B) hospital (C) hotel (D) hobby

( ) 5. "What do you usually do on _____?" "I usually go shopping with my sister."

(A) horses (B) hot dogs (C) holidays (D) hospitals

Unit 20

1. hour
[aʊr]

keep early/good
hours 早睡早起

n. [C] 小時；鐘頭

· Albert spent **hours** playing online games every day.
艾伯特每天都花好幾個小時玩線上遊戲。

· My mom asks me to *keep early/good* **hours** to stay healthy.
我媽媽要我早睡早起以保持健康。

2. house
[haʊs]

n. [C] 房子，房屋；家

· Alex built a big **house** in the country for his family.
艾力克斯在鄉下蓋了一棟大房子給他的家人。

注意

house 與 home 的比較請見單字 home。

H

3. how
[haʊ]

how many/much
有多少(詢問數量、
程度多寡等)

adv. 如何；怎麼（詢問方式、方法、健康狀況等）

· **How** do you go to school every day? By bicycle or by bus?
你每天是怎麼上學的？騎腳踏車或是搭公車？

· "**How** have you been today?" "Fine, thank you."
「你今天過的如何？」「很好，謝謝你。」

· "**How** many people are there in your family?" "Five."
「你家一共有幾個人？」「五個。」

adv. 多麼（用於「讚嘆」或「感嘆」）

· **How** lucky you are!
你是多麼的幸運啊！

· **How** fast the boy runs!
這個男孩跑得多快呀！

注意

how 與 what、when、where、who、why 為基本疑問詞。

4. however
[haʊˋɛvɚ]

adv. 然而；但是

· Ricky is a rich man; **however**, he is not happy.
瑞奇是個有錢人；然而，他並不快樂。

5. hundred

[ˋhʌndrəd]

hundreds of
數以百計的～
(接可數名詞)

n. [C] 一百

· The little girl can count from one to one **hundred**.
這小女孩能從一數到一百。

· We could see *hundreds of* kites flying in the sky.
我們可以看見數以百計的風箏在天空中飛。

adj. 一百的；一百個的

· I spent three **hundred** and twenty dollars on the ticket.
我花三百二十元買那張票。

6. hungry

[ˋhʌŋgrɪ]

be hungry to death
餓死了

be hungry for + N/
Ving 渴望得到～

adj. 餓的，飢餓的 ↔ full [fʊl] 飽的

· The **hungry** man has no money to buy any food.
那飢餓的男人沒錢可以買任何食物。

· I am *hungry to death*. Give me something to eat.
我餓死了，給我點吃的。

adj. 渴望的；渴求的

· Jim *is hungry* for a new bike.
吉姆渴望得到一輛新腳踏車。

7. hurry

[ˋhɝɪ]

Hurry up!
快點!

in a hurry
匆忙地

v.i. 趕忙

· If you don't **hurry**, you will miss the train.
如果你不快一點，你就會錯過火車。

· *Hurry up*! We have to catch the bus!
快一點! 我們得趕上公車。

v.t. 催促

· The mom **hurried** her son to put on his shoes.
這個媽媽催促她兒子穿好鞋子。

n. [U] 急忙；匆促；忙亂

· Austin was going to be late, so he ate his breakfast *in a hurry*.
奧斯汀快遲到了，所以他早餐吃得很匆忙。

H

8. hurt

[hɜt]

過去式	過去分詞	現在進行式
hurt [hɜt]	hurt [hɜt]	hurting [ˋhɜtɪŋ]

v.t. 傷害；使受傷；使疼痛

- Don't **hurt** the poor little animal.
  不要傷害這隻可憐的小動物。
- The cheap shoes **hurt** my feet.
  那雙便宜的鞋子把我的腳弄痛了。

be/get hurt
受傷

- Be careful not to *be*/*get* **hurt** when you cut the meat.
  在你切肉的時候要小心，不要受傷了。
- Ray *was*/*got* **hurt** in the game and was sent to the hospital.
  雷在比賽中受了傷，並被送往醫院。

v.i. 疼痛

- Ouch! You are stepping on my toe; it really **hurts**.
  唉唷！你踩到我的腳指了，真的好痛喔！

n. [C][U] 傷痛；傷害（精神上或肉體上的傷害都可用此字）

- Being cheated by her best friend was a real **hurt** to Janet.
  被最好的朋友欺騙對珍妮而言真的是個傷害。

9. husband

[ˋhʌzbənd]

n. [U] 先生；丈夫；老公 ↔ wift [waɪf] 妻子；老婆

- Barbara met her **husband** when she was twenty.
  芭芭拉在她二十歲的時候遇見她的老公。

10. ice

[aɪs]

n. [U] 冰

- When it is below 0°C, the water will turn to **ice**.
  當攝氏零度以下的時候，水就會變成冰。

adj. 冰的；冰製的

- Would you please give me a glass of **ice** water?
  請你給我一杯冰水好嗎？

I

練習題 (一)

Exercise 1

I. 字彙翻譯

1. 鐘頭 ＿＿＿＿＿＿＿＿
2. 如何 ＿＿＿＿＿＿＿＿
3. 百 ＿＿＿＿＿＿＿＿
4. 傷害 ＿＿＿＿＿＿＿＿
5. 冰 ＿＿＿＿＿＿＿＿

II. 字彙填充

＿＿＿＿＿＿＿＿ 1. I was tired and h＿＿＿＿y after walking for two hours.

＿＿＿＿＿＿＿＿ 2. Mr. Lin invited us to a party in his big h＿＿＿＿e on the hill.

＿＿＿＿＿＿＿＿ 3. The h＿＿＿＿d and wife love and take care of each other.

＿＿＿＿＿＿＿＿ 4. The boy did his homework in a h＿＿＿＿y because he wanted to go out to play.

＿＿＿＿＿＿＿＿ 5. I do want to go to the movies with you; h＿＿＿＿r, I have to work now.

III. 字彙選擇

(　) 1. It cost me five ＿＿＿＿＿ and eighty dollars to buy the book. It is so expensive.
(A) hour (B) hungry (C) hundred (D) husband

(　) 2. ＿＿＿＿＿ do you feel about that movie? Do you like it?
(A) House (B) Hour (C) However (D) How

(　) 3. I have to ＿＿＿＿＿ up now, or I will miss the train.
(A) hurry (B) hurt (C) hungry (D) hundred

(　) 4. I haven't had anything today, and I feel very ＿＿＿＿＿ now.
(A) hungry (B) hurry (C) hundred (D) husband

(　) 5. Cathy married her ＿＿＿＿＿ two years ago, and they have a baby now.
(A) house (B) husband (C) hundred (D) hour

158

11. ice cream
[ˋaɪsˌkrim]

n. [U] 冰淇淋
- I love eating **ice cream** on hot summer days.
  在炎炎夏日，我最愛吃冰淇淋了。

12. idea
[aɪˋdiə]

have no idea
不知道

n. [C] 主意；構想；概念；想法
- Good **idea**.
  好主意。
- Jimmy is a man with a lot of **ideas**.
  吉米是個有很多主意的人。
- I *have no idea* about the computer.
  對於電腦，我一竅不通。

13. if
[ɪf]

if only
但願

conj. 如果（表條件）
- **If** you have enough money, you can buy a sports car.
  如果你有足夠的錢，就可以買一部跑車。

conj. 假如，要是（表假設）
- **If** I were you, I would not buy that expensive ring.
  如果我是你，我就不會買那只昂貴的戒指。

conj. 是否；是不是
- I don't know **if** I should give it up.
  我不知道我是不是應該放棄。
- *If only* I could save all the poor people in Africa.
  但願我能救得了所有非洲可憐的人!

14. important
[ɪmˋpɔrtənt]

adj. 重要的，重大的
- I have something **important** to tell you.
  我有一件重要的事要告訴你。
- I think it's more **important** to understand than to know.
  我認為瞭解比光是知道重要多了。

15. in
[ɪn]

prep. 在～裡面；在～之中 ↔ out [aut] 在～之外
- Can you tell me who is **in** the classroom?
  你能告訴我是誰在教室裡嗎?

I

159

prep. 在～方面

- Tom has lots of experiences *in teaching* math.
  姆姆在教數學方面有很多的經驗。

注意

in 是介系詞，之後的動詞一定要用 Ving。

---

16. **inside**
[ɪn`saɪd]

n. [C] 內部；內側；裡面 ↔ outside [`aut`saɪd] 外部；外側

- The price tag is on the **inside** of the box.
  標價在盒子的內側。

adj. 裡面的；內在的 ↔ outside [`aut`saɪd] 外面的；外在的

- The **inside** wall of the house is painted green.
  房子內部的牆被漆成綠色。

adv. 在裡面；在室內 ↔ outside [`aut`saɪd] 在外面；在室外

- Al stayed **inside** all day long for it was very cold outside.
  因為外面很冷，艾爾整天都待在室內。

I

---

17. **interest**
[`ɪntərɪst]

have an interest in +
N/Ving 對～感興趣

n. [C][U] 興趣

- Paul has lost his **interest** in that game.
  保羅已經失去了他對於那個遊戲的興趣。

- Do you *have any* **interest** in listening to music?
  你對於聽音樂有沒有任何興趣？

v.t. 使～感興趣

- This comic book has **interested** many kids.
  這本漫畫已使許多小孩感到興趣。

---

18. **interested**
[`ɪntərɪstɪd]

be interested in + N/
Ving 對～感興趣

adj. 感興趣的

- Alice *is* very **interested** in singing and dancing.
  艾莉絲對於唱歌跳舞非常感興趣。

- *Are* you **interested** in comic books?
  你對漫畫有興趣嗎？

注意

有關情緒動詞的詳細用法請參閱附錄。

19. **interesting**
[`ɪntərɪstɪŋ]

adj. 有趣的；令人感興趣的

· I saw an **interesting** movie last night; it was really funny.
我昨天看了一部有趣的電影，真的很好笑。

注意
有關情緒動詞的詳細用法請參閱附錄。

20. **Internet**
[`ɪntɚˌnɛt]

n. 網際網路 (the Internet)

· Today, we can find almost anything through the **Internet**.
現在，經由網際網路我們幾乎可以找到任何東西。

I

休息一下喔！

Exercise 2

I. 字彙翻譯

1. 感興趣的 _____
2. 冰淇淋 _____
3. 令人感興趣的 _____
4. 如果 _____
5. 在～裡面 (*prep.*) _____

II. 字彙填充

_____ 1. Watching TV does not i_____t me at all. I like listening to music.

_____ 2. I have no i_____a what to do next.

_____ 3. This watch is very i_____t for me; my grandfather gave it to me.

_____ 4. Don't stay i_____e all day long. You should go out to take some exercise.

_____ 5. Many teenagers like to kill time in the I_____t café.

III. 字彙選擇

( ) 1. If you are _____ in mountain climbing, we can go together this Sunday.
    (A) interest   (B) interested   (C) interesting   (D) interests

( ) 2. I don't like _____, because it will make me fat.
    (A) inside   (B) interest   (C) idea   (D) ice cream

( ) 3. This is a very good _____. Let's just do it.
    (A) interest   (B) Internet   (C) ice   (D) idea

( ) 4. What I am going to say is very _____. You had better write it down.
    (A) important   (B) interested   (C) inside   (D) Internet

( ) 5. It is going to rain. Go _____ as soon as possible.
    (A) interest   (B) inside   (C) important   (D) Internet

Unit 21

1. island
[`aɪlənd]

a traffic island
安全島

n. [C] 島嶼

- Taiwan is an **island** country.
  台灣是個島國。
- He took a vacation on a small **island**.
  他在一座小島上渡假。
- The car hit the *traffic island* because the driver was drunk.
  因為司機喝醉酒，車子撞上了安全島。

2. jacket
[`dʒækɪt]

n. [C] 夾克

- Remember to put on your **jacket**; it is cold outside.
  記得穿上你的夾克，外頭很冷。

注意

coat 與 jacket 的比較請參見 Unit 9 的 coat。

3. jeans
[dʒinz]

a pair of jeans
一條牛仔褲

n. 牛仔褲

- Helen likes to wear (blue) **jeans** when working.
  海倫工作時喜歡穿牛仔褲。
- I bought *a new pair of jeans* in the department store.
  我在百貨公司買了一條新的牛仔褲。

注意

jeans 與 pants（褲子）都是只用複數形的名詞，因此要講幾條牛仔褲時，要用 pair 為單位。

4. job
[dʒɑb]

n. [C] 工作；職業

- Amelia is looking for a new **job** because she was fired.
  愛蜜莉雅正在找新工作，因為她被開除了。

注意

work 與 job 都可以解釋為「工作；職業」，但 job 為「可數名詞」，work 為「不可數名詞」。

J

163

| good job
表現好 | · You did a *good* *job*!
你表現的很好。 |

5. jog
[dʒɑg]

過去式	過去分詞	現在進行式
jogged [dʒɑgd]	jogged [dʒɑgd]	jogging [ˋdʒɑgɪŋ]

v.i. 慢跑

· I get up early and **jog** in the park every day.
我每天早起，在公園裡慢跑。

go jogging
去慢跑

· Since you want to exercise, let's *go* *jogging*.
既然你想運動，那我們就去慢跑吧。

n. [U] 慢跑

· **Jog** is a good exercise which can make you healthier.
慢跑是一項好運動，可以讓你更健康。

6. join
[dʒɔɪn]

v.t. 參加；加入；成為～的成員

· How much should I pay to **join** your club?
我應該付多少錢才能加入你們的俱樂部？

· Besides studying, I want to **join** more activities in school.
除了唸書，我想要多參加一些學校的活動。

7. joy
[dʒɔɪ]

n. [U] 喜悅；高興；歡樂

· Spending the weekend with my friends brings me a lot of **joy**.
和朋友們共度週末帶給我許多歡樂。

8. juice
[dʒus]

n. [U] 果汁

· Which do you like? Orange or apple **juice**?
你喜歡哪一個？柳橙汁還是蘋果汁？

a glass of juice
一杯果汁

· I like to have *a glass of* orange **juice** every morning.
我喜歡每天早上喝一杯柳橙汁。

9. jump
[dʒʌmp]

v.i. 跳；跳躍

· Hannah runs fast and **jumps** high. She is good at sports.
漢娜跑得快又跳得高。她很擅長於運動。

v.t. 跳過；越過

· The horse **jumped** the wall and ran to the grass.
那馬兒跳過牆，朝著草地跑去。

10. **junior high school**

[ˌdʒunjɚˈhaɪ ˌskul]

n. [C][U] 國中；初級中學

· My sister is thirteen and still studies in **junior high school**.
我妹妹現在十三歲，還在國中就讀。

· junior　年紀輕輕的；資淺的

J

休息一下喔！

Exercise 1

I. 字彙翻譯

1. 職業 _____
2. 參加 _____
3. 果汁 _____
4. 跳躍 _____
5. 喜悅 _____

II. 字彙填充

_____ 1. Taiwan is a beautiful i_____d, which is also called "Formosa."

_____ 2. More and more people like to go j_____gging to stay healthy.

_____ 3. Wear your j_____s when you go camping in the mountains.

_____ 4. You had better put on a j_____t. It's pretty cold outside.

_____ 5. Students in j_____r high school always have lots of tests and homework.

III. 字彙選擇

( ) 1. Little Johnny _____ on the bed like a monkey and laughed loudly.

    (A) joined   (B) jogged   (C) jumped   (D) juice

( ) 2. Don't be lazy anymore, or you will soon lose your _____.

    (A) job   (B) jump   (C) jog   (D) joy

( ) 3. Karen's heart is filled with _____ because she gave birth to a baby last week.

    (A) juice   (B) joy   (C) job   (D) jog

( ) 4. We are going to play basketball. Do you want to _____ us?

    (A) join   (B) jog   (C) jump   (D) juice

( ) 5. I like to drink orange _____. It's better for my health than Coke.

    (A) jeans   (B) juice   (C) jacket   (D) joy

J

11. **just**
[dʒʌst]

adv. 只是，僅僅 = only [ˋonlɪ]

· I spent **just** a few minutes to finish the easy job.
我只花了短短幾分鐘做完這簡單的工作。

· Don't take it too seriously. I was **just** kidding.
不要太嚴肅。我只是開玩笑。

adv. 正要，剛要

· Anderson came to my house when I **just** wanted to call him.
當我正要打電話給安德森的時候，他來到我家。

just now　剛才

· I finished my job *just* now.
我剛剛才做完我的工作。

12. **keep**
[kip]

過去式	過去分詞	現在進行式
kept [kɛpt]	kept [kɛpt]	keep [ˋkipɪŋ]

v.t. 持有；保有

· Sally **keeps** the letter her boyfriend wrote to her all the time.
莎莉一直都保有著她男朋友寫給她的那封信。

v.t. v.i. 保持；持續不斷

· When you get into the library, you should **keep** quiet.
當你進入圖書館時，你應該保持安靜。

· It has **kept** raining for more than two weeks.
已經持續下雨超過兩個星期了。

注意
keep 當「保持」或「持續」時，後面接形容詞或 Ving。

v.t. 阻止；妨礙；使不能～

keep + N + from + N/Ving　使遠離～

· Parents should *keep* their children *from* fire.
父母應該讓小孩子離火遠些／無法接近火。

keep away from
不接近～；離開～

· Teenagers should *keep* away from bad friends.
青少年應該遠離壞朋友。

v.t. 記（日記、帳本等）

keep (one's / a / the) diary　寫日記

· Do you have the habit of *keeping a diary*?
你有寫日記的習慣嗎?

K

v.t. 撫養；飼養

- My family **keep** two dogs and three rabbits in the house.
  我家人在屋子裡養了兩隻狗和三隻兔子。

13. **key**
[ki]

n. [C] 鑰匙

- I forgot to bring my **keys**, so I could not open the door.
  我忘了帶鑰匙，所以我沒辦法開門。

n. [C] 祕訣

the key to + N/Ving
～的祕訣

- Working hard is *the key to* success.
  努力工作是成功的祕訣。

adj. 關鍵的；主要的

- Please find out the **key** word in this sentence.
  請找出這個句子裡的關鍵字。

14. **kick**
[kɪk]

v.t. 踢

- You shouldn't **kick** the dog like that.
  你不該那樣子踢這隻狗。

kick out
解雇～；踢～出去

- Celia was *kicked* out for she was lazy.
  希莉雅被解雇了，因為她很懶惰。

K

15. **kid**
[kɪd]

n. [C] 小孩子 = child [tʃaɪld]

- Dolly is a good **kid**; all teachers like her.
  桃莉是個好孩子；所有的老師都喜歡她。

v.i. 取笑；戲弄

- Are you **kidding**?
  你是在開玩笑吧?

16. **kill**
[kɪl]

v.i., v.t. 殺；宰；致死

- Kim was afraid when he saw his mother **killing** the fish.
  當金恩看到他媽媽在殺魚時，他很害怕。

- Three people were **killed** in the typhoon.
  有三個人在颱風中喪生了。

· These medicines could **kill** if you take too much of it.
如果你服用太多這種藥物，就可能會致死。

v.t. 消磨（時間）

kill time
消磨時間

· I like to read some books to *kill* time on Sunday afternoon.
禮拜天的下午，我喜歡閱讀來消磨時間。

---

17. **kilogram**
[`kɪləˌgræm]

n. [C] 公斤 = kg

· Do you know how many **kilograms** an elephant weighs?
你知不知道一隻大象有幾公斤重？

---

18. **kind**
[kaɪnd]

n. [C] 種；種類

· There are many **kinds** of TV programs for you to watch.
有許多種電視節目你可以收看。

all kinds of + N
各式各樣的～

· There are *all kinds* of animals in the zoo.
動物園裡有各式各樣的動物。

adj. 仁慈的；親切的

· Dr. Lin is such a **kind** old man that every kid loves him.
林醫師是個很親切的老先生，每個小孩都喜歡他。

---

19. **king**
[kɪŋ]

n. [C] 國王；君主 ↔ queen [`kwin] 女王；王后

· The **king** has ruled the country for twenty years.
這國王已經統治這個國家二十年了。

K

---

20. **kiss**
[kɪs]

v.t. 親；親吻；接吻

· She **kisses** her husband before he goes to work every morning.
她在她老公每天早上上班之前，都會親他一下。

v.i. 接吻

· The young lovers **kiss** in public.
那對年輕情侶當眾接吻。

n. [C] 吻；親吻

· Mother gave me a **kiss** before I went to bed.
在我睡前，媽媽親了我一下。

Exercise 2

I. 字彙翻譯

1. 鑰匙 _____

2. 小孩 _____

3. 種類 _____

4. 國王 _____

5. 保持（動詞三態） _____ _____ _____

II. 字彙填充

_____ 1. The mom k_____ses her girl to show her love.

_____ 2. Sam is only ten years old but he is fifty k_____ms. I think he is too fat.

_____ 3. John was k_____ked by a horse on the back yesterday.

_____ 4. Don't push him too hard. He is j_____t a ten-year-old boy.

_____ 5. I usually play basketball to k_____l time on Sundays.

III. 字彙選擇

(　　) 1. The baby _____ crying all morning and nothing could stop him.

　　(A) killed 　　　　(B) kissed 　　　　(C) kicked 　　　　(D) kept

(　　) 2. I think the _____ to the problem has not been found.

　　(A) key 　　　　(B) kid 　　　　(C) king 　　　　(D) kiss

(　　) 3. He is so _____ that we all like him.

　　(A) kiss 　　　　(B) kind 　　　　(C) kick 　　　　(D) king

(　　) 4. Fire might _____ you if you don't use it carefully.

　　(A) keep 　　　　(B) kick 　　　　(C) kill 　　　　(D) kiss

(　　) 5. We are _____ friends. You don't have to think too much.

　　(A) juice 　　　　(B) just 　　　　(C) jump 　　　　(D) junior

K

Unit 22

1. kitchen
[`kɪtʃɪn]

n. [C] 廚房
- Mother was preparing our dinner in the **kitchen**.
  媽媽正在廚房裡準備我們的晚餐。

2. kite
[kaɪt]

fly a kite
放風箏

n. [C] 風箏
- Do you see those colorful **kites** in the sky?
  你有沒有看見天空中那些色彩鮮豔的風箏?
- My dad taught me how to *fly a kite*.
  我爸爸教我怎麼放風箏。

3. knee
[ni]

on one knee
單膝下跪

n. [C] 膝蓋; 膝部
- The young woman wears a skirt above her **knees**.
  那名年輕女子穿了一件長度不到膝蓋的裙子。
- Jack got down *on one knee* and asked Rose to marry him.
  傑克單膝跪在地上,要求蘿絲嫁給他。

注意
　　單膝下跪叫做 on one knee,如果兩隻腳都下跪,就叫做 on the knees(雙腳下跪)或者 on one's knees(某人雙腳下跪)。

4. knife
[naɪf]

n. [C] 刀; 小刀; 菜刀(複數: knives)
- The cook cut the meat into small pieces with a **knife**.
  那廚師用一把菜刀把肉切成小塊。
- When you eat steak, you have to use a **knife** and a fork.
  當你吃牛排的時候,你需要使用刀叉。

5. knock
[nɑk]

knock out + sb
擊倒～

v.t. v.i. 敲; 擊; 打; 敲打
- Somebody is **knocking** (at/on) the door. Go and see who it is.
  有人在敲門。去看看是誰吧。
- Rocky *knocked* the black man *out* in thirty seconds.
  洛基在三十秒內就擊倒了那個黑人。

K

補完

knock out 兩字可合併為一個字：knockout，此時可當及物動詞或名詞，同樣是「擊倒」的意思，可簡稱為 KO。

n. [C] 敲；敲打

- I felt a **knock** on my head and after that, I passed out.
  我感覺到頭被敲了一下，在那之後，我就昏倒了。

6. **know**
[no]

過去式	過去分詞	現在進行式
knew [nju]	known [non]	knowing [`noɪŋ]

v.t. v.i. 知道；得知

- How could I **know** the fact if nobody told me?
  如果沒人告訴過我的話，我怎麼可能知道事實？

v.i. 瞭解，懂得

know about/of
瞭解～

- I don't **know** much *about/of* cameras.
  我對照相機瞭解的不多。
- Nobody **knows** what the movie is talking about?
  沒人懂得那部電影在說些什麼。

v.t. 認識

- Do you **know** the tall boy with a blue hat?
  你認識那個戴著藍帽子的高個子男孩嗎？

7. **knowledge**
[`nɑlɪdʒ]

n. [U] 知識；學識；學問

- **Knowledge** is power.
  知識就是力量。

8. **lake**
[lek]

n. [C] 湖泊

- There are many fish in the **lake** near the mountain.
  在那山旁邊的湖裡有許多的魚。

9. **lamp**
[læmp]

n. [C] 燈；燈火

- Father turned on the desk **lamp** and started to read.
  爸爸打開書桌上的燈，開始閱讀。

L

10. **land**
[lænd]

n. [U] 土地；陸地

- Do you know how much **land** Mr. Wang owns in the country?
  你知不知道王先生在鄉下擁有多少土地？
- Elephants are the biggest animals on **land**.
  大象是陸地上最大的動物。

v.i. 登陸；降落

- The plane **landed** and everyone was safe and sound.
  飛機降落，且每個人都安然無恙。

休息一下喔！

L

Exercise 1

I. 字彙翻譯

1. 膝蓋 _____　　2. 敲打 _____　　3. 土地 _____

4. 湖泊 _____　　5. 知道（三態） _____ _____

II. 字彙填充

_____ 1. The more books we read, the more k_____e we get.

_____ 2. Reading without a l_____p at night would hurt your eyes.

_____ 3. There are a lot of foods and drinks in the k_____n.

_____ 4. Keep the k_____e away from small children. It's very dangerous.

_____ 5. Do you know how to fly a k_____e high in the sky?

III. 字彙選擇

( ) 1. The mother put _____ in a high place, so her kids could not play with them.

　　(A) kitchens　　　　(B) knees　　　　(C) knives　　　　(D) kings

( ) 2. I _____ lots of new friends in the English Camp last week.

　　(A) kissed　　　　(B) knew　　　　(C) knocked　　　　(D) kicked

( ) 3. I don't want to leave my country _____ all my life.

　　(A) lamp　　　　(B) land　　　　(C) lake　　　　(D) late

( ) 4. If you want to get more _____ about Chinese history, you can have a talk with Mr. Wang.

　　(A) knowledge　　　(B) kitchen　　　(C) kilogram　　　(D) knife

( ) 5. Some people believe that _____ on the wood will bring them good luck.

　　(A) knowing　　　　(B) knocking　　　(C) kissing　　　(D) kicking

L

11. language

[`læŋgwɪdʒ]

mother language
母語

n. [C] 語言

- Janet can speak several **languages** like English and French.
  珍納會說好幾種語言，像是英文和法文。
- Joe is an American, and his *mother **language*** is English.
  喬是美國人，他的母語是英語。

12. large

[lɑrdʒ]

adj. 大的；寬大的 = big [bɪg]

- That was really a **large** box; I can put all my things in it.
  那真是一個好大的箱子，我可以把我所有的東西裝進去。

13. last

[læst]

at last = finally
最後；終於

adj. 最後的 ↔ first [fɜˑst] 第一的

- Peter was the **last** one to arrive at school; he was late.
  彼得最後一個到校，他遲到了。

adv. 最後；上一次

- When did you **last** see your elementary school teacher?
  你上一次看到你的小學老師是何時?

- After five years, the writer finished her book *at **last***.
  五年之後，那個作家終於寫完了她的書。

v.i. 持續

- The meeting **lasted** for hours, and everyone felt tired.
  會議持續了幾個小時，每個人都累了。

L

14. late

[let]

be late for + N
於～場合遲到

adj. 晚的；遲的；遲到的 ↔ early [`ɜˑlɪ] 早的

- You had better go home quickly. It's very **late** now.
  你最好快回家。現在很晚了。

- If you *are **late** for* work again, you will be fired.
  如果你再上班遲到，你就會被開除。

adv. 晚；遲到

- Kelly got up too **late** this morning and couldn't catch the bus.
  凱莉今天早上太晚起床，所以趕不上公車。

15. **later**
[ˋletɚ]

adv. 較晚地；更晚地

- I am very busy now; I will call you **later**.
  我現在很忙。我晚一點會打給你。
- I will come home **later** today. Don't wait for me.
  我今天會比較晚回家。不用等我了。

adv. 以後；後來

- It was the last time I saw him; I haven't seen him **later**.
  那是我最後一次看到他，後來我就沒再見過他了。

adj. 以後的

- We will learn more knowledge in the **later** classes.
  在以後的課程中，我們將會學到更多知識。

比較

later [ˋletɚ]	*adj.* 以後的；較晚的；更晚的 ↔ earlier [ˋɝlɪr]
	• In my **later** life, I want to live in the country. 在我的晚年，我希望在鄉下生活。
latter [ˋlætɚ]	*adj.* 後面的；（兩者中）後者的 ↔ former [ˋfɔrmɚ]
	• The latter part of the story is more interesting than the former. 這個故事的後半部份比前半部份要有趣。

◎這兩個字在拼字及意義上都很容易混淆，要特別注意。

16. **laugh**
[læf]

laugh at + sb
嘲笑某人

v.i. 笑 ↔ cry [kraɪ] 哭

- We all **laughed** when we heard the funny joke.
  當我們聽到這個好笑的笑話時，全都笑了。
- You should help the poor boy, not *laugh* at him.
  你應該幫助這個可憐的男孩，而不是嘲笑他。

17. **lazy**
[ˋlezɪ]

adj. 懶惰的；怠惰的

- You should study hard. Girls do not like **lazy** boys like you.
  你應該用功讀書。女孩子們不喜歡像你一樣懶惰的男孩。

L

18. **lead**
[lid]

過去式	過去分詞	現在進行式
led [lɛd]	led [lɛd]	leading [ˋlidɪŋ]

v.t. v.i. 領導；帶領

- The waiter **led** me into the dining room.
  侍者領著我進入飯廳。

lead to + N/Ving
導致～

- The strong typhoon *led to* the heavy rain for days.
  強烈颱風導致連續好幾天的豪雨。

19. **leader**
[ˋlidɚ]

n. [C] 領導者；領隊

- A **leader** should be wiser than the common people.
  一個領導者必須比一般人更有智慧。

a class leader
班長

- Anne is our *class leader*. She is smart and popular.
  安是我們的班長，她既聰明又受歡迎。

20. **learn**
[lɝn]

v.t. v.i. 學習

- I want to **learn** new things every day.
  我希望每天都能學習到新的東西。

- You should **learn** from mistakes, not repeat them.
  你應該從錯誤中學習，而不是重複犯同樣的錯誤。

v.t. 得知 = know [no]

- I was so surprised when I **learned** that Mike is my brother.
  當我得知邁可是我兄弟時，我很驚訝。

L

Exercise 2

I. 字彙翻譯

1. 較晚地 _____ 2. 語言 _____ 3. 懶惰的 _____

4. 最後的 _____ 5. 領導（動詞三態） _____ _____ _____

II. 字彙填充

_____ 1. I need a l_____e box to put all these heavy books.

_____ 2. He is a bad boy. He always l_____hs at others.

_____ 3. The teacher told John not to be l_____e for school again.

_____ 4. Paul is a good l_____r; we believe that he could bring us a better life.

_____ 5. I have l_____ned English for several years.

III. 字彙選擇

( ) 1. Tim is a _____ man. He does nothing but eat and sleep all day long.

    (A) last   (B) late   (C) lazy   (D) large

( ) 2. Don't worry. I will help you with your homework _____.

    (A) lamp   (B) late   (C) last   (D) later

( ) 3. Drunken driving often _____ to car accidents.

    (A) laughs   (B) leads   (C) lasts   (D) learns

( ) 4. Norman is the _____ person who knows the news.

    (A) last   (B) late   (C) later   (D) lazy

( ) 5. Joe could speak Chinese very well, even though it is not his mother _____.

    (A) language   (B) land   (C) leader   (D) lamp

L

Unit 23

1. **least**
[list]

原級	比較級	最高級
little [ˋlɪtḷ]	less [lɛs]	least [list]

adj. 最少的，最小的 ↔ most [most] 最多的

- She has the **least** money among us.

  她在我們之中錢最少。

adv. 最少地；最小地

- He is the **least** hard-working man of us; he is very lazy.

  他是我們之中最不努力工作的；他很懶惰。

at least
至少

- Don't be too sad. You have tried your best *at least*.

  別太難過。至少你已經盡力了。

2. **leave**
[liv]

過去式	過去分詞	現在進行式
left [lɛft]	left [lɛft]	leaving [ˋlivɪŋ]

v.t. v.i. 離開 ↔ stay [ste] 留下

- Don't **leave** us without saying goodbye.

  不要沒說一聲再見就離開我們。（不要與我們不告而別。）

leave for + N
前往～（某地）

- Diana will *leave for* New York to study art in two weeks.

  黛安娜將在兩個禮拜內前往紐約學習藝術。

v.t. 忘了帶～；丟下～

- I can't find my key. Maybe I **left** it in the office.

  我找不到我的鑰匙。也許我把它留在辦公室了。

leave behind + N
忘了帶～；留下～

- I *left* my umbrella *behind* this morning and it is raining now.

  今天早上我忘了帶我的傘而且現在下雨了。

v.t. 留給～（某人）（某物）

- The father **left** his son nothing after he died.

  那位父親死後沒有留給他兒子東西。

注意

　　葉子 (leaf) 的複數是 leaves，跟以第三人稱單數為主詞時所使用的動詞「離開」(leaves) 一樣，請不要搞混。

L

3. **left**
[lɛft]

v.t. v.i. leave（離開）的「過去式」和「過去分詞」

· I **left** the party early for I felt tired.
因為我覺得疲倦，所以提早離開了宴會。

adj. 左邊的 ↔ right [raɪt] 右邊的

· Turn right and you will see the church on the **left** side.
右轉，然後你就會在左（手）邊看到那間教堂。

adv. 向左；在左邊

· Should I turn **left** or right at the traffic light?
在我走到紅綠燈的時候，應該向左還是向右轉？

4. **leg**
[lɛg]

on one's legs
站著

n. [C] 腿；小腿

· Max got hurt in his left **leg** and could not walk now.
馬克斯的左腿受傷了，所以沒辦法走路。

· The salesman has to work *on his legs* all day.
那個店員必須一整天都站著工作。

5. **lemon**
[ˋlɛmən]

lemonade
檸檬水

n. [C][U] 檸檬

· Few people eat **lemon** because it is very sour.
很少人會吃檸檬，因為它非常酸。

· I ordered a glass of **lemonade** in the tea shop.
我在茶館點了一杯檸檬水。

6. **lend**
[lɛnd]

lend sb sth
借給某人某物
lend sth to sb
將某物借給某人

過去式	過去分詞	現在進行式
lent [lɛnt]	lent [lɛnt]	lending [ˋlɛndɪŋ]

v.t. 借；借出

· I forgot to bring my money. Could you **lend** me some?
我忘了帶錢。你可以借我一點嗎？

· I *lent* a pencil *to* Tom.
我借了一支鉛筆給湯姆。

注意

borrow 與 lend 的比較請參見 Unit 5 的 borrow。

L

7. **less**

[lɛs]

原級	比較級	最高級
little [`lɪtl̩]	less [lɛs]	least [list]

adj. 較少的；較小的 ↔ more [mor] 較多的

- I have **less** time than I thought, so I can't finish the job in time.
  我有的時間比我預料的少，所以我不能及時完成這項工作。

adv. 較少地；較小地

- The blue T-shirt is not bad; besides, it is **less** expensive.
  這件藍運動衫不錯；此外它也比較不貴。

8. **lesson**

[`lɛsn̩]

n. [C] 課程

- Pamela'll have her piano **lesson** at three p.m.
  潘蜜拉下午三點要上鋼琴課。

n. [C] （課本中的）一課

- **Lesson** One talks about how to learn English well.
  第一課講的是如何把英文學好。

n. [C] 教訓，訓誡

- The poor grades will be a good **lesson** for Tom to study hard.
  這壞成績將給湯姆一個很好的教訓，讓他用功唸書。

9. **let**

[lɛt]

過去式	過去分詞	現在進行式
let [lɛt]	let [lɛt]	letting [`lɛtɪŋ]

L

v.t. 讓；使

- My mom would never **let** me stay outside after 10 o'clock p.m.
  我媽媽絕不會讓我在晚上十點以後還待在外面。

let's = let us
[口語] 讓我們～

- "Do you want to play basketball?" "Sure, *let's* go".
  「你想打籃球嗎?」「當然，我們走吧。」

注意
let 為「使役動詞」，故後面的動詞用原形動詞。

let + sb + down
使～失望

- I believe you can make it. Don't *let* me *down*.
  我相信你辦的到。不要讓我失望。

10. **letter**
[`lɛtɚ`]

n. [C] 信，信件 = mail [mel]

· Write a **letter** to me when you arrive in New York City.

在你抵達紐約市的時候，寫封信給我。

n. [C] 字母

· There are twenty-six **letters** in the English language.

英文裡有二十六個字母。

休息一下喔！

L

Exercise 1

I. 字彙翻譯

1. 小腿 _____

2. 檸檬 _____

3. 左邊的 _____

4. 借出 _____

5. 讓（三態）_____ _____ _____

II. 字彙填充

_____ 1. Don't l_____e your baby at home without anybody else. It is not safe.

_____ 2. I keep in touch with my old friends by writing l_____rs to them.

_____ 3. We didn't make it, but at l_____t we had done our best.

_____ 4. How many l_____ns do you usually have in school every day?

_____ 5. You should spend more time on your studies and l_____s time on TV.

III. 字彙選擇

( ) 1. I didn't wear my glasses, so I couldn't see the _____ on the blackboard.

(A) leaves (B) leaders (C) lemons (D) letters

( ) 2. I _____ some interesting books to Amy.

(A) lent (B) learned (C) let (D) learned

( ) 3. Peter can write with both his _____ and right hand.

(A) lemon (B) least (C) left (D) less

( ) 4. Bill is studying _____ Eight because he will have a test on it tomorrow.

(A) Lesson (B) Lemon (C) Letter (D) Leader

( ) 5. At _____ five classmates will come to John's birthday party, and there might be more.

(A) last (B) least (C) less (D) late

L

11. library
[ˋlaɪˏbrɛrɪ]

n. [C] 圖書館（複數：libraries）

- Amy went to the **library** to borrow some books.
  艾咪去圖書館借一些書。

12. lie
[laɪ]

v.i. 說謊

過去式	過去分詞	現在進行式
lied [laɪd]	lied [laɪd]	lying [ˋlaɪɪŋ]

lie to + sb
對～說謊

- Don't **lie** *to* me. Tell me what happened.
  不要對我說謊了。告訴我發生什麼事。

n. [C] 謊話 ↔ fact [fækt] 事實

- What he said was a **lie**.
  他說的是謊話。

tell a lie
說謊話

- If you *tell a lie* to me again, I will never believe you.
  如果你再對我說謊話，我就永遠不會相信你了。

a white lie
白色謊言；善意的
／無惡意的謊言

- When Maria asked how I felt about her work, I told *a white lie*.
  當瑪麗亞問我對她的作品有什麼感想的時候，我說了一個善意的謊言。

v.i. 躺；臥

過去式	過去分詞	現在進行式
lay [le]	lain [len]	lying [ˋlaɪɪŋ]

- **Lie** down in the bed if you don't feel well.
  如果你覺得不太舒服，就到床上躺著。

13. life
[laɪf]

n. [C] 一生（複數：lives [laɪvz]）

- Potter's **life** was full of surprise.
  波特的一生充滿了驚奇。

n. [C] 性命（複數：lives [laɪvz]）

- The doctor saved the kid's **life** in time.
  那醫生及時救了這小孩一命。

L

live/lead a... life
過著～的生活

n. [C][U] 生活（複數：lives [laɪvz]）

- I like to *lead a* quiet *life* in the country.
  我喜歡在鄉村過著安靜的生活。

n. [U] 生命；生存

- Make good use of your time, because **life** is short.
  好好利用你的時間，因為生命是短暫的。

14. **light**
[laɪt]

n. [U] 光；光線；光亮

- It would hurt your eyes if you read without enough **light**.
  如果你在沒有足夠光線的狀況下閱讀，就會損壞你的眼睛。

n. [C][U] 燈

turn on/off the light
打開／關上燈

- It's getting dark. Please *turn on the* **light**.
  天色暗了。請開燈。

adj. 輕的 ↔ heavy [ˋhɛvɪ] 重的

- This box is very **light**; I can move it easily.
  這箱子很輕，我可以輕易地移動它。

v.t. v.i. 點燃；照亮

過去式	過去分詞	現在進行式
lighted [ˋlaɪtɪd]; lit [lɪt]	lighted [ˋlaɪtɪd]; lit [lɪt]	lighting [ˋlaɪtɪŋ]

- The man **lit** the fire to keep himself warm.
  那男人點燃了爐火，讓自己保持溫暖。

light up + N
點燃～；照亮～

- There is an old English song called "You *Light Up* My Life."
  有一首英文老歌叫做「你照亮我的生命」。

15. **like**
[laɪk]

v.t. 喜歡～

- Mary **likes** the doll very much and wants to buy it.
  瑪莉非常喜歡那個洋娃娃，並希望能夠買下它。

- Susan **likes** to go shopping on weekends.
  蘇珊喜歡在週末的時候去逛街。

if you like
如果你樂意

- You can go to the movies with me *if you like*.
  如果你樂意的話，可以和我一起去看電影。

prep. 像～

- The boy looks so much **like** his father.
  這個男孩看起來好像他爸爸。

16. line
[laɪn]

n. [C] 線；界線

- The **line** between good and evil is not always clear.
  善與惡之間的界線並不總是清楚明顯的。

n. [C] 列；排；行列

- There is a long **line** of people waiting in front of the restaurant.
  在這間餐廳前面有一長排的人在等著。

n. [C] （詩文的）行

- He wrote some **lines** on a piece of paper.
  他在一張紙上寫下了幾行詩。

read between the lines
領悟言外之意

- He didn't mean what he said; you must *read between the lines*.
  他說的並不是他想表達的，你必須領悟他的言外之意。

line up
排隊

v.i. 排隊

- We should *line up* when getting on the bus.
  我們上公車時應該排隊。

17. lion
[ˋlaɪən]

n. [C] 獅子

- **Lions** and tigers are the most dangerous animals in the zoo.
  獅子和老虎是動物園裡最危險的動物。

18. lip
[lɪp]

n. [C] 嘴唇（通常用複數，因為有上下兩片）

- The man kissed the woman on the **lips**.
  那男人親吻了女人的嘴唇。

- Mary is a beautiful woman with big eyes and sexy **lips**.
  瑪麗是個有大眼睛和性感雙唇的美女。

L

19. **list**
[lɪst]

n. [C] 條列；名冊；清單

· Could you give me the **list** of the students?
你可以把學生名冊給我嗎?

· The teacher wrote down the name of the student in the **list**.
老師在名冊裡寫下這個學生的名字。

v.t. 把～編成表；把～編入目錄；把～列成清單

· Mother **listed** the things she wanted to buy on a piece of paper.
媽媽把她想買的東西在紙上列成清單。

20. **listen**
[`lɪsn̩]

v.i. 聽；傾聽；仔細聽

· **Listen**/Hear! There is a strange noise outside.
聽! 外面有一個怪聲。

注意

hear 和 listen 的比較請參見 Unit 18 的 hear。

v.i. 聽從

listen to + N
聽～；聽從～

· Be sure to *listen* to what your teacher says in class.
務必聽從老師在課堂上所說的話。

listen to music
聽音樂

· I always *listen* to music when I study.
我總是邊唸書邊聽音樂。

L

187

Exercise 2

I. 字彙翻譯

1. 獅子 _____

2. 嘴唇 _____

3. 清單 _____

4. 界線 _____

5. 躺；臥（三態） _____ _____ _____

II. 字彙填充

_____ 1. Please l_____n to me when I talk to you.

_____ 2. It is too dark in the room. Would you please turn on the l_____t?

_____ 3. If you feel it too noisy in the classroom, you can go to the l_____y to study.

_____ 4. Several l_____es were taken away by the big fire.

_____ 5. The two girls look l_____e each other. They must be sisters.

III. 字彙選擇

( ) 1. If you want to buy the movie ticket, please _____ up.

    (A) list   (B) lie   (C) line   (D) lip

( ) 2. Don't believe that little girl again. She has _____ to me several times.

    (A) lay   (B) lied   (C) lain   (D) lies

( ) 3. _____ what you want to buy in the market, and I will buy them for you.

    (A) List   (B) Listen   (C) Line   (D) Light

( ) 4. James _____ to play basketball. He plays it almost every day.

    (A) lines   (B) likes   (C) lights   (D) lies

( ) 5. It is not good to tell a _____ to your parents.

    (A) line   (B) life   (C) lion   (D) lie

L

Unit 24

1. little
[ˋlɪtḷ]

adj. 小的
- This is my **little** sister; she is only three months old.
  這是我小妹，她才三個月大而已。

adj. 少的；幾乎沒有的

原級	比較級	最高級
little [ˋlɪtḷ]	less [lɛs]	least [list]

- There is **little** rice left; it would not be enough for all of us.
  只剩下很少的米了，這不夠我們全部的人吃。

注意

few 以及 a few 後面接可數名詞 *n.* [C]，little 和 a little 後接不可數名詞 *n.* [U]，四者間的比較可參見 Unit 1 的 a few。

adv. 少；毫不
- Ron eats **little** in order to be thin.
  為了要變瘦，朗吃的很少。

little by little
逐漸地
- Ben ate more and more and grew fat *little by little*.
  班吃的越來越多，所以逐漸地變胖了。

2. live
[lɪv]

v.i. 居住
- I was born in Taipei, but I have **lived** in Hsin-chu for ten years.
  我在台北出生，但是我住在新竹已經十年了。

live with + sb
與～同住
- Mary *lived with* her grandfather when she was a kid.
  瑪麗在她小時候跟她的祖父住在一起。

v.i. 活著 ↔ die [daɪ] 死
- Few people in the town **lived** after the fire.
  在火災之後，在那村子裡幾乎沒有人還活著。

v.t. 過～生活

live a + Adj + life
過著～的生活
- The old man *lives a* simple *life* in the mountain.
  那個老人在山中過著簡樸的生活。

L

[laɪv]

adj. 實況轉播的；現場的

· Ted watched a **live** baseball game last Sunday.

泰德上星期日看了一場實況轉播的棒球賽。

3. **living room**

[ˋlɪvɪŋ͵rum]

n. [C] 客廳

· 3LDK means a house with three bedrooms, a **living room**, a dining room and a kitchen.

3LDK 的意思是指有三間臥室、一個客廳、一個餐廳和一個廚房的房子。

· Jack is watching TV in the **living room**.

傑克正在客廳裡看電視。

4. **lonely**

[ˋlonlɪ]

adj. 孤單的；寂寞的

· Joe feels **lonely** for there is no one he can talk to.

喬覺得寂寞，因為沒人可以跟他說話。

· Joan has been feeling **lonely** since her pet dog got lost.

自從瓊的寵物狗狗失蹤之後，她一直覺得很孤單。

5. **long**

[lɔŋ]

adj. （距離）長的；遠的 ↔ short [ʃɔrt] 短的

· Cheer up. We have still a **long** way to go.

振作起來。我們還有很遠的路要走呢。

adj. （時間）長久的

· **Long** time ago, there was a witch living in the forest.

很久以前有一個巫婆住在森林裡。

· Henry has been waiting for his girlfriend for a **long** time.

亨利已經等他女朋友很久了。

6. **look**

[lʊk]

v.i. 看

· **Look**! There is an airplane flying high.

看！有架飛機在高處飛翔。

look at + N
看著～

· Please **look** *at* me when I am talking to you.
當我在跟你說話時，請看著我。

look [ˋlʊk]	*v.i.* 看 (+ at)
	· **Look** at that picture. It is a beautiful garden. 看那幅畫，是一個漂亮的花園。
see [si]	*v.t.* 看；看見
	· I will see a movie tonight. 我今天晚上要去看電影。
watch [watʃ]	*v.t.*, *v.i.* 看；觀看
	· I don't like to watch TV. I like reading books. 我不喜歡看電視，我喜歡唸書。

◎雖然中文都是翻譯為「看」，但「看一幅畫」用的動詞是 look at，「看電影」用的動詞是 see，「看電視」用的動詞是 watch，可不能搞混喔！

v.i. 看起來～；好像～

· Howard **looked** very sad after he knew his grades in math.
霍華在知道自己的數學成績之後，看起來非常難過。

· The woman is so beautiful; she **looks** like a movie star.
這個女人很美，看起來像個電影明星。

v.i. 注意；留神

Look out!
小心！注意！
look after + N
照顧～
look for + N
尋找～
look forward to + N/
Ving 盼望～
look up + N
查詢～

· **Look** *out*! There is a car coming.
小心！有輛車過來了。

· I **looked** *after* my little sister when my parents were not home.
我父母不在家的時候，我照顧我的小妹妹。

· I am **looking** *for* my blue T-shirt. Did you see it today?
我正在找我的藍色 T 恤。你今天有看到它嗎?

· We **look** *forward to* your coming every day.
我們每天都盼望著你的到來。

· You can **look** *up* the new words in the dictionary.
你可以在字典裡查這些新字。

L

7. **lose**
[luz]

過去式	過去分詞	現在進行式
lost [lɔst]	lost [lɔst]	losing [ˋluzɪŋ]

v.t. v.i. 未贏得～；輸～；失敗

- The Lakers **lost** the game by only two points.
  湖人隊以兩分之差輸了那場比賽。
- I won, and you **lost**.
  我贏，而你輸了。

v.t. 遺失～；把～弄丟了

- Winnie **lost** her ring when she went shopping last Friday.
  維妮上禮拜五去逛街的時候，把她的戒指弄丟了。

v.t. 失去～；喪失～ ↔ get [gɛt] 得到

- I don't want to **lose** you; please give me a chance to make it up.
  我不想失去你。請給我一個補償的機會。

lose one's job
失業

- Carl *lost his job* and stayed at home all day long.
  卡爾失業了，所以整天待在家裡。

lose one's way = get
lost　迷路

- Diane *lost her way*/got lost in the city and found no way out.
  黛安在城市裡迷了路，找不到路出去。

lose (one's) weight
減肥

- Matthew is too fat now so he wants to *lose* (*his*) *weight*.
  馬修現在太胖了，所以他想要減肥。

L

8. **loud**
[laʊd]

adj. 大聲的；響亮的

- The kids outside made a **loud** noise so I could not sleep well.
  在外面的小孩子製造很大（聲）的噪音，所以我睡不好。

adv. 大聲地；響亮地

- We should not speak **loud** in the library.
  我們在圖書館裡不該大聲說話。

9. **love**
[lʌv]

v.t. 愛；喜愛；喜歡 ↔ hate [het] 討厭；恨

- All parents **love** their kids no matter they are good or bad.
  所有的父母都愛自己的小孩，無論他們是好是壞。
- Mary Jane **loves** to go shopping on weekends.
  瑪莉‧珍喜歡在週末的時候逛街。

n. [U] 愛

- My **love** for you will never change. Let's get married.
  我對妳的愛永遠不會改變。我們結婚吧。
- The pretty girl *fell in love with* the handsome young man.
  那漂亮的女孩愛上了那英俊的年輕人。

fall in love with +
sb 愛上～

10. **low**
    [lo]

adj. （相對位置）低的 ↔ high [haɪ] 高的

- Water flows from high places to **low** places.
  水從高的地方往低的地方流。

adj. （在量、度、價值等方面）低的；小的；少的

- I bought lots of books at **low** prices.
  我買了一大堆廉價的書。

adj. （聲音）低沈的；低聲的

- He spoke to me in a **low** voice so that others couldn't hear him.
  他低聲的對我說話，所以其他人聽不到他說話。

adv. （相對位置）低地；向下地

- The plane flew **low** and landed in the airport.
  飛機低飛並降落在機場。

L

Exercise 1

I. 字彙翻譯

1. 居住 _____ 2. 喜愛 _____ 3. 低的 _____

4. 客廳 _____ 5. 遺失（三態）_____ _____ _____

II. 字彙填充

_____ 1. The little boy cried l_____d, but no one was there to help him.

_____ 2. Mia lives by herself in America and sometimes she feels l_____y.

_____ 3. L_____g time ago, people didn't know how to use fire.

_____ 4. When I was still a l_____e kid, I liked to play with my dolls.

_____ 5. L_____k at the picture. It is really beautiful, isn't it?

III. 字彙選擇

( ) 1. The price of this T-shirt is quite _____. You can buy it now.

    (A) loud   (B) little   (C) low   (D) long

( ) 2. Anna is very sad because she _____ her favorite pet dog last night.

    (A) losed   (B) lost   (C) loved   (D) loud

( ) 3. I usually watch TV and eat some snacks with my family in the _____.

    (A) loud room   (B) live room   (C) long room   (D) living room

( ) 4. I'm sorry for being late. How _____ have you been waiting here?

    (A) long   (B) lonely   (C) loud   (D) low

( ) 5. Turn the radio _____, please. I can't hear the news.

    (A) low   (B) loud   (C) long   (D) love

L

11. lucky
[ˋlʌkɪ]

adj. 幸運的 ↔ poor [pʊr] 不幸的

- You win the lottery. What a **lucky** man you are!
  你中了樂透。你是多幸運的一個人啊!
- You are **lucky** to have so many good friends.
  你能擁有這麼多好朋友真是幸運。

12. lunch
[lʌntʃ]

n. [C][U] 午餐

- Do you want to have **lunch** with me this noon?
  你今天中午想跟我一起吃午餐嗎?
- What will we have for **lunch** today? Rice or noodles?
  我們今天午餐要吃什麼? 飯還是麵?

lunchbox
便當; 飯盒

- I have two sandwiches and a banana in my **lunchbox**.
  我的便當裡有兩個三明治和一根香蕉。

13. machine
[məˋʃin]

n. [C] 機器; 機械

- I am a human, not a **machine**. I can't work around the clock.
  我是人,不是機器。我不能日以繼夜的工作。

washing machine
洗衣機
vending machine
自動販賣機
answering machine
電話答錄機

- Most people use the *washing **machine*** to clean their clothes.
  大部分的人都用洗衣機清潔他們的衣物。
- I bought some cold drinks from the *vending **machine***.
  我在自動販賣機買了些冷飲。
- There is no message left in the *answering **machine***.
  電話答錄機裡沒有任何留言。

14. magic
[ˋmædʒɪk]

n. [U] 巫術; 魔法; 魔術

- I have no **magic**, so I can not go back to the past.
  我並沒有魔法,所以我無法回到過去。

n. [U] 魔力; 魅力

- The **magic** of love can make a wise man stupid.
  愛情的魔力可以讓一個聰明人變笨。

adj. 魔術的; 有魔力的

- The fairy turned the cat into a lion with her **magic** wand.
  那個仙女用她的魔杖把那隻貓變成了老虎。

M

15. **mail**

[mel]

mailbox
郵件信箱

n. [C][U] 郵件，信 = letter [`lɛtɚ]

· There is no new **mail** in my **mailbox**.
在我的郵件信箱裡沒有新信。

n. [U] 郵遞

· Please send the letter by air **mail** for me.
請幫我用航空郵遞寄這封信。

v.t. 郵寄 = send [sɛnd]

· Would you please **mail** these packages for me? Thank you.
可以請你幫我郵寄這些包裹嗎? 謝謝。

16. **mailman**

[`mel,mæn]

n. [C] 郵差；郵遞員 = mail carrier [`mel,kærɪr]

· Abel is a **mailman**; it is his job to send letters.
亞伯是個郵差，他的工作是遞送信件。

注意

mailman 是美式英文，postman [`postmən] 是英式英文。

17. **make**

[mek]

過去式	過去分詞	現在進行式
made [med]	made [med]	making [`mekɪŋ]

v.t. 做；製造

· Grace **made** a cake by herself for her mom's birthday.
葛蕾絲為了媽媽的生日自己做了一個蛋糕。

be made of + N
由～製成

· The window *is **made*** of glass.
那個窗戶是由玻璃所製成。

v.t. 使～做～；使得；讓（使役動詞）

· The sad movie **made** a lot of people cry.
這部哀傷的電影讓許多人哭泣。

· The police's questions **made** the thief afraid.
警察的質問讓小偷害怕。

注意

make 當「使役動詞」時，後面加 V 或 Adj。

v.t. 使成為～

· Her interest in singing **made** her a singer.

她對歌唱的興趣使她成為一名歌手。

v.t. 賺取；贏得；獲得

· Bruce **makes** twenty five thousand dollars a month.

布魯斯一個月賺兩萬五千塊錢。

v.t. 構成；組成

be made up of + N
由～所製成

· The cup *is **made** up of* glass.

這杯子是由玻璃所製作。

---

18. **man**
[mæn]

n. [C] 男人（成年男子）；人（複數：men [mɛn]）↔ woman [`wʊmən] 女人（複數：women [`wɪmɪn]）

· The **man** saved his wife and kids from the fire.

那男人從火災現場中救出他的妻子和孩子。

n. [U] 人類

· In the history of **man**, this kind of thing happens again and again.

在人類的歷史中，這類的事情一再的發生。

M

19. **many**
[`mɛnɪ]

原級	比較級	最高級
many [`mɛnɪ]; much [mʌtʃ]	more [mor]	most [most]

adj. 許多的；很多的

· I can't talk to you now. I have **many** things to do.

我現在不能和你說話。我有很多事情要做。

比較

	adj. 許多的；很多的
many [`mɛnɪ]	◎ many 後面一律接可數名詞。
	· There are **many** books in the library. 圖書館裡有許多的書。

much [mʌtʃ]	*adj.* 許多的；大量的
	◎ much 後面一律接不可數名詞。
	· How much time do you spend on studying a day? 你一天花多少時間唸書？
◎ a lot of 的意思也是「許多的；大量的」，但其後面可以接「可數名詞」，也可以接「不可數名詞」。	

20. **map**

[mæp]

read a map
看地圖

n. [C] 地圖

· You should bring a **map** with you or you might get lost.
你應該隨身帶著一張地圖，不然你可能會迷路。

· You'll find the park if you know how to *read the **map***.
如果你懂得看地圖的話，就找得到公園。

休息一下喔！

M

Exercise 2

I. 字彙翻譯

1. 郵件 _____
2. 許多的 _____
3. 製造 _____
4. 地圖 _____
5. 男人（單數）_____（複數）_____

II. 字彙填充

_____ 1. If I had a time m_____e, I would go to see what the future would be like.

_____ 2. The m_____m sent a package to me this morning.

_____ 3. It's almost noon. What do you want to eat for l_____h?

_____ 4. David turned a ball into a flower. I didn't know how he played the m_____c.

_____ 5. Ben is really a l_____y man to have such a happy family.

III. 字彙選擇

( ) 1. I don't know how to read this _____. Can you just tell me where the park is?

    (A) map   (B) mail   (C) magic   (D) man

( ) 2. The funny story _____ me laugh for several minutes.

    (A) man   (B) map   (C) mailed   (D) made

( ) 3. It was really a _____ time when we first kissed.

    (A) lunch   (B) magic   (C) map   (D) machine

( ) 4. _____ people enjoy watching the movie "Harry Potter."

    (A) A lot   (B) Many   (C) Much   (D) Little

( ) 5. I have to fix this _____. It is broken.

    (A) machine   (B) mailman   (C) magic   (D) map

M

Unit 25

1. mark
[mɑrk]

n. [C] 記號；符號
- The fire left a **mark** on his body.
  那次火災在他身上留下了記號。

v.t. 做記號於～；標明～
- The toy was **marked** for kids over five years old.
  這玩具上標明了適用於五歲以上的兒童。

n. [C] 成績；分數
- Peter got high **marks** on the math test yesterday.
  彼得昨天數學測驗考了高分。

2. market
[`mɑrkɪt]

a night market
夜市

n. [C] 市場；市集
- Mother went to the *market* to buy some eggs and beef.
  媽媽到市場去買了一些雞蛋和牛肉。
- You can eat all kinds of delicious food in the *night markets*.
  在夜市你可以吃到各種美味的食物。

3. married
[`mærɪd]

get married with sb
和某人結婚

adj. 結婚的，已婚的
- Linda is **married** and has two kids.
  琳達已婚，而且有兩個孩子。
- Amy *got married* with the man she loved last month.
  愛咪上個月和她所愛的男人結婚了。

M

4. math
[mæθ]

n. [U] 數學 = mathematics [ˌmæθəˈmætɪks]
- Kids learn how to count numbers in the **math** class.
  孩子們在數學課學數數字。

5. matter
[`mætɚ]

as a matter of fact
事實上；實際上

n. [C] 事情；問題
- I'll finish the work. It's just a **matter** of time.
  我會把工作完成的。這只是時間的問題。
- *As a **matter** of fact*, he is not as smart as he looks.
  實際上，他並沒有他看起來這麼聰明。

a matter of life and death
生死攸關的事情

- Bring the doctor here right now; this is *a **matter** of life and death*.
  馬上把醫生帶過來，這是生死攸關的事情。

no matter how/who/what/where/when
無論如何／誰／什麼／哪裡／何時

- *No **matter** how* hard he tried, he could not win the game.
  無論他多努力地嘗試，他還是無法贏得比賽。

- *No **matter** what* you say, I would not change my mind.
  無論你說什麼，我都不會改變我的心意。

- *No **matter** where* you go, I will go with you.
  無論你到哪裡，我都會跟著你。

n. [C] 麻煩事

- What's the **matter** with you? = What's wrong with you?
  你怎麼了？你有什麼麻煩事？

6. **may**
[me]

aux. 可能；也許；或許（過去式：might [maɪt]）

- It **may** rain tomorrow, but I'm not sure.
  明天可能會下雨，但我不確定。

aux. 可以

- I've put on my clothes. You **may** enter now.
  我已經穿好衣服，你可以進來了。

aux. 祝；願

- **May** you have a good day.
  祝你有愉快的一天。

注意
may 為「助動詞」，後面一律接原形動詞。

7. **maybe**
[`mebi]

adv. 大概；可能；或許 = perhaps [pɚ`hæps]

- It looks cold outside. **Maybe** I should put on my jacket.
  外面看起來很冷，也許我該穿上我的外套。

M

8. meal
[mil]

n. [C] 一餐；餐點

· Most people have three **meals** a day.
大部分人一天都吃三餐。

· My dad took us to a nice restaurant to enjoy a big **meal**.
我爸爸帶我們去一家很好的餐廳，享用一頓大餐。

9. mean
[min]

v.i. 意指；意思是

· I'm sorry. I didn't **mean** to hurt you.
對不起。我並不是有意要傷害你。

adj. 小氣的，吝嗇的

· Mr. Chang is so **mean** that no one can get a cent from him.
張先生很小氣，沒有人能從他那兒得到一分錢的。

10. meat
[mit]

white meat
白肉

red meat
紅肉

n. [U] 肉

· Some animals like tigers and lions eat **meat** only.
有些動物，像是老虎和獅子，是只吃肉的。

· I only eat *white meat* like chicken or fish.
我只吃白肉，像是雞肉或魚肉。

· Some wine goes well with *red meat* like beef or pork.
有些葡萄酒跟紅肉，像是牛肉或豬肉，搭配起來很不錯。

M

Exercise 1

I. 字彙翻譯

1. 一餐 _____   2. 記號 _____   3. 數學 _____

4. 可以 _____   5. 肉 _____

II. 字彙填充

_____ 1. Mother is not home. She went to the m_____t to buy some fresh fruit.

_____ 2. Jane got m_____d with Alex five years ago, and now they have a kid.

_____ 3. What's the m_____r with Tom? He looks so angry.

_____ 4. I don't know the answer to this question. M_____e you should ask your teacher.

_____ 5. If you don't know what this word m_____ns, you can look it up in the dictionary.

III. 字彙選擇

( ) 1. It is a _____ of life and death. You have to take it seriously.

    (A) map   (B) mail   (C) matter   (D) math

( ) 2. Jeff slept in class today. _____ he went to bed too late last night.

    (A) Meal   (B) Math   (C) May   (D) Maybe

( ) 3. I have to buy some food in the _____. What do you want to eat tonight?

    (A) mark   (B) market   (C) matter   (D) meal

( ) 4. The teacher asked his students to answer the _____ question in five minutes.

    (A) math   (B) many   (C) make   (D) married

( ) 5. You have to eat both _____ and vegetables if you want to be healthy.

    (A) meat   (B) market   (C) mail   (D) mailman

M

11. medicine
[ˋmɛdəsn̩]

take (the) medicine
服藥；吃藥

n. [C][U] 藥，藥物

- This **medicine** doesn't work on me. I don't feel better at all.
  這藥對我沒有作用。我一點也不覺得比較好。
- If you want to get better, you must *take medicine* on time.
  如果你想身體好轉，就一定要按時吃藥。

12. medium
[ˋmidɪəm]

adj. 中間的；適中的

- The shirt is too small. Please give me a **medium** one.
  這件襯衫太小了。請給我一件中號的。
- Please give me a beef hamburger and a **medium** coke.
  請給我一個牛肉漢堡和一杯中杯可樂。

adj. 中等熟度的

- "How would you like your steak?" "**Medium**."
  「您牛排要幾分熟?」 「五分熟。」

注意

排餐的熟度分為：well done（全熟）、medium well（七分熟）、medium（五分熟）、medium rare（三分熟）、rare（生的）。

13. meet
[mit]

過去式	過去分詞	現在進行式
met [mɛt]	met [mɛt]	meeting [ˋmitɪŋ]

v.t. 遇見

- I **met** my high school teacher by chance yesterday.
  我昨天意外地遇見我的高中老師。

v.t. 碰面

- I'll **meet** you in the park at 3:00 p.m. Don't be late.
  我下午三點在公園跟你碰面，別遲到了。

14. meeting
[ˋmitɪŋ]

n. [C] 會議；集會

- An important **meeting** will be held at ten a.m. today.
  今天早上十點將舉行一個重要的會議。
- The boss cannot see you now. He is at a **meeting**.
  老闆現在不能見你，他正在開會。

M

15. **menu**
[ˋmɛnju]

n. [C] 菜單

- This is the **menu**. You can order anything you want to eat.
  這是菜單，你可以點任何你想吃的東西。
- Is my favorite dish "sweet and sour chicken" on the **menu**?
  我最喜歡的菜餚「醣醋雞」有沒有在菜單上？

16. **mile**
[maɪl]

n. [C] 英里；哩

- The hospital is ten **miles** away from here.
  醫院離這裡有十英里之遠。
- Don't drive too fast. It's almost eighty **miles** an hour now.
  別開太快，現在時速已經將近80英哩了。

17. **milk**
[mɪlk]

n. [U] 牛奶；乳

- A glass of **milk** every morning is good for you.
  每天早上一杯牛奶對你有好處。

18. **million**
[ˋmɪljən]

n. [C] 百萬；百萬元

- Ten thousand times one hundred is one **million**.
  一萬乘以一百（一百的一萬倍）是一百萬。

millions of + N
上百萬的～

- There are *millions of* books in the national library.
  在這個國家圖書館裡，有上百萬的書刊。

adj. 百萬的

- There are more than two **million** people living in Taipei.
  有超過兩百萬的人住在台北。

19. **mind** [maɪnd]

n. [C] 主意；意見；想法

change one's mind
改變主意

make up one's mind
下定決心

out of one's mind
精神不正常，發瘋

- I know what I have said but I *change my **mind*** now.
  我知道我說過什麼，但我現在改變主意了。
- I've *made up my **mind*** to buy that game; don't try to stop me.
  我已經下定決心要買那款遊戲，別試著阻止我。
- He must be *out of his **mind*** to talk back to his boss.
  他一定是瘋了才會跟他老闆頂嘴。

M

keep + N + in mind 把～記在腦海裡	· I'll *keep* the rule *in mind* and try not to break it again. 　我會把這規定記住，並試著不要再犯。

v.t. v.i. 介意

· I will sit here if you don't **mind**.
　如果你不介意，我就坐在這裡了。

· Do you **mind** *opening* the door for me?
　你介意幫我開個門嗎？

never mind 沒關係	· "I'm so sorry that I am late." 　"*Never **mind**.*" 　「很抱歉我遲到了。」 　「沒關係。（不要放在心上）」

注意

　　mind 當「介意」時，後面的動詞一律用 Ving。

20. **minute** [`mɪnɪt]	*n.* [C] 分鐘 · I can hold my breath for more than five **minutes**. 　我能憋住呼吸超過五分鐘。
in a minute 一會兒	· Don't talk. The teacher will come back *in a minute*. 　不要說話。老師一會兒就回來了。

M

Exercise 2

I. 字彙翻譯

1. 遇見 _____   2. 菜單 _____   3. 英里 _____

4. 牛奶 _____   5. 適中的 _____

II. 字彙填充

_____ 1. Don't forget to take the m_____e, or you won't get better.

_____ 2. The boss will hold a m_____g tomorrow morning. You must be present.

_____ 3. Wait a m_____e. I will be back soon.

_____ 4. The rich man paid three m_____n dollars to buy a sports car.

_____ 5. I want to open the windows if you don't m_____d. It's so hot inside.

III. 字彙選擇

(   ) 1. If you want to be tall, you have to drink more _____ and play basketball more often.

     (A) map   (B) milk   (C) magic   (D) man

(   ) 2. How do you like your steak? Well-done, _____, or rare?

     (A) million   (B) meeting   (C) medium   (D) medicine

(   ) 3. The movie theater is five _____ away from here. You can go there by bus.

     (A) miles   (B) meals   (C) minds   (D) meets

(   ) 4. Sir, this is our _____. The special meal today is steak.

     (A) meat   (B) menu   (C) meet   (D) mind

(   ) 5. Keep my words in _____, and don't make the same mistake again.

     (A) meat   (B) mile   (C) milk   (D) mind

M

Unit 26

1. miss
[mɪs]

n. [C] 小姐（首字母大寫）
- I want to see **Miss** Wu. Is she here?
  我想見吳小姐。她在這兒嗎？

v.t. v.i. 錯過；未擊中 ↔ catch [kætʃ] 趕上
- I **missed** the bus, so I was late for school.
  我錯過那班公車，所以我上學遲到了。
- I tried to hit the ball again but I still **missed** it.
  我再一次試著擊中球，不過我仍然沒打到。

v.t. 想念
- I **missed** my family so much when I studied in the U.S..
  當我在美國唸書的時候，我非常想念我的家人。

2. mistake
[mə`stek]

make a mistake
犯錯

n. [C] 錯誤
- Find the **mistake** in this sentence and correct it.
  找出這句子中的錯誤並修正它。
- Everybody *makes* *mistakes*, but you must learn from them.
  每個人都會犯錯，但你必須從錯誤中學習。

3. modern
[`mɑdə-n]

adj. 現代的；現代化的
- It is not easy to understard the **modern** art.
  要瞭解現代藝術並不容易。

adj. 時髦的；最新的
- Girls like to spend money on new **modern** clothes.
  女孩子們喜歡把錢花在時髦新裝上。

4. moment
[`momənt]

at any moment
隨時

n. [C] 時刻；片刻
- All the tests are over; now it's the **moment** to have fun.
  所有的考試已結束，現在該是歡樂的時刻了。
- The sky is dark; it could rain *at any* *moment*.
  天色陰暗，隨時都可能會下雨。

M

hold on a moment 等一下（電話用語） wait a moment 等一下	• "May I speak to Mr. Li?" "*Hold on a **moment***. I'll get him." 「我可以和李先生講話嗎？」「稍等一下，我去叫他。」 • Please *wait a **moment***. The show will begin in minutes. 請稍待片刻。表演幾分鐘之內就要開始了。

5. money
[ˋmʌnɪ]

n. [U] 錢；金錢
• If I had a lot of **money**, I would travel around the world.
  如果我有很多錢，我就會去世界各地旅遊。
• **Money** talks.
  [諺語]金錢萬能。

lose money
賠錢；輸錢
make money
賺錢

• It is common to *lose **money*** when doing business.
  做生意時賠錢是很平常的。
• Sam *makes* lots of ***money*** by selling computers.
  山姆賣電腦賺了很多錢。

6. monkey
[ˋmʌŋkɪ]

n. [C] 猴子
• **Monkeys** love bananas and are good at climbing trees.
  猴子愛吃香蕉且擅長爬樹。

7. month
[mʌnθ]

n. [C] 月
• There are twelve **months** in one year.
  一年總共有十二個月份。

month after month
月復一月

• Working **month** *after* **month**, Natalie got bored and tired.
  月復一月地工作下來，娜塔莉感到既無聊又疲倦。

注意
十二個月的個別名稱可參考附錄。

8. moon
[mun]

n. [C] 月亮；月球
• Don't point your finger at the **moon**, or your ears would be cut.
  不要用手指指月亮，否則你的耳朵會被割到。

moon cake
月餅

• We eat *moon* cakes on the **Moon** Festival.
  我們在中秋節吃月餅。

M

9. **more**
[mor]

	原級	比較級	最高級
	many [`mɛnɪ]; much [mʌtʃ]	more [mor]	most [most]

adj. 較多的；更多的 ↔ less [lɛs] 較少的

· I could not finish the job in one hour; I need **more** time.
　我沒辦法在一小時內完成這項工作，我需要更多時間。

adv. 更；更多；更加

· It is **more** convenient to take the MRT than to take the bus.
　搭捷運要比搭公車更加方便。

more...than...
比起～更～

· May is **more** interested in movies *than* in TV programs.
　跟電視節目比起來，梅對電影更感興趣。

more and more
越來越～

· The girl becomes **more and more** beautiful in these years.
　那女孩這幾年來變得愈來愈漂亮。

not...any more
不再～

· Joan doesn't play with dolls *any more* after she was ten.
　十歲之後，瓊就不再玩洋娃娃了。

10. **morning**
[`mɔrnɪŋ]

n. [C][U] 早上；上午

· Amy likes to go jogging before breakfast every **morning**.
　艾咪喜歡在每天早上吃早餐以前先去慢跑。

Good morning.
早安。

· Mother said "*good morning*" to me when I woke up.
　媽媽在我起床的時候，向我道了聲「早安」。

in the morning
在早上

· It is good for you to take some exercise early *in the morning*.
　在早晨做些運動對你有益。

M

Exercise 1

I. 字彙翻譯

1. 錯過 _____
2. 早晨 _____
3. 更多的 _____
4. 月亮 _____
5. 時刻 _____

II. 字彙填充

_____ 1. There are three m_____hs in one season.

_____ 2. Computers become more and more important in the m_____n world.

_____ 3. Those m_____ys are very excited when they see the bananas.

_____ 4. Cathy spent a lot of m_____y buying the beautiful dress.

_____ 5. I made a big m_____e, and I hope I can make it up in time.

III. 字彙選擇

(　　) 1. If you need any help, I am right here at any _____.

(A) monkey　　　　(B) mistake　　　　(C) morning　　　　(D) moment

(　　) 2. This skirt is _____ expensive than that one.

(A) moon　　　　(B) more　　　　(C) month　　　　(D) modern

(　　) 3. Peter got up too late this _____ and was late for school again.

(A) morning　　　　(B) moment　　　　(C) month　　　　(D) moon

(　　) 4. There are clouds all over the sky, so we can't see the _____ and the stars.

(A) monkey　　　　(B) month　　　　(C) moon　　　　(D) more

(　　) 5. Jerry has not seen his wife for a week. He _____ her very much.

(A) minds　　　　(B) misses　　　　(C) milks　　　　(D) minds

M

11. **most**
[most]

	原級	比較級	最高級
	many [`mɛnɪ]; much [mʌtʃ]	more [mor]	most [most]

adj. 大部分的；多數的

- **Most** students hate tests and love holidays.
  大部分的學生都討厭考試，喜歡放假。

adj. 最多的 ↔ least [list] 最少的

- Michael got the **most** points in the game; he was the winner.
  邁克在比賽中得到最多的分數，他是勝利者。

adv. 最

- You are the **most** beautiful woman I have ever met.
  你是我見過最美麗的女人。

12. **mother**
[`mʌðɚ]

n. [C] 母親；媽媽 = mom [mɑm] = mommy [`mɑmɪ]

- My **mother** met my father when she was twenty.
  我媽媽在她二十歲的時候，遇到了我爸爸。

13. **motorcycle**
[`motɚˌsaɪkl̩]

n. [C] 摩托車；機車

- Before eighteen years old, you could not ride a **motorcycle**.
  在你未滿十八歲之前，你不能騎摩托車。

14. **mountain**
[`maʊntn̩]

n. [C] 山，山脈

- I like to climb **mountains**/go **mountain** climbing on Sundays.
  我喜歡在禮拜天去爬山。

注意

mountain 與 hill 的比較請參見 Unit 19 的 hill。

15. **mouse**
[maʊs]

n. [C] 老鼠（複數：mice [maɪs]）

- My cat likes to run after **mice**.
  我的貓喜歡追老鼠。

n. [C] 滑鼠（複數：mice [maɪs]）

- It is easy to use the computer with the **mouse**.
  用滑鼠操作電腦非常簡單。

16. **mouth**
[mauθ]

n. [C] 嘴；嘴巴
- Open your **mouth**. I must check your teeth.
  張開你的嘴巴。我得檢查一下你的牙齒。

17. **move**
[muv]

v.t. 移動
- The man is badly hurt; you had better not **move** him.
  這個人受傷嚴重，你最好不要移動他。

v.i. 搬家
- Kelly **moved** to New York and began a new life there.
  凱莉搬到紐約，在那裡開始新的生活。

18. **movie**
[`muvɪ]

n. [C] 電影
- My dream is to become a **movie** star like Harrison Ford.
  我的夢想是成為一個像哈里遜・福特一樣的電影明星。

see a movie
看電影
- Jimmy asked the girl he liked to *see a movie* with him.
  吉米邀請他喜歡的女生和他去看電影。

19. **much**
[mʌtʃ]

原級	比較級	最高級
many [`mɛnɪ]; much [mʌtʃ]	more [mor]	most [most]

M

adj. 許多的；大量的
- Jack is rich and he makes **much**/lots of money.
  傑克很富有，他賺很多錢。

adv. 很；非常；太（大量；多）
- Don't eat too **much**, or you will get fat.
  不要吃太多，否則你會變胖。

pron. 許多；大量
- **Much** of the water was drunk by Tom.
  許多的水都被湯姆給喝掉了。

注意
(1) many 與 much 的比較請參見 Unit 24 的單字 many。
(2) much 當形容詞時，後面接不可數名詞。

20. museum

[mju`ziəm]

n. [C] 博物館

· We could see many famous art works in the **museum**.
  在博物館裡，我們可以看到許多著名的藝術作品。

· You can learn a lot when you visit the **museum**.
  你在參觀博物館的時候，可以學到很多東西。

休息一下喔！

M

214

Exercise 2

I. 字彙翻譯

1. 母親 _____
2. 嘴巴 _____
3. 移動 _____
4. 許多的 (+ n. [U]) _____
5. 老鼠（單數）_____ （複數）_____

II. 字彙填充

_____ 1. I visited an art show of Picasso（畢卡索） in the m_____m yesterday.

_____ 2. It is sunny but not too hot today. Let's go m_____n climbing.

_____ 3. Have you seen the latest m_____e by Sandra Block?

_____ 4. Jeff is the m_____t polite boy in my class.

_____ 5. I traveled the island by riding a m_____e last summer.

III. 字彙選擇

( ) 1. The box is so heavy that no one is able to _____ it.

    (A) movie   (B) move   (C) more   (D) miss

( ) 2. We don't have _____ water left.

    (A) little   (B) few   (C) many   (D) much

( ) 3. Ted's _____ loves him very much, because he is her only son.

    (A) mother   (B) mouse   (C) museum   (D) monkey

( ) 4. Karen visited the _____ last Sunday and saw lots of art work.

    (A) mother   (B) museum   (C) much   (D) mountain

( ) 5. My cat is good at catching _____.

    (A) mice   (B) mouse   (C) mouth   (D) month

M

N

Unit 27

1. music
[ˋmjuzɪk]

n. [U] 音樂

- What kind of **music** do you like?
  你喜歡哪一種音樂?

listen to music
聽音樂

- I like to *listen to **music*** when I study.
  我喜歡在唸書時聽音樂。

face the music
勇敢接受懲罰

- We have to *face the **music*** if we do something wrong.
  如果我們做錯了事,就應該勇敢接受應得的懲罰。

2. must
[mʌst]

aux. 必須;得~ = have to(表示命令、必要或強制)

- You **must**/have to clean your room, or mom will be angry.
  你一定要打掃你的房間,不然媽媽會生氣的。

aux. 一定;八成是(表示肯定推測)

- If May is not home, she **must** be in the movie theater.
  如果梅不在家,她八成就是在電影院。

注意

must 為「助動詞」,後面一律接「原形動詞」。

3. name
[nem]

n. [C] 名字

- My **name** is Edward. What is yours?
  我的名字叫愛德華,你的呢?

v.t. 命名;取名字

- I **named** my pet cat "Tiger", because he is strong and quick.
  我把我的寵物貓命名為「老虎」,因為他既強壯又敏捷。

name after + sb
依照(某人的名字)
~命名

- The little baby was **named** *after* his grandfather.
  這小寶寶被取了跟他爺爺一樣的名字(依照他爺爺的名字為他命名)。

N

4. **national**
[ˈnæʃən!]

national holiday
國定假日

adj. 國家的；全國性的
- You can find New York city on the **national** map of the U.S.
  你可以在美國的國家地圖上找到紐約市。
- We don't have to work on *national* holidays.
  國定假日我們不必去工作。

5. **near**
[nɪr]

prep. 在～附近
- I live **near** the park and usually take a walk there.
  我住在公園附近，所以常去那裡散步。

adv. 附近；接近
- Nancy came **near** to me and kissed me on the face.
  蘭西向我靠近，然後在我的臉上親了一下。

adj. 附近的；接近的
- Could you buy me some drinks in the **near** shop?
  你能幫我到附近的店買些飲料嗎？

6. **neck**
[nɛk]

break one's neck
（折頸）致死

n. [C] 頸；脖子
- Does a snake have a **neck**?
  蛇有脖子嗎？
- You might *break your neck* if you fell from the tree.
  如果你從樹上掉下來，可能會摔斷你的脖子。

7. **need**
[nɪd]

in need
在窮困中的

v.t. 需要
- I **need** some eggs and milk to make a cake.
  我需要一些雞蛋和牛奶來做蛋糕。

n. [U] 需要；需求
- People have a **need** to love and to be loved.
  人們有愛及被愛的需求。
- Parents should care the **need** of their kids.
  父母應該關心孩子們的需求。
- Everybody should care about those *in need*.
  每個人都應該關心那些在窮困中的人。

8. never
[ˋnɛvɚ]

adv. 從未；永不；絕不
- I have **never** seen this man before. I don't know him.
  我以前從未見過這個人。我不認識他。
- I will **never** do anything to hurt you.
  我絕不會做出任何會傷害你的事。

adv. 不要；別
- **Never** put your dirty clothes on my white sofa.
  絕不要把你的髒衣服放在我的白色沙發上。

never mind
別介意
- "I am so sorry for being late." "*Never mind.*"
  「真的很抱歉我遲到了。」「不用介意。」

9. new
[nju]

adj. 新的；新型的；新鮮的 ↔ old [old] 舊的
- My shoes are old; I need to buy a **new** pair (of shoes).
  我的鞋子舊了，我得去買雙新的。

adj. 新發現的；新加入的；新任的
- Lilly is a **new** student, and we don't know much about her.
  莉莉是這裡新加入的學生，所以我們對她所知不多。

adj. 沒有經驗的；陌生的

be new to + sb
對～而言是陌生的
- Pan just moved here and everything is *new to* her.
  潘才剛搬來這兒，所以每樣東西對她而言都是陌生的。

10. news
[njuz]

n. [U] 新聞；消息
- You can read the hottest **news** about NBA on the Internet.
  你可以在網路上看到有關 NBA 的最熱門新聞。

in the news
被報導；上了新聞
- The new husband of that singer was *in the news*.
  那名歌手的新老公上了新聞。

Exercise 1

I. 字彙翻譯

1. 脖子 _____
2. 附近的 _____
3. 從不 _____
4. 新的 _____
5. 新聞 _____

II. 字彙填充

_____ 1. English is a n_____l language in the United States and many other countries.

_____ 2. Alice gave birth to a new baby girl yesterday, and she n_____ed her Elizabeth.

_____ 3. No one can help you with your homework; you n_____d to do it by yourself.

_____ 4. I enjoy listening to all kinds of m_____c.

_____ 5. You m_____t arrive at the airport on time, or you will miss the airplane.

III. 字彙選擇

( ) 1. _____ lie to me again, or I won't believe you any more.

    (A) Must   (B) Never   (C) Near   (D) Need

( ) 2. You don't _____ to be afraid of the police if you did nothing wrong.

    (A) name   (B) neck   (C) new   (D) need

( ) 3. My watch was lost last weekend, so my dad bought me a _____ one.

    (A) news   (B) music   (C) new   (D) national

( ) 4. David didn't show up in the meeting. He _____ have forgotten it.

    (A) name   (B) near   (C) music   (D) must

( ) 5. The poor animal was hurt in the _____.

    (A) neck   (B) need   (C) news   (D) name

N

11. **next**
[nɛkst]

next to + N
緊鄰著～

next door
在隔壁

adj. 接下來的；下一個的；緊接在後的

· **Next** weekend, my best friend will get married.
下個週末，我最要好的朋友就要結婚了。

adj. 緊鄰的；貼近的；隔壁的

· The wall is thin and the voice from the **next** room is very clear.
牆壁很薄，所以隔壁房間裡的聲音可以聽得非常清楚。

· Tina's seat in the classroom is *next to* Jane's.
蒂娜在教室的位子就在珍的旁邊。

· Today most people don't know those who just live *next door*.
現今大部分的人都不認識就住在隔壁的人。

adv. 接下來；然後

· The poor little girl got lost and didn't know what to do **next**.
這個可憐的小女孩迷了路，不知道接下來該怎麼做。

12. **nice**
[naɪs]

adj. 極好的，愉快的

· Very **nice**. You just hit the point.
好極了，你正好說到了重點。

· **Nice** to meet you. How have you been these days?
見到你真好。最近你過的如何呀？

adj. 好心的；親切的

· It is **nice** of you to help me carry this big box.
你真是好心，幫我搬這個大箱子。

adj. （天氣）宜人的

· The weather is so **nice** that everyone wants to go outside.
天氣如此宜人，以致於每個人都想出門。

13. **night**
[naɪt]

at night
在晚上

n. [C][U] 晚上；夜晚

· I could not sleep all **night**, because I was worried about my sick grandmom.
我整夜都睡不著，因為我擔心著生病的祖母。

· It is late *at night*; kids should not play outside.
現在已經晚上很晚了，小孩子不該還在外面玩。

day and night 日以繼夜地 Good night. 晚安	· He worked *day and **night*** to get the work done on time. 　為了要讓工作準時完成，他日以繼夜地工作。 · The mother kissed her baby and said *good **night*** to her. 　那名母親親了親她的寶寶，並向她道了晚安。 *adj.* 晚上的；夜間的
night market 夜市	· Many foreigners like to visit the ***night*** markets in Taiwan. 　許多外國人喜歡參觀臺灣的夜市。

14. nobody
[`no,badɪ]

pron. 沒有人；無人 ↔ everybody [`ɛvrɪ,badɪ] 每個人

· I thought somebody would do the job, but **nobody** did.
　我以為某個人會去做這個工作，但是卻沒有人做。

n. [C] 小人物；無足輕重的人

· Of course you never heard of me. I am just a **nobody**.
　當然你沒有聽說過我，我只是個小人物。

15. nod
[nad]

過去式	過去分詞	現在進行式
nodded [`nadɪd]	nodded [`nadɪd]	nodding [`nadɪŋ]

v.t. v.i. 點頭（打招呼；表示友好）

· My boss **nodded** to me when I said hello to him.
　當我跟老闆打招呼時，他對我點點頭。

比較

nod (one's head)	*v.t. v.i.* 點頭（表示同意；贊成） · Joe **nodded** (his head) to agree with my point. 　喬點頭表示他同意我的論點。
shake one's head	*phr.* 搖頭（表示反對；不贊同） · When May asked if she could go to the party, her father shook his head. 　當梅問是否能參加宴會時，她的父親搖搖頭。

n. [C] 點頭

· My uncle welcomed us with a friendly **nod**.
　我叔叔友善地點頭以表示歡迎。

N

16. **noise**

[nɔɪz]

make noise
製造噪音

n. [C][U] 噪音；喧鬧聲
- I couldn't sleep because of the **noise** outside.
  因為外面的噪音，我無法睡覺。
- Don't *make* any **noise** in the library.
  在圖書館不要製造任何噪音。

17. **noodle**

[`nudl̩]

beef noodles
牛肉麵

instant noodles
泡麵；速食麵

n. [C] 麵；麵條
- What kind of food do you love most? Rice, **noodles** or steaks?
  你最喜歡吃哪一種食物？是米食、麵食、還是排餐？
- The restaurant is famous for its *beef noodles*.
  那家餐廳以其牛肉麵聞名。
- When I am hungry at midnight, I would eat *instant noodles*.
  我半夜肚子餓的時候，都會吃泡麵。

18. **noon**

[nun]

at noon
在中午；在正午

n. [U] 正午；中午
- All ice creams are sold out before **noon** for the hot weather.
  因為炎熱的天氣,所有的冰淇淋在中午前全賣光了。
- It is the hottest hour *at noon*.
  正午是最熱的時間。

19. **north**

[nɔrθ]

North Pole
北極

n. [U] 北；北方
- Some say that a house should sit in **north** and face the south.
  有人說房子應該座北朝南。

adj. 北的；北方的
- Polar bears only live in the *North Pole*.
  北極熊只生活在北極。

adv. 在北方；向北方
- You should drive **north** if you want to go to Keelung.
  如果你想去基隆，（你的車）就應該朝北方開。

N

20. **nose**
[noz]

pick one's nose
挖鼻孔

n. [C] 鼻子

- She is a beauty with bright eyes, thin lips and a high **nose**.
  她是一個有著明亮雙眼、薄薄嘴唇和高挺鼻子的美人兒。
- Don't *pick* your **nose** in public.
  別當眾挖你的鼻孔。

注意

其他有關鼻子的片語還有很多，例如 have a stuffed-up nose（鼻子不通）、have a running nose（流鼻涕；流鼻水）、blow one's nose（擤鼻涕）、a flat nose（扁鼻子；塌鼻子）、the bridge of the nose（鼻樑）、hold one's nose（捏住鼻子）等等。

休息一下喔！

Exercise 2

N

I. 字彙翻譯

1. 麵條 ＿＿＿＿＿＿＿＿＿＿   2. 中午 ＿＿＿＿＿＿＿＿＿＿   3. 點頭 ＿＿＿＿＿＿＿＿＿＿

4. 接下來 ＿＿＿＿＿＿＿＿＿＿   5. 北方 ＿＿＿＿＿＿＿＿＿＿

II. 字彙填充

＿＿＿＿＿＿＿＿＿＿ 1. N＿＿＿＿y answers the door. Maybe they are all out.

＿＿＿＿＿＿＿＿＿＿ 2. Johnny was very angry with Tom and he hit him on the n＿＿＿＿e.

＿＿＿＿＿＿＿＿＿＿ 3. I heard a loud n＿＿＿＿e . Do you know what happened?

＿＿＿＿＿＿＿＿＿＿ 4. I said good n＿＿＿＿t to my family before I go to bed.

＿＿＿＿＿＿＿＿＿＿ 5. The weather is n＿＿＿＿e today. Let's go picnicking.

III. 字彙選擇

( ) 1. Don't make any ＿＿＿＿＿. The teacher is coming.

　　　(A) next 　　　　(B) noise 　　　　(C) night 　　　　(D) north

( ) 2. Did you know what happened ＿＿＿＿＿ after Ted left home?

　　　(A) nice 　　　　(B) night 　　　　(C) north 　　　　(D) next

( ) 3. It is very quiet at ＿＿＿＿＿ in the country.

　　　(A) night 　　　　(B) north 　　　　(C) noise 　　　　(D) nice

( ) 4. The clock will knock twelve at ＿＿＿＿＿.

　　　(A) nice 　　　　(B) noon 　　　　(C) nod 　　　　(D) noise

( ) 5. What do you want for dinner, rice or ＿＿＿＿＿?

　　　(A) night 　　　　(B) noon 　　　　(C) noodles 　　　　(D) nobody

Unit 28

1. notebook
[`not,bʊk]

n. [C] 筆記本；手冊

- I wrote down what the teacher said in my **notebook**.
  我把老師說的話寫在我的筆記本裡。

n. [C] 筆記型電腦

- **Notebooks** are easier to carry than PCs.
  筆記型電腦比個人電腦更方便隨身攜帶。

2. nothing
[`nʌθɪŋ]

n. [U] 沒有東西；沒有事情

- There is **nothing** in the room.
  房間裡什麼東西都沒有。（沒有東西在房間裡。）
- **Nothing** can stop Mary from going to New York to study art.
  沒有什麼事情能夠阻擋瑪莉去紐約學習藝術。

have nothing to do with + N　與～無關

- I *have* **nothing** *to do with* that man; I don't even know him.
  我跟那個人完全無關，我甚至不認識他。

3. notice
[`notɪs]

v.t. 注意

- The teacher has **noticed** that Gina is a little strange today.
  老師注意到吉娜今天有一點奇怪。

n. [U] 注意

- The boy took away the watch without anyone's **notice**.
  那男孩在沒有任何人注意到的情況之下，拿走了那隻錶。

n. [C] 公告；通知；貼示

- A **notice** before the restaurant says, "No Smoking!"
  那家餐廳外有個公告寫著：「禁止吸煙」。

without notice
不預先通知地

- The boss fired several workers *without* **notice**.
  那個老闆在未預先通知的情況下，解雇了好幾名工人。

4. now
[naʊ]

adv. 現在；此刻

- Sara is playing the piano in her room **now**.
  莎拉現在正在房間裡彈鋼琴。

225

right <u>now</u>/away 立刻；馬上	· Hand in your paper *right **now***, or you must stay after school. 立刻交出你的報告，不然你放學後就得留下來。
from now on 從現在開始	· *From **now** on* I will stop playing and start to study hard. 從現在開始，我會停止玩樂，開始用功唸書。
just now 剛才；現在	· I got up *just **now***; I still want to sleep. 我剛剛才起床，還好想睡喔。 · Mother is cooking *just **now***, and later we can eat dinner. 媽媽現在正在煮飯，待會兒我們就可以吃晚餐了。
up to now 到目前為止	· *Up to **now***, everything is fine, so you don't have to worry. 到目前為止，一切都很順利，所以你不必擔心。

5. **number**
[ˋnʌmbɚ]

n. [C] 數目；數字

· The **number** of students in our class is forty-two.
我們班上學生的數目是四十二個。

a number of
一些～

· There are only *a **number** of* restaurants open on Sundays.
禮拜天只有一些餐廳開門營業。

numbers of
許多～

· ***Numbers** of* kids are playing basketball in the park.
許多孩子正在公園裡打籃球。

n. [C] 第～號（縮寫為 No.）

· Julia lives at **No.** 358, Chung Hsiao East Road, Section 3.
茱莉亞住在忠孝東路三段 358 號。

n. [C] 號碼

phone number
電話號碼

· Please remember that my ***phone** number* is 02-8765-4321.
請記住我的電話號碼是 02-8765-4321。

6. **nurse**
[nɝs]

n. [C] 護士

· As a **nurse**, Amy's job is to take care of patients.
身為一個護士，艾咪的工作就是去照顧病人。

7. **o'clock**
[əˋklɑk]

adv. ～點鐘

· The TV show will start at seven **o'clock** p.m.; I won't miss it.
那個電視節目會在晚上七點鐘開始，我是不會錯過它的。

O

8. **off** [ɔf]
turn off
關掉

adv. 切掉；關掉

· Please *turn off* the light when you leave the room.
你要離開房間時，請把燈關掉。

adv. 離開；走開

· Sam went **off** without saying goodbye to us.
山姆沒有跟我們道別就走了。

take off
脫下～；移去～
take off
起飛

· I *took off* my coat because it was hot.
因為天氣熱，所以我把外套脫掉。

· The airplane will *take off* on time.
飛機將會準時起飛。

prep. 折價

· These books are forty percent **off**; I think they are very cheap.
這些書打六折，我覺得很便宜。

注意

　　中文跟英文打折的說法並不相同，英文說 thirty percent off 是指將售價減去原本售價的百分之三十，也就是中文所說「打七折」的意思。

9. **office**
[`ɔfɪs]

n. [C] 辦公室

· The boss asks us not to talk too loud in the **office**.
老闆要我們在辦公室講話不要太大聲。

10. **officer**
[`ɔfəsɚ]

n. [C] 警官；軍官；官員

· The little boy wants to be a police **officer** when he grows up.
這個小男孩長大之後想當一名警官。

Exercise 1

I. 字彙翻譯

1. 辦公室 _____

2. 離開 _____

3. 現在 _____

4. 筆記本 _____

5. 護士 _____

II. 字彙填充

_____ 1. The o_____r ordered some policemen to catch the bad man.

_____ 2. I have eaten n_____g since the noon. I'm hungry now.

_____ 3. The first class in our school begins at eight o_____k every morning.

_____ 4. Ben tried to tell us the news, but no one n_____ed him.

_____ 5. What is your lucky n_____r? Mine is seven.

III. 字彙選擇

( ) 1. After taking a bath, be sure to turn _____ the gas.

    (A) off   (B) nothing   (C) now   (D) office

( ) 2. Jerry was called to the teachers' _____ because he was late for school again this morning.

    (A) officer   (B) notebook   (C) office   (D) o'clock

( ) 3. The _____ in this hospital are very kind and helpful.

    (A) nothing   (B) officers   (C) notebooks   (D) nurses

( ) 4. The girl is playing the piano _____.

    (A) number   (B) nurse   (C) now   (D) off

( ) 5. Did you _____ a smile on his face?

    (A) notice   (B) number   (C) nurse   (D) now

O

11. often
[`ɔfən]

adv. 常常

- Ryan is good at math and he **often** gets high grades in the tests.
  雷恩數學很好，他常常在考試中得到高分。
- Men are **often** stronger than women.
  男人通常都比女人強壯。

注意
　頻率副詞的比較請參考 Unit 2 的 always。

12. oil
[ɔɪl]

n. [U] 油（泛指各種油）

- There is some **oil** on the floor. You had better clean it.
  地板上有些油。你最好把它清乾淨。

n. [U] 石油；汽油

- My car is running out of **oil**, so I must go to the gas station.
  我的車子沒油了，所以我得去一趟加油站。

13. OK
[`o`ke]

adj. （口語）可以的；不錯的 = O.K. = okay

- It would be **OK** to meet you at noon; I will be free then.
  我中午可以見你，那時候我有空。

adj. （口語）很好的

- The plan is **OK** with me. I don't have any problem.
  這計畫我覺得很好。我沒有任何問題。

adv. （口語）尚可；挺好

- "Do you want to see a movie tonight?"
  "**OK**, let's meet at 7:00 p.m."
  「你今天晚上想看電影嗎?」
  「好，我們就約晚上七點碰面吧。」

14. old
[old]

adj. ～歲大的

- "How **old** are you?" "I am twenty-eight years **old**."
  「你幾歲?」「我二十八歲。」
- Tommy is a ten-year-**old** boy.
  湯米是個十歲的男孩。

adj. 老的；上了年紀的 ↔ young [jʌŋ] 年輕的

· My grandpa is eighty, and he is too **old** to live by himself.

　我爺爺八十歲了，他已經老的沒辦法靠他自己一個人生活。

adj. 破的；舊的 ↔ new [nju] 新的

· Your shoes look very **old**; I think you should buy a new pair.

　你的鞋子看起來好破舊了，我覺得你該買雙新的了。

adj. 多年的；長時間的；舊交的

· Charles is my **old** friend; I have known him for twenty years.

　查爾斯是我多年的朋友，我已經認識他二十年了。

adj. 古代的；古時候的；過時的

· In the **old** days, there were no telephone or Internet.

　在古時候，沒有電話也沒有網際網路。

---

15. **on**

[ɑn]

prep. 在～之上

· There is a bee **on** your shoulder.

　你的肩膀上有一隻蜜蜂。

· There is a beautiful picture **on** the wall.

　有一幅漂亮的畫掛在牆上。

on TV
在電視上
on the TV
在電視機上

· Look, my daughter is *on TV*; she looks like a real star.

　你看，我女兒上電視了耶，她看起來就像個真的明星。

· I put my keys *on the TV* and forgot to take them.

　我把鑰匙放在電視機上，忘了拿了。

prep. 在～之上（地點；交通工具）

· There is only one hospital **on** the small island.

　在那座小島上只有一家醫院。

· Tim is **on** the airplane/bus/train now.

　提姆現在正在飛機／公車／火車上。

prep. 在～之日（特定的日子、早晨、下午、晚上等）

· I will give you a very special present **on** your birthday.

　在你的生日，我將會給你一個很特別的禮物。

adv. 穿戴～在身上

O

put on
穿戴上～

- It is cold; *put on* your coat if you want to go out.

  天氣很冷，如果你要出門，就穿上你的外套。

adv. 搭上～

get on
搭上～（交通工具）

- We *got on* the school bus to go home.

  我們搭校車回家。

prep. 關於～；有關～

- I don't want to talk **on** this. Don't ask any more.

  關於這件事我不想談。不要再問了。

prep. 正在做，在～中

on fire
失火的；著火的

- The apartment is **on** *fire*; luckily there is nobody in it.

  那棟公寓失火了，所幸並沒有人在裡面。

on sale
廉售中；拍賣中

- Yes, these books are **on** *sale*. Do you want to buy some?

  是的，這些書正在拍賣。你想買一些嗎？

on the way to
在前往～的途中

- Molly is **on** *the way to* school.

  茉莉正在前往學校的途中。

adv. 運轉

turn on
打開；使～運轉

- *Turn* **on** the light.

  打開電燈。

- The worker *turned* the machine **on** and started to work.

  那工人打開機器使其運轉，然後開始工作。

prep. 用～（工具）；以～（手段）

- Did you hear the news **on** (the) radio? A typhoon is coming.

  你有聽到收音機上的新聞嗎？颱風要來了。

prep. 在～之後，立即

- **On** hearing the good news, everyone was very excited.

  在一聽到這個好消息之後，每一個人都非常興奮。

prep. 接近；在～分界處；臨，沿著；在～的一側

- Larry lives in a house **on** the road, so there is noise of traffic.

  賴瑞住在馬路邊的房子裡，所以會有車輛經過造成的噪音。

- The town is **on** the other side of the river.

  市鎮在河的另外一側。

231

16. once

[wʌns]

once in a while
有時候；偶爾
once more/again
再一次
at once = right now
立刻；馬上

adv. 一次；一回

- I have been to London **once** several years ago.
  我幾年前去過倫敦一次。
- Doing some exercise *once* in a while is good for you.
  偶爾做做運動對你有好處。
- Please tell me your name *once* more; I didn't hear just now.
  請再跟我說一次你的名字，我剛才沒聽到。
- The house is on fire. Please call 119 *at once*.
  房子失火了，請馬上打一一九。

17. one

[wʌn]

a one-way road
單行道
a one-way ticket
單程票

number one
第一名；最棒的

one by one
一個（接）一個地

adj. 一個的

- Please give me **one** hamburger and **one** small Coke.
  請給我一個漢堡跟一杯小杯可樂。
- This is *a one*-way road, so you can't drive the same way back.
  這是一條單行道，所以你不能開原路回來。
- Sir, do you want *a one*-way ticket or a return ticket?
  先生，請問您是要單程票還是來回票？

n. 一

- **One** and two are three.
  一加二等於三。
- You won the game; you are *number* one.
  你贏得了比賽，你是最棒的。

pron. 一個；一塊；一枝～

- You are the only **one** who can help me.
  你是唯一一個可以幫我的人。
- "Do you want **one** or two cakes?"
  "I am not hungry. **One** would be enough."
  「你想吃一兩塊蛋糕嗎?」
  「我不餓，一塊蛋糕應該就夠了。」
- The hungry boy ate all the cakes *one by one* without stop.
  那飢餓的男孩一個一個地吃掉了所有的蛋糕，毫無停頓。

18. only
[`onlɪ]

adj. 唯一的

· You are the **only** person I care about.
你是我唯一關心的人。

adv. 只；僅

· What I **only** want is to take a rest. I'm too tired.
我想要的就只有休息，我太累了。

19. open
[`opən]

v.t. 打開 ↔ close [kloz] 關

· Joe **opened** the door and let his friends come into the house.
喬打開門，讓他的朋友們進屋子。

· May I **open** the windows to make the air fresher?
我可以打開窗子，讓空氣清新些嗎？

adj. 開著的

· The door is **open**; please come in.
門是開著的（沒鎖），請進來。

v.t. v.i. 營業；開張

· Mr. Chang **opened** a bookstore last year.
張先生去年開了一家書店。

adj. 營業中的

· The department store is **open** from 11:00 a.m. to 10:00 p.m.
那家百貨公司從上午十一點營業到晚上十點。

20. or
[ɔr]

conj. 或者

· What do you want? Coffee, tea **or** juice?
你想要什麼？咖啡、茶或是果汁？

· You **or** he has to do the job.
你或他必須做這項工作。

either A or B
不是 A，就是 B

· *Either* you *or* I am wrong.
不是你就是我錯了。

conj. 否則；要不然

· Don't be late for school, **or** you'll miss the first class.
上學不要遲到，否則你就會錯過第一堂課。

Exercise 2

I. 字彙翻譯

1. 曾經 _____ 2. 在～上面 _____ 3. 好的 _____

4. 一個 _____ 5. 或者 _____

II. 字彙填充

_____ 1. O_____n your book and read page 45, class.

_____ 2. "How o_____d are you?" "Ten."

_____ 3. I need some o_____l to cook eggs. Would you please take some for me?

_____ 4. My sister and I o_____n go shopping on Saturday night.

_____ 5. O_____y men above thirty can enter this club.

III. 字彙選擇

( ) 1. Not _____ I but also Tom saw the movie.

   (A) only   (B) once   (C) or   (D) other

( ) 2. Please turn the radio _____ ; I want to hear the morning news.

   (A) once   (B) only   (C) on   (D) old

( ) 3. Clio _____ talks to her American friends in English, so she is good at speaking English.

   (A) old   (B) often   (C) OK   (D) once

( ) 4. Hurry up, _____ you'll be late for school again.

   (A) once   (B) only   (C) on   (D) or

( ) 5. He has been to Australia _____ .

   (A) once   (B) one   (C) on   (D) or

Unit 29

1. orange

[ˋɔrɪndʒ]

orange juice
柳橙汁

n. [C] 柳橙

- I love juicy fruits, like **oranges**.
  我喜歡多汁的水果，像是柳橙。
- Please give me a cup of iced ***orange* *juice***. It is so hot.
  請給我一杯冰柳橙汁，好熱呀。

adj. 橙色的；橘黃色的

- The **orange** belt goes well with the pink skirt.
  這條橘黃色的腰帶跟這粉紅色裙子搭配起來很好看。

2. order [ˋɔrdɚ]

in order
按順序；按次序
out of order
發生故障；雜亂的
in order to + V
為了～

n. [U] 順序

- Tim's room is so clean and everything is put *in **order***.
  提姆的房間非常整齊，每樣東西都依次序擺放。
- Since my car is *out of **order***, I could only go to work by bus.
  既然我的車子故障了，我也只能搭公車上班了。
- ***In order*** to pass the test, Jane studied very hard.
  為了通過考試，珍非常努力地用功讀書。

v.t. 命令；指揮

- The officer **ordered** the police to catch the man.
  警官命令警察逮住那個男人。

v.t. 點餐

- I'd like to **order** a steak and a salad. Thank you.
  我想點一客牛排跟一份沙拉，謝謝。

3. other

[ˋʌðɚ]

adj. 另一個；其餘的

- No **other** boy is as tall as Tom in my class.
  = Tom is taller than any **other** boy in my class.
  = Tom is the tallest boy in my class.
  我班上沒有其他男孩子和湯姆一樣高。
  = 湯姆比我班上任何其他男孩子都高。
  = 湯姆在我班上是最高的男孩子。

adj. 其他的；別的；更多的

- I can not move this table; I need **other** people's help.

  我搬不動這張桌子，我需要其他人的幫忙。

in other words
換句話說

- I find a job; *in other* words, I can make money by myself.

  我找到工作了；換句話說，我可以靠自己賺錢了。

pron. 另一個；其餘的

others = other + N
其餘的

- Jack is here. Where are all the **others**?

  = Jack is here. Where are all the **other** persons?

  傑克在這裏。那其他人呢?

注意

　　other 和 another 的比較請參考 Unit 2 的 another。

---

4. out
[aut]

adv. 在外；外出；不在家

- He went **out** for a walk.

  他出門去散步。

- "May I speak to Ken?"

  "He is **out** now. Could you call later?"

  「我可以跟肯說話嗎?」

  「他現在不在家，你可以晚點再打來嗎?」

prep. 通過～出去

- I looked **out** the window and saw the garden.

  從窗戶看出去，我看到了花園。

adv. 顯露；出現；洩漏

- The moon came **out** after the rain stopped.

  雨停之後，月亮顯露了出來。

adv. 出局；出界 ↔ safe [sef] 安全上壘

- The baseball game is over after the third hitter is **out**.

  在第三位打者出局之後，棒球比賽就結束了。

adv. 出聲地；大聲地

- The alarm rang **out** and everyone ran out of the house.

  警鈴大聲地響，所有人都跑出了房子。

O

adv. （用）完

- Time is running **out**; you have to answer the question now.
  時間快用完了，你必須立刻回答出這個問題。

adv. 去掉

- The dirty mark on your clothes would be hard to wash **out**.
  你衣服上的髒污會很難洗掉。

---

5. **outside**
[`aut`saɪd]

n. 外表；外部；外側 ↔ inside [`ɪn`saɪd] 內部

- The word on the **outside** of the package is not clear.
  包裹外側的字不是很清楚。

adj. 外面的；外部的；外來的 ↔ inside [`ɪn`saɪd] 裡面的

- The **outside** wall of the school was painted white.
  學校的外牆被漆成白色。

adv. 在外面 ↔ inside [`ɪn`saɪd] 在裡面

- I hate to go **outside** on rainy days.
  我討厭在下雨天出門（到外面去）。

---

6. **over**
[`ovɚ]

adj. 結束的

- The vacation is **over**, and we must go to school again.
  假期結束了，我們又得去上學。

- "Where are you, **over**?" "I'm at the park, **over**."
  「你在哪裡，OVER？」「我在公園裡，OVER。」

- Game **over**. = The Game is **over**.
  遊戲結束。

adv. 再一次；重複地

over and over again
一次又一次地

- He tried *over* and *over* again to hit the other man but in vain.
  他一次又一次地試著想打擊另一個人，但終究徒勞無功。

prep. 在～上面；在～上方

- The bridge **over** the river was great for lovers to take a walk.
  河流上方的這座橋很適合情人散步。

P

prep. 超過；多餘

- You have studied **over** three hours; you should take a rest.
  你已經唸書超過三小時了，你應該休息一下。

prep. 遍及；到處

all over + N
～到處都是

- Clean your room right now; the garbage is *all over* the ground.
  馬上清理你的房間，地板上到處都是垃圾。

---

7. own [on]

of one's own
屬於自己的
on one's own
獨力地

adj. 獨自的；自己的

- A teenager should have a room *of his/her own*.
  一個青少年應該有一個屬於他／她自己的房間。
- Gary finished the job *on his own*.
  蓋瑞自己獨力完成了工作。

v.t. 擁有

- The rich man **owns** several houses in Taipei.
  這有錢人在台北擁有好幾棟房子。

---

8. p.m.
[`pɪ`ɛm]

abbr. 下午 = post meridiem（拉丁文）的縮寫 = after noon

- I often watch the evening news at 7:00 **p.m.** when I eat dinner.
  在吃晚餐的時候，我通常會看下午七點的晚間新聞。

注意
p.m. 和 a.m. 的比較請參考 Unit 1 的 **a.m.**。

---

9. pack
[pæk]

n. [C] 包裹；背包

- Sam put all the things in his **pack** quickly and went outside.
  山姆很快地把東西放進他的背包裡，然後就出門去了。

n. [C]（一）包；（一）捆

a pack of + Ns
一包～

- Leon used to eat *packs* of candies every day.
  里昂以前習慣一天吃好幾包糖果。

v.t. v.i. 打包

- You have to take the airplane tomorrow morning, so don't forget to **pack** tonight.
  你明天一早就得搭飛機，所以今晚別忘了要打包。

10. **package**
[ˋpækɪdʒ]

n. [C] 包裹

· "Jack sent a **package** to you and I put it on your desk."
"Thanks."

「傑克寄了一個包裹給你，我把它放在你桌上了。」
「謝啦!」

n. [C]（一）包;（一）捆

a package of + Ns
一包（裹）的～

· Quincy sent me *a **package** of* books from U.S. last month.
昆西上個月從美國寄了一包裹的書給我。

P

休息一下喔!

Exercise 1

I. 字彙翻譯

1. 外出 _____

2. 擁有 _____

3. 打包 _____

4. 下午 _____

5. 在～上面 _____

II. 字彙填充

_____ 1. The kid has no o_____r questions.

_____ 2. Having a glass of o_____e juice every morning is good for you.

_____ 3. What would you like to o_____r, sir?

_____ 4. The kids were playing o_____e the house.

_____ 5. Ray carried a p_____e home from his office.

III. 字彙選擇

( ) 1. Mom sent me a large _____ of food from Taiwan.

(A) package   (B) other   (C) orange   (D) own

( ) 2. Father went _____ to go fishing in the early morning.

(A) own   (B) over   (C) out   (D) pack

( ) 3. William did his homework on his _____.

(A) pack   (B) order   (C) other   (D) own

( ) 4. Last night, I forgot I had a date with Rebecca at 7:00 _____.

(A) p.m.   (B) a.m.   (C) over   (D) out

( ) 5. The movie was _____ ten minutes ago.

(A) own   (B) over   (C) outside   (D) package

P

11. page
[pedʒ]

n. [C] 頁
- Class, open the book to **page** thirty one.
  同學們，把書翻到第三十一頁。

12. paint
[pent]

v.t. 用油漆塗以～顏色
- I **painted** the wall light yellow.
  我把牆壁塗成淡黃色。

v.t. 畫～
- The kid is **painting** a monkey on the paper.
  那孩子正在紙上畫一隻猴子。

n. [U] 顏料；油漆
- Don't sit on the chair. The **paint** is still wet.
  別坐在這張椅子上。油漆未乾。

13. pair [pɛr]

a pair of + Ns
一雙／對／副～

n. [C] 雙；對；副
- My shoes are worn out. I need to buy *a* new *pair of* ones.
  我的鞋子穿壞了，我得去買一雙新的。

14. pants
[pænts]

n. 褲子；寬鬆的長褲
- Your coat goes well with the **pants**.
  你的外套和褲子很搭。
- I bought two pairs of **pants** and a pretty dress as I got my pay.
  我拿到薪水的時候，就去買了兩件褲子跟一套漂亮的洋裝。

注意

　　pants 較常見複數形式，只有在當複合詞的第一要素時，才會出現單數，如 pant legs（褲子的褲腳部分）。

15. paper [`pepɚ]

a piece of paper
一張紙

n. [C] 紙
- I need *a piece of* **paper** to take some notes.
  我需要一張紙記些筆記。

n. [C] 報紙
- My father likes to read **papers** when he eats breakfast.
  我爸爸喜歡在吃早餐的時候看報紙。

P

n. [C] 考卷；答案卷

- Time is up. Put down your pen and pass the **papers** to me.
  時間到。將你的筆放下，並將考卷傳給我。

16. **parent**
[`pɛrənt]

n. [C] 雙親

- Most **parents** want their children to have a better life.
  大部分的雙親都希望他們的孩子能夠有更好的生活。

注意

parents 通常用複數，使用單數時則指父母其中一人。

17. **park**
[pɑrk]

n. [C] 公園；遊樂場

- Many old people like to get up early and exercise in the **park**.
  很多老人家都喜歡早早起床，到公園裡運動。

v.t. v.i. 停車

- You can't **park** your car here; this is my land.
  你不能把你的車停在這兒，這是我的土地。

a parking space
停車位

- I drove around for hours to find *a **parking** space*.
  我在這附近開車繞了好幾個小時找停車位。

a parking lot
停車場

- When you are in a traffic jam, the road is like *a **parking** lot*.
  當你遇到塞車的時候，馬路就像是一個停車場。

18. **part**
[pɑrt]

n. [C][U] （一）部分

- Some **parts** of his story is ture.
  他所說的故事裡，有某些部份是真的。

- The first **part** of the book is about how to use time well.
  本書的第一個部分是有關如何善加利用時間。

take part in + N
參加～

- Because I caught a cold, I couldn't *take **part** in* the game.
  因為感冒，所以我無法參加比賽。

19. **party**
[`pɑrtɪ]

n. [C] 派對；聚會

- We had a great time at the birthday **party**.
  我們在這生日派對上玩得很愉快。

注意

不同「聚會」定義之比較請參閱 Unit 10 的 dance。

n. [C] 政黨；黨派

· There are voices from different **parties** in a modern country.
   在現代國家裡會有不同黨派所表達的意見。

---

20. **pass**
   [pæs]

   pass by
   經過；過去

   pass away
   過世

   pass the test
   通過考試

v.t. v.i. 經過；穿過；越過；超過（＋地點）

· Before the bridge there is a mark saying "No **Passing**."
   在那座橋之前，有一個標誌寫著「不准超車」。

· When I *passed* by the bakery, I bought some bread.
   在我經過那家麵包店的時候，買了一些麵包。

· The bus just *passed* by; you have to wait for the next bus now.
   巴士剛過去，現在你得等下一班了。

· The old man *passed* away at the age of one hundred and six.
   那個老先生在一百零六歲的時候過世。

v.t. v.i. 通過，及格（＋考試，測驗）

· Did you successfully *pass* the test?
   你成功通過考試了嗎？

v.t. v.i. 傳遞；（球類運動中的）傳球

· Would you please **pass** me the salt?
   請把鹽遞給我好嗎？

· Peter **passed** the ball to John and made him get two points.
   彼得將球傳給約翰，讓他得了兩分。

n. [C] 通行證；護照；入場證

· Without the **pass**, you can't enter this factory.
   沒有通行證，你不能進入這家工廠。

Exercise 2

I. 字彙翻譯

1. 公園 _____ 2. 部分 _____ 3. 油漆 _____

4. 通過 _____ 5. 派對 _____

P

II. 字彙填充

_____ 1. Have you read the sports p_____es of the newspaper?

_____ 2. The old man in black p_____ts is my father.

_____ 3. Kay bought me a p_____r of gloves as a gift.

_____ 4. My p_____ts ask me to sleep before 10:00 p.m.

_____ 5. Before you hand in the test p_____r, remember to check it again.

III. 字彙選擇

( ) 1. You can't _____ your car around the house.

    (A) pass   (B) park   (C) paint   (D) part

( ) 2. The first _____ of the novel is my favorite.

    (A) paint   (B) paper   (C) part   (D) pass

( ) 3. Father _____ the wall for a whole week.

    (A) painted   (B) passed   (C) parted   (D) parked

( ) 4. We are going to have fun at the Christmas _____.

    (A) party   (B) page   (C) pair   (D) pants

( ) 5. Though he studied hard for the test, he still didn't _____ it.

    (A) paper   (B) part   (C) pants   (D) pass

Unit 30

1. **past**
[pæst]

adj. 過去的；之前的

· The winter is **past** and the spring is coming.
　冬天過去了，而春天即將來臨。

· I was sleeping in the **past** few hours. What happened?
　之前的幾小時我都在睡覺。發生什麼事啦？

n. 過去；昔日；往事 (the S)↔ future [`fjutʃ⁀] 未來

· In the **past**, people went to bed early for there was no light.
　在過去，因為沒電燈，人們早早就上床睡覺。

· The older people are, the more often they think about the **past**.
　人們越老，越常去想往事。

prep. （範圍；程度；能力等）超過

· It's ten **past** five.
　現在是五點十分。

2. **pay**
[pe]

過去式	過去分詞	現在進行式
paid [ped]	paid [ped]	paying [`peɪŋ]

v.t. v.i. 付錢；償還

· In some restaurants, you have to **pay** before eating.
　在某些餐廳，你必須在用餐前就付帳。

pay for + N
為～付出代價

· The bad man has to *pay* *for* what he did.
　這個壞人必須為他所做過的事付出代價。

v.i. （工作等）有報酬

· I like the job. It is what I'm interested in and it **pays** well.
　我喜歡這份工作。它是我感興趣的東西而且薪水還蠻高。

n. [U] 薪水、工資

· Everyone listens carefully when the boss talks about the **pay**.
　當老闆提到薪水的時候，每個人都專心地聽。

P

3. **PE**
[ˋpiˋi]

n. [C] 體育課 = physical education [ˋfɪzɪkḷ͵ɛdʒəˋkeʃən]
- We played basketball in **PE** class today.
  今天我們體育課打籃球。

4. **pen**
[pɛn]

n. [C] 筆；鋼筆；原子筆
- I need a **pen** to write down the words.
  我需要一隻筆把這些字寫下來。

  - a ballpoint pen 圓珠筆

5. **pencil**
[ˋpɛnsḷ]

n. [C] 鉛筆
- You can erase the words written with a **pencil** easily.
  你可以輕易地擦掉這些用鉛筆寫的字。

6. **people**
[ˋpipḷ]

n. 人們
- Most **people** love to be easy and comfortable but hate to work.
  大部分人都喜愛安逸、舒適，討厭工作。
- Some rich **people** are not happy; they also have troubles.
  有些有錢人並不快樂。他們也會有煩惱。

注意

people 指兩個以上的人，後面接複數動詞。

7. **perhaps**
[pɚˋhæps]

adv. 或許；大概；可能
- I am not sure where John is; **perhaps** he is in the library.
  我不確定約翰在哪裡，他可能在圖書館。

8. **person**
[ˋpɝsṇ]

n. [C] 人
- You are kind; it's hard to find a nice **person** like you.
  你真仁慈，現在很難找到像你一樣好的人了。

in person
親自

- The king will welcome those foreigners *in **person***.
  國王將親自迎接那些外國人。

P

person 為泛稱，所有成人 (adult)、青少年 (teenager)、兒童 (kid, child)、男子 (man)、女子 (woman)、男孩 (boy)、女孩 (girl) 等都可泛稱為 person，person 的複數為 persons 或 people，用 person(s) 時表示較重視不同「個體」間的差異性，而用 people 時則較偏向指稱某一「群體」。

---

9. **pet**
[pɛt]

keep + N + as a pet
養～當寵物
the teacher's pet
老師寵愛的人

n. [C] 寵物

· People can't keep any **pet** in this apartment.
在這棟公寓，是不准任何人養寵物的。

· I have *kept* a cat *as a **pet*** for about seven years.
我已經養一隻貓當寵物大約七年之久了。

· Sally is *the teacher's **pet***, and sometimes I think she is proud.
莎莉是老師最寵愛的人，有時候我會覺得她太傲慢。

---

10. **piano**
[pɪˋæno]

play the piano
彈鋼琴

n. [C] 鋼琴

· I love music and have a **piano** in my living room.
我喜愛音樂，而且在我家客廳裡有一架鋼琴。

· Hannah likes *playing the **piano*** and she wants to be a pianist.
漢娜喜歡彈鋼琴，並希望能成為一個鋼琴家。

補充

· pianist [pɪˋænɪst]　鋼琴家

Exercise 1

I. 字彙翻譯

1. 寵物 _____

2. 體育課 _____

3. 付錢 _____

4. 鉛筆 _____

5. 原子筆 _____

II. 字彙填充

_____ 1. The market is full of p_____e especially on weekends.

_____ 2. The young girl is good at playing the p_____o.

_____ 3. The student p_____s found the answer to the question.

_____ 4. In the p_____t, people led a simple life.

_____ 5. Don't talk to any strange p_____n.

III. 字彙選擇

( ) 1. Jack worked sixteen hours a day in the _____ week. He is tired out now.

(A) past   (B) pay   (C) perhaps   (D) pet

( ) 2. Can I keep a cat as a _____?

(A) person   (B) pet   (C) pencil   (D) pay

( ) 3. Students play basketball in _____ class.

(A) past   (B) piano   (C) people   (D) PE

( ) 4. The bad boss didn't _____ the worker anything.

(A) piano   (B) pay   (C) pen   (D) perhaps

( ) 5. He is the nicest _____ that I have ever known.

(A) person   (B) people   (C) pet   (D) pay

11. **pick**

[pɪk]

pick + sth + up
撿起某物
pick + sb + up
接某人

v.t. 挑選

· I don't know which cake tastes better. Can you **pick** one for me?
我不知道哪個蛋糕比較美味。你能幫我挑選一個嗎？

· Don't put your garbage at will; *pick it up.*
別隨意亂放你的垃圾，把它撿起來。

· "Can you *pick me up* at seven o'clock p.m.?"
"Sure, see you tonight."
「你晚上七點能來接我嗎？」
「當然，今晚見。」

12. **picnic**

[`pɪknɪk]

go on/have a picnic
= go picnicking
去野餐

n. [C] 野餐

· The weather is great for *going on a picnic* in the park.
天氣好極了，很適合到公園去野餐。

v.i. 野餐

過去式	過去分詞	現在進行式
picnicked [`pɪknɪkt]	picnicked [`pɪknɪkt]	picnicking [`pɪknɪkɪŋ]

· We **picnicked** beside the river and had a good time.
我們到河邊野餐，玩得很愉快。

13. **picture**

[`pɪktʃɚ]

take a picture
拍照
get the picture
瞭解情況

n. [C] 相片；圖畫

· The kid drew a **picture** of his house and his family.
那孩子畫了一張裡面有他房子跟他家人的圖。

· Smile, and I will *take a picture* of you with my camera.
笑一個，我用我的相機幫你拍一張照片。

· I was hurt on the leg and could not go to the party. Do you *get the picture* now?
我腿受傷了，不能參加那個宴會。你現在瞭解狀況了嗎？

v.t. 想像

· It's funny to **picture** the world in the future.
想像未來的世界是什麼樣子，是很有趣的一件事。

14. pie

[paɪ]

n. [C] 派

· The apple **pie** is very delicious.

蘋果派很好吃。

n. [C] 極簡單之事；不堪一擊的對手

as easy as pie
很容易；易如反掌

· It is *as easy as pie* for me to answer this math question.

對我而言，回答這個數學問題根本就是易如反掌。

> **注意**
>
> pie（派）有很多種，有甜的，像是 apple pie（蘋果派）、fruit pie（水果派）、cream pie（奶油派），也有鹹的，像是 meat pie（肉派）等等。

15. piece [pis]

a piece of + N
一張～；一片～

break into pieces
成為碎片

n. [C] 一張；一片；一塊

· I need *a piece of* paper to write down the phone number.

我需要一張紙把電話號碼記下來。

· The bottle fell down on the ground and *broke into pieces*.

那個瓶子掉到地上，摔成了碎片。

16. pig

[pɪg]

when pigs fly
不可能；決不

n. [C] 豬

· **Pigs** and chickens are usually kept to be eaten.

豬和雞通常被養來吃。

· Paul is so mean; he will treat you only *when pigs fly*.

保羅如此小氣，不可能請你吃飯。

17. pink

[pɪŋk]

in the pink
非常健康

adj. 粉紅的

· The little girl's room is painted **pink**; it looks very warm.

那小女孩的房間被漆成粉紅色，看起來很溫暖。

· The cute girl has a **pink** face.

那可愛的女孩有一張粉紅色的臉蛋。

n. [C][U] 粉紅色；最佳狀態

· My grandpa is already ninety but is still *in the pink*.

我爺爺已經九十歲了，不過他的身體仍然非常健康。

18. pizza
[ˋpitsə]

n. [C] 比薩；披薩；義大利肉餡餅

- I want to order a big **pizza** and two small Cokes.
  我想點一個大披薩和兩杯小杯可樂。

19. place
[ples]

all over the place
到處

take place
發生；舉行

n. [C] 地方

- The poor man has no food to eat and no **place** to go.
  那可憐的人沒食物可以吃，也沒地方可以去。
- Toys are *all over the **place*** in the boy's room.
  那男孩的房間裡到處都是玩具。

n. [C] 住所

- There is a party in my **place** tonight; welcome to join us.
  今天晚上在我的居所會有一個宴會，歡迎加入。
- All people woke up when the fire *took **place***.
  火災發生的時候，所有人都醒過來了。

v.t. 放置

- I don't remember where I **placed**/put my notebook.
  我不記得我把筆記型電腦放到哪兒去了。

20. plan
[plæn]

plan to + V
計劃做～

n. [C] 計劃

- "Do you have any **plan** this weekend?"
  "I want to see a movie."
  「你這個週末有任何計劃嗎?」
  「我想去看場電影。」

v.t. v.i. 計劃；打算；策劃

過去式	過去分詞	現在進行式
planned [plænd]	planned [plænd]	planning [ˋplænɪŋ]

- We ***plan*** *to* do some shopping in the afternoon.
  我們計劃下午要做些採購。

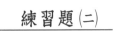
Exercise 2

I. 字彙翻譯

1. 一片；一張 _____   2. 派 _____   3. 挑選 _____

4. 粉紅色 _____   5. 豬 _____

II. 字彙填充

_____ 1. My class went for a p_____c at the beach on the weekend.

_____ 2. Don't go to that p_____e alone at night. It may be dangerous.

_____ 3. We had p_____a and coke for lunch.

_____ 4. We took a lot of p_____es when we were in Sydney.

_____ 5. Jack had a wonderful p_____n for the vacation.

III. 字彙選擇

( ) 1. Mom made a cherry _____ herself.

     (A) pig   (B) pie   (C) pink   (D) piece

( ) 2. Tina wrote something on a _____ of paper.

     (A) pie   (B) pink   (C) piece   (D) place

( ) 3. Alvin bought 99 _____ roses for his girlfriend.

     (A) pink   (B) pieces   (C) pies   (D) pizza

( ) 4. When should I _____ you up?

     (A) pick   (B) picture   (C) pink   (D) plan

( ) 5. Jessica _____ to shop in the department store tonight.

     (A) picks   (B) picnics   (C) places   (D) plans

Unit 31

1. play

[ple]

play with + N
玩～；與～逗玩

v.t. v.i. 玩

· Brad **played** cards with his friends after dinner.
晚餐後，布萊德和他的朋友一起打牌。

· The kids are ***playing*** with toys.
那些孩子正在玩著玩具。

v.t. 打（～球）

· Jeff **plays** tennis very well.
傑夫網球打得很好。

v.t. 演奏（樂器）

· Sue **plays** the piano in the school band.
蘇在學校的樂隊裡彈鋼琴。

v.t. 播放（音樂）

· You shouldn't **play** the music too loud.
你不該把音樂播放的太大聲。

v.t. 演出（某角色）

n. [C] 戲劇；劇本

· "I will **play** a tree in the **play**."
"That must be very interesting."
「我要在戲劇裡演出一棵樹。」
「那一定很有趣。」

n. [U] 遊戲；玩耍

· All work and no **play** makes Jack a dull boy.
[諺語] 只會用功不玩耍，聰明孩子也變傻。

2. player

[`pleɚ]

n. [C] 球員；選手

· Iverson is a great basketball **player**.
艾佛森是個優秀的籃球選手。

n. [C] 播放器；唱機；隨身聽

· I listen to music with my CD **player**.
我用我的CD隨身聽聽音樂。

P

3. **playground**
[`ple,graund]

n. [C] 操場；遊樂場

· We have a lot of fun at the **playground**.
  我們在遊樂場玩得很開心。

4. **please**
[pliz]

interj. 請

· **Please** pass me the bread, thanks.
  請把麵包傳給我，謝謝。

v.t. 使～高興；使～滿意；取悅～

· Tina is angry, and I am trying to **please** her.
  蒂娜在生氣，而我正試著要取悅她。

be pleased with + N
對～感到滿意

· My father *is* **pleased** *with* my grades.
  父親對我的成績感到滿意。

5. **point**
[pɔɪnt]

n. [C] 分數

· We got nine **points** and won the baseball game.
  我們得了九分並贏了那場棒球賽。

v.t. 指向

point + sth + at + sb
把～指向～

· Don't **point** your fingers *at* other people; it's not polite.
  別用手指指別人，這樣子不禮貌。

6. **police**
[pə`lis]
the police
警方（後面須接複數動詞）

n. [U] 警察

· Maria called *the* **police** to find her missing daughter.
  瑪麗亞打電給警方，請他們協尋她失蹤的女兒。

· *The* **police** are looking for her missing daughter.
  警方正尋找她失蹤的女兒。

7. **polite**
[pə`laɪt]

adj. 有禮貌的

· Everyone likes **polite** kids.
  每個人都喜歡有禮貌的小孩。

be polite to + sb
對～有禮貌

· A good kid should *be* **polite** *to* his/her parents.
  好小孩應該對父母有禮貌。

P

8. poor
[pʊr]

the poor
窮人 (接複數動詞)

adj. 貧窮的 ↔ rich [rɪtʃ] 富有的
- The **poor** man doesn't even have food to eat.
  那貧窮的人甚至連食物都沒得吃。
- *The **poor** need our help.*
  窮人需要我們的幫助。

adj. 粗劣的；蹩腳的
- He speaks **poor** English.
  他的英文說的很糟。

adj. 不幸的；可憐的
- Nobody wants to take care of the **poor** old woman.
  沒有人願意照顧這個可憐的老婦人。

9. popcorn
[ˋpɑpˌkɔrn]

n. [U] 爆玉米花
- I like to eat some **popcorn** when I see a movie.
  我在看電影時喜歡吃點爆米花。

10. popular
[ˋpɑpjələ]

be popular with + sb
受～歡迎的

adj. 流行的；廣為流傳的
- Cell phones are very **popular** now; almost everybody has one.
  手機現在很流行，幾乎每個人都有一支。
- Ray loves listening to **popular** music.
  雷喜歡聽流行樂。

adj. 受歡迎的；得人心的
- The movie star *is* very ***popular** with* fans around the world.
  這位電影明星很受全球各地影迷的歡迎。

Exercise 1

I. 字彙翻譯

1. 警察 _____
2. 選手 _____
3. 貧窮的 _____
4. 請 _____
5. 玩 _____

II. 字彙填充

_____ 1. Students have lots of fun during the ten-minute break at the p_____d.

_____ 2. It's p_____e to say "hi" to other people.

_____ 3. Which kind of p_____n do you like, salty（鹹的）or sweet?

_____ 4. Our handsome PE teacher is p_____r with girl students.

_____ 5. My mother is so happy, because I got one hundred p_____ts in the math test.

III. 字彙選擇

( ) 1. You should call the _____ if your husband hits you.
  (A) polite　　　　(B) police　　　　(C) point　　　　(D) popcorn

( ) 2. Could you open the window for me, _____?
  (A) please　　　　(B) point　　　　(C) polite　　　　(D) police

( ) 3. Johnny is _____ with his dog and having a lot of fun.
  (A) popular　　　　(B) poor　　　　(C) playing　　　　(D) pointing

( ) 4. Erwin always helps the _____.
  (A) poor　　　　(B) play　　　　(C) point　　　　(D) popcorn

( ) 5. Jordan is the best basketball _____ I have ever known.
  (A) play　　　　(B) playground　　　　(C) please　　　　(D) player

P

11. pork
[pork]

n. [U] 豬肉

· We cooked some **pork** and beef for dinner.
我們煮了些豬肉和牛肉當晚餐。

· I ordered a **pork** steak in the restaurant.
我在餐廳裡點了一客豬排。

12. possible
[`pɑsəbḷ]

adj. 可能的 ↔ impossible [ɪm`pɑsəbḷ] 不可能的

· It is **possible** to rain, so don't forget your umbrella.
可能會下雨，所以別忘了帶你的傘。

as + Adj/Adv + as
possible　儘可能~

· We have no time, so please finish the job *as* soon *as* **possible**.
我們沒有時間了，所以請儘快完成這項工作。

13. post office
[`post͵ɔfɪs]

n. [C] 郵局

· I went to the **post office** to send my letters.
我到郵局去寄信。

注意

post [post] 為不可數名詞，是郵寄，郵件的意思。

14. postcard
[`post͵kɑrd]

n. [C] 郵政明信片

· I will send you some **postcards** when I go to America.
我去美國的時候，會寄些明信片給你。

15. pound
[paʊnd]

n. [C] 磅（重量單位）

· I am a little too fat now; I want to lose some **pounds**.
我現在有點太肥，我想減個幾磅。

n. [C] 英鎊（英國幣制單位）

· One **pound** is about two US dollars.
一英鎊大約等於兩美元。

16. practice
[`præktɪs]

v.t. v.i. 練習

· You must **practice** more if you want to join the baseball team.
如果你想加入棒球隊，你得再多加練習。

P

practice + Ving 練習～	· I *practiced* *swimming* four hours a day before the game. 在比賽之前，我一天練習游泳四小時。 *n.* [U] 練習 · **Practice** makes perfect. [諺語] 練習造就完美。（熟能生巧。）
17. **prepare** [prɪ`pɛr] prepare for + N/to V 為～做準備	*v.t. v.i.* 準備；預備 · I have to *prepare* *for* the math test tomorrow. 我必須準備明天的數學小考。 · Kate is *preparing* *to* go to the America. 凱特正在為去美國作準備。
18. **present** [`prɛzn̩t] at present 目前；現在	*n.* [C] 禮物 = gift [gɪft] · I got many **presents** on my birthday. 在我生日那天，我收到很多禮物。 *n.* 現今；目前 · We should forget the past and hold the **present**. 我們應該忘了過去，把握現在。 · All I want *at* *present* is cold drinks; I am so thirsty. 現在我想要的只有冷飲；我好渴呀。 *adj.* 出席的 · Jason was not **present** at the party yesterday. 傑森沒有出席昨天的宴會。
19. **pretty** [`prɪtɪ]	*adj.* 漂亮的 = beautiful [`bjutəfəl] · Rose is a **pretty** girl. Many boys like her. 蘿絲是個漂亮的女孩。很多男生都喜歡她。 *adv.* 相當地；非常地 · Jack is **pretty** good at English. 傑克相當地擅長英語。
20. **price** [praɪs]	*n.* [C] 價錢 · I want to buy this pair of shoes. What is the **price** of it? 我想買這雙鞋。它的價錢是多少？

- I bought the book at a low **price**.
  我以低價買到那本書。

補充

價錢的高低以 high 或 low 表示；high price（高價）。

n. 代價（當「代價」解釋時只用單數形）

pay a price for
為～付出代價
at any price
不計任何代價

- You have to *pay a **price** for* your mistake.
  你必須為你的錯誤付出代價。
- Thomas will win the game *at any **price***.
  湯瑪士會不計任何代價贏得那場比賽。

P

休息一下喔！

Exercise 2

I. 字彙翻譯

1. 豬肉 _____
2. 禮物 _____
3. 價錢 _____
4. 可能的 _____
5. 郵局 _____ _____

II. 字彙填充

_____ 1. I sent a p_____d to my friend when I was in London.

_____ 2. If you want to speak English well, you must p_____e every day.

_____ 3. The cook bought ten p_____ds of beef.

_____ 4. Tom worked hard to p_____e for the coming test.

_____ 5. Linda is not only a p_____y girl but also nice to everybody.

III. 字彙選擇

( ) 1. The _____ steak at the restaurant tastes really good.

    (A) possible   (B) pork   (C) postcard   (D) pretty

( ) 2. I will finish the paper work as soon as _____.

    (A) price   (B) present   (C) prepare   (D) possible

( ) 3. How did you lose ten _____ in one month?

    (A) pounds   (B) presents   (C) prices   (D) practices

( ) 4. I bought the cap at a good _____.

    (A) pound   (B) price   (C) pretty   (D) present

( ) 5. Willy had a special birthday _____ for you.

    (A) price   (B) pretty   (C) present   (D) pound

Unit 32

1. problem
[`prɑbləm]

n. [C] 問題
- "Could you lend me a pencil?" "No **problem**."
  「你能借我一隻鉛筆嗎?」「沒問題。」
- Traffic has become a serious **problem** in big cities.
  交通已經成為大都市的嚴重問題。

2. program
[`progræm]

n. [C] 節目;表演
- There will be a special **program** on TV tonight.
  今天晚上電視會播一個特別節目。

3. proud
[praʊd]

adj. 驕傲的;得意的
- Jenny is too **proud**, so nobody likes her.
  珍妮太驕傲了,所以沒人喜歡她。

be proud of + sb
以～為榮
- The father *is* very ***proud*** of his excellent son.
  那位父親非常以自己優秀的兒子為榮。

4. public
[`pʌblɪk]

adj. 公眾的
- People can't smoke in many **public** places in Taiwan.
  人們在臺灣很多的公共場所都是不能抽煙的。

in public
公開地;當眾
- Some people don't like to speak *in* ***public***; they are too shy.
  有些人不喜歡當眾發表演說,他們太害羞了。

n. 公眾,大眾 (the public)
- The museum is open to the **public** six days a week.
  博物館一個禮拜有六天對大眾開放。

5. pull
[pʊl]

v.t. v.i. 拉 ↔ push [pʊʃ] 推
- He should **pull** the door open, not push it.
  他應該拉開門,不是用推的。

pull out + N
拔出
- My bad tooth was ***pulled*** out.
  我的蛀牙昨天被拔掉了。

| pull + N + over | · The officer asked the driver to **pull** his car *over*. |
| 把車開到路邊停下 | 警官要求那名司機把車開到路邊停下。 |

P

6. **purple**
[ˋpɝp!]

adj. 紫色的

· The **purple** shirt goes well with the blue jeans.
　這紫色襯衫搭配藍色牛仔褲很好看。

· Denny just fell over; his knee hurt and turned **purple**.
　丹尼剛才跌倒了，他的膝蓋痛而且變成紫色的（淤青）。

n. [C][U] 紫色

· **Purple** is the color of fresh grapes.
　紫色是新鮮葡萄的顏色。

7. **push**
[puʃ]

v.t. v.i. 推 ↔ pull [pul] 拉

· I **push** the door open and walk into the room.
　我推開門，然後走進房間。

v.t. v.i. 按

· Don't **push** the red button at will.
　不要隨意就按下那個紅色按鈕。

v.t. 逼迫；促使

· Don't **push** the kid too hard.
　別把那孩子逼的太緊。

8. **put**
[put]

過去式	過去分詞	現在進行式
put [put]	put [put]	putting [ˋputɪŋ]

v.t. v.i. 放；放下

· Where did you **put** the car keys?
　你把車鑰匙放到哪兒了？

put down + N	· I **put** *down* the book and take a rest.
放下～	我把書放下，休息一會兒。
put on + N	· **Put** *on* your jacket before going out. It's cold outside.
穿上	外出前先穿上外套。外面很冷。

| put off
拖延 | · Don't ***put off*** till tomorrow what can be done today.
[諺語] 別把今天能做的事拖延到明天。（今日事今日畢。） |

9. **queen**
[kwin]

n. [C] 女王；皇后
· Elizabeth is one of the most famous **queens** of England.
伊莉莎白是英國最有名的女王之一。

10. **question**
[ˋkwɛstʃən]

n. [C] 問題
· If you have any **question**, please tell me.
如果你們有任何問題，請告訴我。
· The answer to this **question** is fifty one. Am I right?
這個問題的答案是 51，我說對了嗎？
v.t. 對～提出質疑；質疑～
· I will finish the work on time. Don't **question** my words.
我會準時完成工作。不要質疑我說的話。

Q

休息一下喔！

Exercise 1

I. 字彙翻譯

1. 公眾的 _____   2. 驕傲的 _____   3. 女王 _____

4. 問題 _____   5. 推 _____

II. 字彙填充

_____ 1. You have to face the p_____m yourself.

_____ 2. There are many good p_____ms on TV tonight.

_____ 3. The picture was painted with dark colors like p_____e and brown.

_____ 4. Jack p_____led the door hard, but couldn't open it.

_____ 5. I remember p_____ting my pen here, but it's gone.

III. 字彙選擇

( ) 1. Natalie is very _____ of her son.

　　(A) purple　　　　(B) pull　　　　(C) proud　　　　(D) put

( ) 2. I cannot start my car. Could you help me to _____ it?

　　(A) push　　　　(B) put　　　　(C) question　　　　(D) proud

( ) 3. Don't talk so loud in a _____ place.

　　(A) purple　　　　(B) pull　　　　(C) proud　　　　(D) public

( ) 4. Can I ask you some _____, sir?

　　(A) questions　　(B) problems　　(C) programs　　(D) queens

( ) 5. The _____ is popular with her people. Everyone likes her a lot.

　　(A) problem　　　(B) queen　　　(C) program　　　(D) put

11. **quick**

[kwɪk]

adj. 快速的；敏捷的
- You must be **quick** or you will be late.
  你動作一定要快，不然你就會遲到。

adv. 快速地 = quickly [`kwɪklɪ]
- He runs as **quick** as a horse.
  他跑的像馬一樣快。

12. **quiet**

[`kwaɪət]

adj. 安靜的
- Be **quiet**! The baby is sleeping.
  安靜！小寶寶正在睡覺。
- It is very **quiet** at night; we could only hear the wind.
  晚上非常安靜，我們只聽的到風的聲音。

13. **quite**

[kwaɪt]

quite a/an + N
相當～的

adv. 相當地
- It is **quite** stupid to water flowers on a rainy day.
  在下雨天澆花是相當蠢的。
- It is *quite* a strange experience to see the garden in the sea.
  觀看海中花園的景象是相當不可思議的經驗。

14. **rabbit**

[`ræbɪt]

n. [C] 兔子
- **Rabbits** have long ears and could jump very fast.
  兔子有著長長的耳朵，而且跳得非常快。

15. **radio**

[`redɪ,o]

turn on/off the radio
打開／關掉收音機

n. [C][U] 無線電廣播；收音機
- I used to listen to the music program on the **radio** when I drove.
  我過去時常在開車的時候收聽廣播裡的音樂節目。
- Jack *turned on the radio* and listened to the news.
  傑克打開收音機，收聽新聞。

v.t. v.i. 用無線電發送訊息
- The pilot **radioed** the airport and asked to land.
  飛行員透過無線電向機場聯絡，請求降落。

R

16. **railway**
[`rel,we]

n. [C] 鐵路

• Leave the **railway** right now; the train is coming.
馬上離開鐵路，火車就要來了。

> **注意**
>
> railway 為英式用法，美式用法則為 railroad [`rel,rod]。

17. **rain**
[ren]

v.i. 下雨

• It is **raining** now. Get in the house or you will be all wet.
下雨了。進屋子裡來，不然你會全身濕答答。

n. [U] 雨；雨水

• The flowers are dying for there has been no **rain** for months.
因為已經好幾個月沒有雨水，所以那些花都快死了。

18. **rainbow**
[`ren,bo]

n. [C] 彩虹

• After the rain, we could see the **rainbow** in the sun.
雨停之後，我們可在陽光下看到彩虹。

19. **rainy**
[`renɪ]

adj. 下雨的

• The **rainy** season in Taiwan falls in April and May.
台灣的雨季在四月和五月。

20. **read**
[rid]

read the papers /
comic books/a book
看報紙／漫畫／書

過去式	過去分詞	現在進行式
read [rɛd]	read [rɛd]	reading [`ridɪŋ]

v.t. 閱讀～

• My father likes to *read the papers* when he eats breakfast.
我爸爸喜歡在吃早餐的時候看報紙。

v.i. 讀書；閱讀

• I love **reading**, and my favorite is "The Catcher in the Rye."
我喜歡閱讀，而我最愛的一本書就是「麥田捕手」。

Exercise 2

I. 字彙翻譯

1. 安靜的 _____　　2. 相當地 _____　　3. 下雨 _____

4. 彩虹 _____　　5. 鐵路 _____

II. 字彙填充

_____ 1. Nick turned the r_____o on to listen to music.

_____ 2. Leo keeps a r_____t as a pet.

_____ 3. Move q_____k, or you won't catch up with others.

_____ 4. Amy likes to r_____d books before going to bed.

_____ 5. It's a r_____y day. Bring an umbrella with you.

III. 字彙選擇

(　) 1. Have you _____ the first book of *Harry Potter*?

　　(A) read　　　　(B) readed　　　　(C) reads　　　　(D) reading

(　) 2. Keep _____ ; the baby is sleeping.

　　(A) quite　　　　(B) quiet　　　　(C) quick　　　　(D) queen

(　) 3. We had a lot of _____ here last night.

　　(A) read　　　　(B) rainy　　　　(C) rain　　　　(D) railway

(　) 4. The weather is _____ hot today.

　　(A) quiet　　　　(B) quite　　　　(C) queen　　　　(D) quick

(　) 5. There are seven different colors in a _____ .

　　(A) real　　　　(B) ready　　　　(C) rain　　　　(D) rainbow

Unit 33

1. ready
[`rɛdɪ]
be ready for + N/to
V 準備好～

adj. 準備好的

· *Are* you **ready** *for* the coming test?
   對於即將來臨的考試，你準備好了嗎？
· *Are* you **ready** *to* go shopping?
   你準備好去逛街了嗎？

R

2. real
[`riəl]

adj. 真的；真正的

· Everything I told you is **real**. I didn't lie.
   我告訴你的每件事都是真的，我沒說謊。

adj. 實際的；現實的

· Sometimes the **real** life is more interesting than a story book.
   有時候現實的人生比故事書還要來的有趣。

adj. 完全的；十足的

· You are a **real** fool if you think it is cool to smoke.
   如果你覺得抽煙很酷，那你就是個十足的傻瓜。

3. really
[`riəlɪ]

adv. 真正地；確實地；實際上

· I don't **really** know the answer. I just guess.
   我並不是真正地知道答案，我只是猜的。

adv. 很；十分；全然

· Father was **really** angry when he saw my poor grades.
   當爸爸看到我的壞成績時，他十分地生氣。

adv. 實在；其實（用於加強語氣）

· I should **really** have got up earlier.
   我其實應該早點起床的。

adv. 真的嗎？（表示驚訝、疑問）

· "In fact, Jay doesn't love Jolin."
   "Oh, my god. **Really**?"
   「其實，傑並不愛裴琳。」
   「喔，我的天啊！真的嗎？」

4. **red**

[rɛd]

turn red with anger
因生氣而臉紅

in red
穿紅衣服的

adj. 紅色的

- Do you like a green apple or a **red** apple?
  你喜歡青蘋果呢？還是紅蘋果？
- May *turned **red** with anger* when Ben made fun of her hair.
  當班取笑她的髮型時，梅因為生氣而臉紅。

n. [C][U] 紅；紅色

- **Red** is the color of fire, tomato, and an angry face.
  紅色是火、蕃茄和生氣的臉的顏色。
- The girl (dressed) *in red* is my daughter.
  那個穿著紅衣服的女孩是我女兒。

5. **refrigerator**

[rɪˋfrɪdʒəˏretɚ]

n. [C] 冰箱

- Today, people use **refrigerators** to keep their food fresh.
  現今人們都用冰箱來保持食物新鮮。

　　冰箱可簡稱為 fridge [frɪdʒ]，這是比較口語化的用法。另外像是 freezer [ˋfrizɚ] 和 icebox [ˋaɪsˏbɑks] 指的也是冰箱。

6. **remember**

[rɪˋmɛmbɚ]

remember to + V
記得要去做某事
remember + Ving
記得曾做過某事

v.t. v.i. 記得 ↔ forget [fɚˋgɛt] 忘記

- I **remember** that you don't eat beef, do you?
  我記得你是不吃牛肉的，是嗎？
- ***Remember** to turn* off the light when you leave the room.
  在你離開房間的時候，記得要關燈。
- I *remember seeing* this man, but I forget where I saw him.
  我記得我看過這個男人，但我忘了是在哪兒看過的。

v.t. v.i. 記住；牢記

- **Remember** this word; it is very important.
  記住這個單字，它很重要。

v.t. v.i. 想起；回憶起

- Sorry, but I just can't **remember** your name.
  抱歉，但我就是想不起你的名字。

R

7. **repeat**
[rɪ`pit]

v.t. v.i. 重複

· Don't **repeat** the same mistake.

不要重複犯同樣的錯誤。

v.t. v.i. 重說；照著說

· "**Repeat** this word two times after me. 'Nice.'"

"'Nice.' 'Nice.'"

「跟著我說兩遍這個字，'Nice'。」

「'Nice'。'Nice'。」

8. **rest**
[rɛst]

n. 其餘的（人或物）；剩下的（人或物）；剩餘部分 (the rest)

· I ate some cake and put the **rest** of it in the refrigerator.

我吃了一些蛋糕，然後把剩下的放冰箱。

n. [C][U] 休息

take a rest
休息

· You have worked for hours. You should *take a rest*.

你已經工作好幾個小時了。你應該休息一下。

v.i. 休息

· I have to **rest** for minutes after walking for so long.

走了這麼遠的路之後，我需要休息幾分鐘。

9. **restaurant**
[`rɛstərənt]

n. [C] 餐廳

· Do you want to eat at home or go to a **restaurant**?

你想在家裡吃飯還是要去餐廳吃?

10. **restroom**
[`rɛst͵rum]

n. [C] 廁所；洗手間；盥洗室 = rest room

· May I use your **restroom**? I want to wash my hands.

我可以借用一下你的洗手間嗎? 我想洗個手。

注意

廁所除了可以叫做 restroom 之外，常用的還有 ladies'
room（女生廁所）、men's room（男生廁所）、bathroom（浴室；
廁所）、toilet（廁所）、lavatory（廁所）等等。

Exercise 1

I. 字彙翻譯

1. 真的 _____
2. 廁所 _____
3. 紅色 _____
4. 餐廳 _____
5. 重複 _____

II. 字彙填充

_____ 1. Does Jack r_____y leave without saying goodbye?

_____ 2. I don't r_____r what I did last night.

_____ 3. We are r_____y to go now.

_____ 4. If you are thirsty, you can take a bottle of ice water out of the r_____r.

_____ 5. You look tired. Why not take a r_____t?

III. 字彙選擇

( ) 1. I will let you know when I get _____.

　　(A) real 　　　　(B) really 　　　　(C) ready 　　　　(D) red

( ) 2. The baby girl looks like _____, but in fact, it is a doll.

　　(A) real 　　　　(B) really 　　　　(C) repeat 　　　　(D) ready

( ) 3. John is not in the office now; he might go to the _____.

　　(A) rest 　　　　(B) repeat 　　　　(C) red 　　　　(D) restroom

( ) 4. The food in that _____ is great and not expensive.

　　(A) restroom 　　(B) restaurant 　　(C) ready 　　　　(D) repeat

( ) 5. Please _____ the sentence after me.

　　(A) repeat 　　　(B) remember 　　(C) rest 　　　　(D) really

11. rice

[raɪs]

fried rice
炒飯

n. [U] 稻米；米飯；稻穀

· Americans seldom eats **rice**; they usually eat fast food.
美國人很少吃米飯，他們通常都吃速食。

· It's hard to cook delicious *fried* **rice**.
要做出美味的炒飯是困難的。

12. rich

[rɪtʃ]

the rich
有錢人

be rich in + N
有豐富的～

adj. 有錢的；富有的 ↔ poor [pʊr] 貧窮的

· The businessman became **rich** from selling drinks.
這名商人靠著賣飲料致富。

· Some people say *the* **rich** should pay more taxes.
有些人說，有錢人應該繳比較多的稅。

adj. 富於～的；有很多的～

· The country *is* **rich** *in* oil.
這國家有豐富的石油。

13. ride

[raɪd]

過去式	過去分詞	現在進行式
rode [rod]	ridden [ˋrɪdn̩]	riding [ˋraɪdɪŋ]

v.t. v.i. 騎（摩托車、腳踏車、馬等）

· **Riding** a motorcycle without a helmet is dangerous.
騎摩托車不戴安全帽是危險的。

· You must be careful when you **ride** a bicycle.
你騎腳踏車的時候一定要小心。

· I have never **ridden** a horse.
我從未騎過馬。

注意
　　drive 與 ride 的比較請參見 U12 的 drive。

n. [C] 搭乘

give someone a ride
載某人一程

· I am going to be late for school. Could you *give me a* **ride**?
我上學快要遲到了，可以載我一程嗎?

272

R

14. right
[raɪt]

adj. 對的；正確的 = correct [kə`rɛkt]

- It's not **right** to tell a lie.

  說謊是不對的。

adj. 右邊的 ↔ left [lɛft] 左邊的

- Some people write with their **right** hand but some don't.

  有些人用右手寫字，有些則否。

adv. 向右地 ↔ left [lɛft] 向左地

- Turn **right** at the next traffic light and you'll find the theater.

  下一個紅綠燈右轉，你就會看到電影院。

n. [C] 右邊 (the right) ↔ left [lɛft] 左邊

- The man sitting on the **right** of Ginger is her older brother.

  坐在金潔右邊的那個男人是她哥哥。

n. [C][U] 權利

the right to + V
做～的權利

- Don't forget you have *the **right*** to say "no."

  別忘了你有說「不」的權利。

15. ring
[rɪŋ]

過去式	過去分詞	現在進行式
rang [ræŋ]	rung [rʌŋ]	ringing [`rɪŋɪŋ]

v.t. v.i. （電話、電鈴、警鈴、鐘等）響，鳴；使～鳴，響

- The phone was **ringing** when I walked into the living room.

  當我走進客廳時，電話正在響。

- I **rang** the bell, and soon Linda came to open the door.

  我按了門鈴，然後很快地琳達就來開門了。

n. [C] 環狀物；戒指

- Buck showed the **ring** and asked Camilla to marry him.

  巴克把戒指拿出來，並要求卡蜜拉嫁給他。

16. river
[`rɪvɚ]

n. [C] 江；河

- We liked to catch fish in the **river** when we were still kids.

  在我們還是小孩的時候，我們喜歡到河裡面去抓魚。

17. road
[rod]

the road/way to + N
～的途徑；手段

n. [C] 路；道路
- The department store is on the Park **Road**.
  那家百貨公司在公園路上。

n. [C] 途徑；手段
- All **roads** lead to Rome.
  [諺語] 條條大路通羅馬。
  (引申為「成功的途徑眾多，不需拘泥於某一種。」)
- Working hard is *the* only **road** *to* success.
  努力工作是成功的唯一途徑。

18. room
[rum]

n. [C] 房間
- You can sleep in this **room** when you stay here.
  你待在這裡的期間，可以睡在這個房間。

n. [U] 空間；位置
- There is not enough **room** to put a new sofa here.
  這裡沒有足夠的空間可以擺一張新沙發。

n. [U] 餘地；機會
- Poor grades mean you still have **room** to be better.
  壞成績表示你還有進步的空間。

19. rose
[roz]

n. [C] 玫瑰；薔薇
- Mary got a bunch of **roses** from Jim on their first date.
  在他們第一次約會的時候，瑪莉收到一束吉姆送的花。

20. round
[raund]

adj. 圓的
- The fat cat looks as **round** as a ball.
  那隻胖貓看起來就跟球一樣圓。
- The circle is not very **round** so I draw it again.
  這圓圈不是很圓所以我又重畫了一次。

R

Exercise 2

I. 字彙翻譯

1. 道路 ＿＿＿＿＿＿＿　　2. 河 ＿＿＿＿＿＿＿　　3. 房間＿＿＿＿＿＿＿

4. 騎 ＿＿＿＿＿＿＿　　5. 鳴響（三態）＿＿＿＿＿＿＿ ＿＿＿＿＿＿＿ ＿＿＿＿＿＿＿

II. 字彙填充

＿＿＿＿＿＿＿＿＿ 1. I like eating r＿＿＿＿e more than noodles.

＿＿＿＿＿＿＿＿＿ 2. You may be r＿＿＿＿t this time, so I listen to you.

＿＿＿＿＿＿＿＿＿ 3. Green vegetables are r＿＿＿＿h in vitamins（維他命）. You should eat more.

＿＿＿＿＿＿＿＿＿ 4. My family have dinner at the r＿＿＿＿d table in the dining room.

＿＿＿＿＿＿＿＿＿ 5. Julia got beautiful r＿＿＿＿es from her boyfriend.

III. 字彙選擇

(　　) 1. I ＿＿＿＿ my bike to school every day.

    (A) rice　　　　(B) ride　　　　(C) rich　　　　(D) ring

(　　) 2. The doorbell ＿＿＿＿ while I was talking on the phone.

    (A) round　　　　(B) rang　　　　(C) river　　　　(D) rode

(　　) 3. We don't have enough ＿＿＿＿ for all kids.

    (A) rooms　　　　(B) rides　　　　(C) roads　　　　(D) rivers

(　　) 4. We used to catch fish in the ＿＿＿＿.

    (A) road　　　　(B) rest　　　　(C) ring　　　　(D) river

(　　) 5. It is dangerous to play on the ＿＿＿＿.

    (A) ride　　　　(B) rich　　　　(C) road　　　　(D) round

R

Unit 34

1. rule [rul]

make it a rule to V
養成習慣做～
follow the rules
遵守規則

R

n. [C] 規則

- You should not *make it a rule to* smoke; it is not good for you.
  你不該養成抽煙的習慣，那對你沒有益處。

- If you want to play the game, you should *follow the rules*.
  如果你想玩遊戲，你就必須遵守（遊戲）規則。

- We should all *follow* traffic *rules* to keep ourselves safe.
  我們都應該遵守交通規則，以保護我們自己的安全。

v.t. 統治；支配

- The king who **ruled** this country was kind to his people.
  統治這個國家的國王對他的人民很仁慈。

2. ruler [`rulɚ]

n. [C] （直）尺

- I need a **ruler** to draw a line.
  我需要一把尺來畫一條直線。

n. [C] 統治者

- The **ruler** of the country was loved by his people.
  這個國家的統治者受到子民的愛戴。

3. run [rʌn]

過去式	過去分詞	現在進行式
ran [ræn]	run [rʌn]	running [`rʌnɪŋ]

v.i. 跑；跑步

- "How fast can you **run** 100 meters?" "About in 14 seconds."
  「你一百公尺跑多快?」「大約十四秒。」

- Gina got up too late, so she had to **run** to catch the bus.
  吉娜太晚起床了，所以她得跑步才趕得上公車。

v.i. （機器等）運轉；進行

· This new washing machine **runs** quietly.

這台新的洗衣機運轉起來很安靜。

v.i. 經營；管理

· The boss is teaching his son how to **run** a factory.

老闆正在教他兒子如何管理一家工廠。

run into + N

偶然遇到～

· I *ran into* Norman yesterday; he was my classmate years ago.

我昨天偶然遇到了諾曼，他是我幾年前的同班同學。

a running nose

正在流鼻水的鼻子

· Daisy catches a cold and has *a running* nose.

黛西感冒了，而且還流鼻水。

S

4. **sad**

[sæd]

adj. 傷心／難過的；令人傷心／難過的

· The **sad** movie about a dog makes a lot of people cry.

那部有關狗的、令人傷心的電影使很多人都哭了。

· King is **sad** about those who died in the fire.

金恩對於那些死在火災裡的人感到很難過。

5. **safe**

[sef]

adj. 安全的 ↔ dangerous [ˋdendʒərəs] 危險的

· It's not **safe** to drive after drinking.

酒後開車並不安全。

safe and sound

平安無恙的

· It is glad to hear that you are all *safe and sound*.

很高興聽到你們全都平安無恙。

adj. 安全上壘的（棒球用語）

· I thought the player is **safe**, but he is out.

我以為那個球員安全上壘，但他卻被判出局。

n. [C] 保險箱

· You should put your ring into the **safe** but not show it off.

你應該把你的戒指放到保險箱裡，而不是拿出來炫耀。

6. **salad**

[ˋsæləd]

n. [C][U] 沙拉

· I only eat vegetable **salad** at noon; I want to be thinner.

我中午只吃蔬菜沙拉。我想變瘦一些。

7. sale [sel]

for sale
出售中的
on sale
廉價出售中的

n. [C][U] 賣，出售
- You can't buy these art works; they are not *for sale*.
  你不能買這些藝術作品；它們是不出售的。
- Some books are *on sale* in San Min Bookstore; let's buy some.
  三民書局有些書正在拍賣，我們去買一些吧。

8. salt
[sɔlt]

n. [U] 鹽；鹽巴
- The soup tastes too light; you should put more **salt** into it.
  這湯嚐起來太淡，你應該多放點鹽進去。

9. same [sem]

the same + N
相同的～

adj. 同樣的（通常與 the 連用）
- We have *the same* interests, so we could become good friends.
  我們有相同的興趣，所以我們應該能成為好朋友。

10. sandwich
[ˋsændwɪtʃ]

n. [C] 三明治（複數：sandwiches）
- We will have a picnic, so Mother is making **sandwiches** for us.
  我們要去野餐，所以媽媽正在幫我們做三明治。

Exercise 1

I. 字彙翻譯

1. 難過的 ＿＿＿＿＿＿＿＿＿＿ 2. 鹽巴 ＿＿＿＿＿＿＿＿＿＿ 3. 直尺 ＿＿＿＿＿＿＿＿＿＿

4. 同樣的 ＿＿＿＿＿＿＿＿＿＿ 5. 跑步（三態）＿＿＿＿＿＿＿＿ ＿＿＿＿＿＿＿＿ ＿＿＿＿＿＿＿＿

II. 字彙填充

＿＿＿＿＿＿＿＿＿＿ 1. It isn't s＿＿＿＿e to drink the water in the river.

＿＿＿＿＿＿＿＿＿＿ 2. There are some r＿＿＿＿es that you must follow.

＿＿＿＿＿＿＿＿＿＿ 3. Jack had a s＿＿＿＿h for lunch in his office.

＿＿＿＿＿＿＿＿＿＿ 4. I had a s＿＿＿＿d and soup before the steak.

＿＿＿＿＿＿＿＿＿＿ 5. We had a s＿＿＿＿e in our shop yesterday.

III. 字彙選擇

( ) 1. Amy and I were born on the ＿＿＿＿ day but in different years.

(A) ruler (B) safe (C) salt (D) same

( ) 2. Don't be ＿＿＿＿ for the past. You must keep moving on.

(A) same (B) sad (C) safe (D) salad

( ) 3. You can put all your important things in this ＿＿＿＿.

(A) safe (B) ruler (C) salt (D) salad

( ) 4. Too much ＿＿＿＿ and sugar are bad for your health.

(A) ruler (B) run (C) salt (D) sandwich

( ) 5. The bicycle is for ＿＿＿＿. You can buy it.

(A) sad (B) sale (C) same (D) run

11. save
[sev]

save + sb + from + <u>N/Ving</u>
拯救～使免於～

v.t. v.i. 救；挽救

- Thank you for your help; you really **saved** my life.
  謝謝你的幫忙，你真的是救了我一命呢。
- The doctor *saved* me *from* dying.
  那醫生拯救了我，使我免於死亡。
- Sam *saved* the girl *from* the burning house.
  山姆把這女孩從著火的房子裡救出來。

v.t. v.i. 儲蓄；儲存；存錢

- In order to buy a car, I have **saved** money for years.
  為了買輛車，我已經存錢好幾年了。

v.t. v.i. 節省；省去

- It would **save** you much time to go to school by MRT.
  搭捷運上學可以節省你很多時間。

12. say
[se]

過去式	過去分詞	現在進行式
said [sɛd]	said [sɛd]	saying [`seɪŋ]

v.t. v.i. 說

- "How do you **say** goodbye in Japanese?" "Sayonara."
  「要怎樣用日文說再見?」「沙唷哪拉。」
- *It goes without saying that* health is above everything.
  健康重於一切是毫無疑問的。

it goes without saying + that 子句
～是毫無疑問的

比較

	v.t. 說～（話）；（人們）聲稱
say [se]	• Peter **said** that he felt sick, so he couldn't go to school today. 彼得說他人不舒服，所以今天不能來上學。 • People **say**/It is **said** that Jane is married. <u>人們聲稱</u>／<u>據說</u>珍已經結婚了。
speak [spik]	v.t. v.i. 說～（語言） • I don't speak French. 我不會說法文。

talk [tɔk]	*v.i.* 說話；談論	
	• Sue was not angry after I talked to her. 在我跟她談過話之後，蘇已經不生氣了。	
	• They are talking about the new teacher. 他們正在談論那位新來的老師。	
tell [tɛl]	*v.t.* 告訴～；說（故事；謊言）	
	• Holly told me that she doesn't like to eat fish. 荷莉告訴我，她不喜歡吃魚。	
	• Grandpa told (us) a story about the nine suns. 祖父（跟我們）說了一個有關九個太陽的故事。	

S

13. **school**
[skul]

go to school
上學

n. [C][U] 學校

• Get up earlier if you don't want to be late for **school**.
如果你不想上學遲到，就早點起床。

• We don't have to *go to school* on Sunday.
我們禮拜天不用上學。

14. **sea**
[si]

by sea
由海路；經由海運

in the sea
在海洋中

n. [U] 海；海洋 (the sea)

• The blue **sea** always makes me feel free and happy.
藍色海洋總是能讓我感到自由、快樂。

• You could send these mails *by sea*; it is slower but cheaper.
你可以利用海運寄送這些郵件，那比較慢但也比較便宜。

• We saw a big fish swimming *in the sea* by chance.
我們意外地看見一條大魚在海中游。

15. **season**
[ˋsizn̩]

in season
旺季的；當季的

out of season
不合季節

n. [C] 季節

• There are four **seasons** in a year.
一年有四季。

• You should buy the fruit *in season*; it is cheap and fresh.
你應該買當季的水果，既便宜又新鮮。

• Hotels would cost less when it is *out of season*.
在（旅遊）淡季時，旅館費用會比較便宜。

16. seat

[sit]

take/have a seat = sit down 坐下

n. [C] 座位

· Is this **seat** taken?

這座位有人坐嗎?

· *Take a seat*, please.

請坐。

17. second

[`sɛkənd]

adj. 第二的

· If you can't be the first, it would be fine to be the **second**.

如果你當不了第一名,當第二名也不錯。

· I live on the **second** floor.

我住在二樓。

n. [C] 秒

· The game will be over in two minutes and thirty **seconds**.

比賽將會在兩分三十秒內結束。

18. see

[si]

過去式	過去分詞	現在進行式
saw [sɔ]	seen [sin]	seeing [`siɪŋ]

v.t. v.i. 看;看見;看過

· I want to **see** a movie. Do you want to come with me?

我要去看場電影,你要跟我去嗎?

· Have you ever **seen** my father?

你曾經見過我父親嗎?

· **Seeing** is believing.

[諺語] 眼見為信。

see + sb + V/Ving
看見某人做～

· I **saw** Larry play/playing in the park last night.

我昨天晚上看到賴瑞在公園裡玩。

注意

look, see, watch 三者的比較請參考 Unit 24 的單字 look。

v.t. v.i. 理解;瞭解

· "Do you know what I am saying?" "Yes, I **see**."

「你知道我在說什麼嗎?」「是的,我瞭解。」

19. seldom
[ˈsɛldəm]

adv. 很少；不常；難得

· Tom is a good student; he is **seldom** late for school.
湯姆是個好學生，他上學難得遲到。

注意

seldom 屬於頻率副詞，與其他頻率副詞的比較請參見 Unit 2 的 always。

20. sell
[sɛl]

過去式	過去分詞	現在進行式
sold [sold]	sold [sold]	selling [ˈsɛlɪŋ]

S

v.t. v.i. 賣；出售 ↔ buy [baɪ] 買

· Jimmy **sold** me a watch for five hundred dollars.
吉米以五百元的價錢賣給我一隻手錶。

· Morris **sold** his house in the country and moved to Taipei.
莫理斯賣掉他在鄉下的房子，搬去台北。

sell out
賣光

· All the tickets of the hot movie were ***sold*** *out* in one hour.
那部熱門電影的所有票券在一個小時內全被賣光了。

Exercise 2

I. 字彙翻譯

1. 季節 _____   2. 說 _____   3. 海 _____

4. 看 _____   5. 座位 _____

II. 字彙填充

_____ 1. Superman s_____es people's lives.

_____ 2. I usually play baseball with my classmates after s_____l.

_____ 3. Tapes are s_____m used now.

_____ 4. Wait a s_____d, and I'll give you the answer.

_____ 5. Cathy wanted to s_____l her books because she needed money.

III. 字彙選擇

(   ) 1. Winter is my favorite _____.

    (A) sea   (B) school   (C) seat   (D) season

(   ) 2. It is _____ that there are no people living on that island.

    (A) saved   (B) saw   (C) said   (D) sold

(   ) 3. We'd like to _____ a movie tonight. Do you want to join us?

    (A) save   (B) see   (C) say   (D) sell

(   ) 4. Excuse me, is this _____ taken?

    (A) seat   (B) school   (C) season   (D) save

(   ) 5. Little Joe started to _____ money to buy a gift for his mother.

    (A) save   (B) sea   (C) season   (D) seat

Unit 35

1. send
[sɛnd]

過去式	過去分詞	現在進行式
sent [sɛnt]	sent [sɛnt]	sending [ˋsɛndɪŋ]

v.t. 寄送；傳送（郵件；訊息）

- People now can **send** pictures with cell phones.
  現在人們可以用手機傳送相片。

send + sb + sth =
send + sth + to + sb
寄送某物給某人
send off
寄出

- Peter ***sent*** me an e-card this Christmas.
  = Peter ***sent*** an e-card *to* me this Christmas.
  彼得今年聖誕節寄了張電子賀卡給我。
- I finished the letter and ***sent*** it *off* right away.
  我把信寫完，然後立刻就寄出去了。

v.t. 贈送

send + sb + sth =
send + sth + to + sb
送某物給某人

- Kay ***sent*** Samantha a cat as a birthday gift.
  = Kay ***sent*** a cat *to* Samantha as a birthday gift.
  凱送莎曼沙一隻貓當作生日禮物。

2. senior high school
[ˏsinjɚˋhaɪˏskul]

n. [C][U] 高中

- Joe is a **senior high school** student, and he is seventeen.
  喬是個高中生，而且他十七歲。
- Most Taiwanese students go to **senior high school** at sixteen.
  大部分的臺灣學生都在十六歲的時候上高中。

3. sentence
[ˋsɛntəns]

n. [C] 句子

- The **sentence** is good except for one spelling mistake.
  除了有一個拼字上的錯誤之外，這句子寫得很好。

make a sentence
造句

- The teacher asked us to *make a **sentence*** with this new word.
  老師要求我們用這個新學的字造句。

4. serious
[ˋsɪrɪəs]

adj. 嚴重的

- You make a **serious** mistake if you lie to your parents.
  如果你向你的父母說謊，那你就是犯了一個嚴重的錯誤。

adj. 嚴肅的；認真的

· Tom is a **serious** teacher, so many students are afraid of him.
  湯姆是個嚴肅的老師，所以有很多學生都怕他。
· I am **serious**, not kidding.
  我是認真的，不是在開玩笑。

---

5. several
[`sɛvərəl]

adj. 幾個的；數個的

· There are **several** movies on. Which one do you like?
  有好幾部電影正在上映，你喜歡哪一部？

---

6. shall
[ʃæl]

aux. 將；會；可以

· "**Shall** we dance?" "Why not?"
  「我們可以一起跳舞嗎？（可以邀請你跳舞嗎？）」
  「為什麼不呢？」
· We **shall** go to America for business for two weeks.
  我們將要因公務到美國兩個禮拜。

注意
　　shall 做為助動詞，表示「將；會」的時候，只能與第一人稱主詞 I（我）、we（我們）連用。

---

7. shape [ʃep]

in the shape of + N
～的樣子

in shape
良好的健康狀況

n. [C][U] 形狀；樣子

· Mom made the cookies *in the **shape** of* animals.
  媽媽把餅乾做成動物的樣子。
· To keep *in **shape***, you must exercise and not pick at food.
  想保持良好的健康狀況，你就應該做運動而且不挑食。

---

8. share [ʃɛr]

share...with...
與～分享～

v.t. 分享；均分

· It would be great to *share* what you have *with* others.
  能把你所擁有的東西和別人分享是很棒的。

v.t. 共同使用

· When I was a kid, my two older brothers and I **shared** a room.
  當我還是小孩時，我的兩個哥哥跟我共同使用一個房間。

9. **sheep** [ʃip]

a flock of sheep
一群綿羊

the black sheep
害群之馬；敗類

a wolf in sheep's clothing
披著羊皮的狼

n. [C] 羊；綿羊（單複數均為 sheep）

- The dog is leading *a flock of sheep* back to the farm.
  那隻狗正在引導一群羊回到農場。

- You will be *the black sheep* of the class if you cheat.
  如果你作弊，你就會成為班上的害群之馬。

- When I knew he was *a wolf in sheep's clothing*, it was too late.
  當我知道他是一隻披著羊皮的狼時，已經太遲了。

注意
　　sheep 是「單複數同形」的單字，而且複數較為常用。要注意的地方是 sheep 的複數仍然是 sheep。

10. **ship** [ʃɪp]

n. [C] 船；艦（指較大型的船）

- Titanic should be a great **ship** that would never sink.
  鐵達尼號應該是一艘偉大且永不沉沒的船。

注意
　　ship 與 boat 的比較請參見 Unit 5 單字 boat。

v.t. 用船運

- These bikes would be **shipped** to the United States for sale.
  這些腳踏車會被用船運到美國出售。

Exercise 1

I. 字彙翻譯

1. 分享 _____

2. 將；會 _____

3. 船；艦 _____

4. 羊 _____

5. 寄送 _____

II. 字彙填充

_____ 1. "Are you kidding?" "No, I am s_____s."

_____ 2. There is a spelling mistake in this s_____e.

_____ 3. My cousin studies in s_____r high school now.

_____ 4. S_____l students are playing basketball on the playground.

_____ 5. Jenny takes exercise every day and is in pretty good s_____e.

III. 字彙選擇

(　　) 1. We have worked for hours. _____ we take a break?

(A) Shall　　　　(B) Send　　　　(C) Senior　　　　(D) Serious

(　　) 2. This is a _____ problem that you need to face.

(A) shape　　　　(B) several　　　　(C) serious　　　　(D) senior

(　　) 3. My friend _____ me an e-mail two days ago.

(A) share　　　　(B) sent　　　　(C) shared　　　　(D) send

(　　) 4. We don't have enough food for everyone; some of you have to _____.

(A) ship　　　　(B) shape　　　　(C) sheep　　　　(D) share

(　　) 5. They decided to cross the sea by _____.

(A) sheep　　　　(B) shop　　　　(C) ship　　　　(D) shall

S

11. shirt

[ʃɝt]

T-shirt
T 恤

n. [C] 襯衫；男式襯衫

· When you meet the boss, you had better wear your **shirt**.
見老闆的時候，你最好穿上你的襯衫。

· I wear a **T-shirt** to play basketball.
我穿了一件 T 恤去打籃球。

12. shoe(s)

[ʃu(z)]

in one's shoes
處於某人的處境

n. [C] 鞋子

· My **shoes** wear out soon because I play basketball every day.
我的鞋子很快就穿破了，因為我每天都打籃球。

· What would you do if you are *in my shoes*?
如果你處於我的處境的話，你會怎麼做?

注意

shoes 的單位是「雙」，英文的說法是 a pair of shoes（一雙鞋子）。

鞋子的種類很多，以功能來分可以分成 sports shoes（運動鞋 = sneakers）、skating shoes（溜冰鞋）、jogging shoes（慢跑鞋）、multi-function shoes（多功能鞋）等等；以外型來分還有 slippers（拖鞋）、boots（長筒靴）。

13. shop

[ʃɑp]

n. [C] 商店 = store [stor]

· Everything in this **shop** was on sale, so I bought lots of things.
這家店裡每樣東西都在廉價拍賣，所以我就買了很多東西。

v.i. 購物

過去式	過去分詞	現在進行式
shopped [ʃɑpt]	shopped [ʃɑpt]	shopping[ˋʃɑpɪŋ]

go shopping
去購物
go window
shopping
逛展示櫥窗

· It could take hours for a girl to *go shopping*.
一個女孩子逛街可以花好幾個小時。

· Maria likes to *go window shopping*; she just looks around and buys nothing.
瑪麗亞喜歡逛櫥窗；她只是四處看看，什麼都不買。

S

14. shopkeeper
[ˋʃɑpˏkipɚ]

n. [C] 店主；店長 = storekeeper [ˋstorˏkipɚ]（美式用法）

- Sorry, but only our **shopkeeper** could cut the prices.
  抱歉，不過只有我們店長可以降價。

15. short
[ʃɔrt]

in short
簡言之；總之

short of + N
～短缺

adj. 短的；簡短的 ↔ long [lɔŋ] 長的

- This pencil is too **short** to write.
  這隻鉛筆太短了，沒辦法拿來寫字。
- *In short*, it would be a wise choice to buy this book.
  簡言之，買這本書將是個明智的抉擇。

adj. 矮小的 ↔ tall [tɔl] 高大的

- Jenny is a **short** girl and she wants to be taller.
  珍妮是個矮個子的女孩，她希望能變高一些。

adj. 短缺的；不足的

- We were *short* of food, so I went to the market to buy some.
  我們的食物短缺，所以我就到市場去買了一些。

16. should
[ʃʊd]

aux. 應該（表示建議、命令、決定）

- You work too hard; I think you **should** take a rest.
  你工作太努力了，我認為你應該休息一下。
- You **should** not sleep in class. Go to wash your face.
  你不應該在上課時間睡覺，去洗把臉。

aux. 應該（表示義務、責任）

- You **should** finish your homework before you play outside.
  在你出門玩之前，你應該先做完你的家庭作業。

aux. 應該（表示可能性、推測）

- It is very late. I think Donna **should** be home now.
  已經很晚了，我想現在多娜應該是在家裡吧！

aux. 應該（表示徵求同意）

- I don't feel well. **Should** I see a doctor?
  我覺得不太舒服。我應該去看醫生嗎？
- What **should** I do next?
  接下來我該做什麼呢？

17. shoulder

[ˈʃoldɚ]

n. [C] 肩膀

- I patted Joyce on the **shoulder** to wake him up.
  我拍拍喬伊斯的肩膀，叫他起床。

shrug one's
shoulder 聳肩

- Ben *shrugged his shoulder* and said he didn't care.
  賓聳聳他的肩，然後說他不在乎。

shoulder to shoulder
肩並肩

- We work *shoulder* to *shoulder* to build a better tomorrow.
  我們肩併著肩，共同建立更好的明天。

18. show

[ʃo]

v.t. 顯示出

- Jack **shows** great interest in joining our team.
  傑克對於加入我們的隊伍顯示出高度興趣。

show + sb + around
帶領～參觀

- Welcome to the museum; I will *show* you *around*.
  歡迎你們來到博物館，我會帶著你們參觀的。

show off
炫耀

- Stop *showing off* your expensive watch; we are sick of it.
  不要再炫耀你那昂貴的手錶了。我們已經受夠了。

v.i. 出現；露面

show up/one's face
現身；露面

- The singer didn't *show up/her face* until the last moment.
  那位歌手直到最後一刻才露面。

n. [C] 展覽會

- There will be a car **show** in the World Trade Center today.
  今天世貿中心將會有一個車展（汽車展覽會）。

n. [C] 表演；演出節目；秀

show business
演藝圈

- Linda dreams to join the colorful life of *show* business.
  琳達夢想著能夠加入演藝圈的多采多姿生活。

19. shy

[ʃaɪ]

adj. 害羞的；靦腆的

- Danny is a **shy** boy; he is afraid to talk with girls.
  丹尼是個害羞的男生，他不敢跟女孩子講話。

adj. 易受驚的；膽小的

- The **shy** birds flew away when I walked near them.
  當我走近的時候，那些容易受驚的鳥兒就飛走了。

S

· Once bitten, twice **shy**.

[諺語] 一朝被蛇咬，十年怕草繩。

---

20. **sick**

[sɪk]

adj. 生病的

· Bush is **sick**, so he can't go to work today.

布希生病了，所以他今天不能去上班。

call in sick
打電話請病假

· Blair *called in sick* this morning; he said he didn't feel well.

布萊爾今天早上打電話來請病假，他說他覺得不舒服。

adj. 對～感到厭倦的 (+ of)

· I am **sick** of the long winter; when will the spring come?

我已經對這個好長的冬天感到厭倦了。春天何時會來呢?

make sb sick　使某
人感到極為不快

· The boring show really *made* me *sick*, so I turned off the TV.

那個無聊的節目使我極為不快，所以我就把電視關了。

adj. 想嘔吐的；噁心的

· I felt **sick** whenever I see a snake.

每次我看到蛇都會覺得好噁心。

Exercise 2

I. 字彙翻譯

1. 短的 _____

2. 店長 _____

3. 肩膀 _____

4. 害羞的 _____

5. 生病的 _____

II. 字彙填充

_____ 1. The blue s_____t goes well with your black pants.

_____ 2. The s_____p is having a big sale.

_____ 3. Nike is famous for its sports s_____es.

_____ 4. It is very late now. A girl s_____d not go outside at this time.

_____ 5. "How did you do that?" "I will s_____w you."

III. 字彙選擇

(　　) 1. The girl is too _____ to talk with boys.

　　(A) shy　　　　　(B) senior　　　　(C) shall　　　　(D) second

(　　) 2. Put your hands on my _____.

　　(A) shy　　　　　(B) shoulder　　　(C) senior　　　　(D) send

(　　) 3. Bob is _____ than everyone else in the classroom. He is not tall.

　　(A) shower　　　(B) sicker　　　　(C) shyer　　　　(D) shorter

(　　) 4. I went _____ with my mom last weekend.

　　(A) shaping　　　(B) shipping　　　(C) shopping　　　(D) showing

(　　) 5. You _____ not have cheated on the test. Why did you do this?

　　(A) should　　　(B) shoulder　　　(C) shape　　　　(D) sheep

Unit 36

1. **side**
[saɪd]

side by side
肩並肩；一起

to be on the safe side
為了安全起見

n. [C] 邊；側；旁邊
- Kids should not play on the **side** of the road.
  小孩子不應該在馬路旁邊玩。
- Cathy sat on my right **side**, and put her head on my shoulder.
  凱西坐在我的右邊，還把頭放在我的肩膀上。
- We should work *side by side* to face the problem.
  我們應該肩併著肩，共同面對問題。

n. [C] （問題等的）方面；（爭論中的）一方
- You see one **side** of the problem, but you don't see the other.
  你看到了問題的一面，卻沒看到另一面。
- *To be on the safe side*, you should not drive after drink.
  為了安全起見，你不該酒後開車。

2. **sidewalk**
[ˈsaɪdˌwɔk]

n. [C] 人行道
- Drivers should not park their cars on the **sidewalk**.
  駕駛人不應該把他們的車子停在人行道上。

3. **simple**
[ˈsɪmpḷ]

adj. 簡單的，容易的
- I can answer the **simple** math question in ten seconds.
  我可以在十秒之內回答出這個簡單的數學問題。
- The machine is **simple** to use.
  這機器使用起來很容易。

4. **since** [sɪns]
S + have + p.p. +
since + S +Ved
自～起就一直～

conj. 自從～以來；從～至今
- Peter has been interested in music **since** he was only a child.
  從彼得是個小孩子起，他就一直對音樂感到有興趣。

conj. 既然
- **Since** you are so busy, I will call you later.
  既然你這麼忙，那我晚一點再打電話給你。

conj. 因為；由於

- **Since** Frank is kind and wise, everybody likes him.
  因為法蘭克既仁慈又聰明，所以大家都喜歡他。

prep. 自從～以來；從～至今

- We haven't seen each other **since** 1997.
  自從一九九七年起，我們就沒見過彼此。

5. **sing**
[sɪŋ]

過去式	過去分詞	現在進行式
sang [sæŋ]	sung [sʌŋ]	singing [`sɪŋɪŋ]

S

v.t. v.i. 唱～；唱歌

- Today is your birthday, so I will **sing** a song for you.
  今天是你生日，所以我要為你唱一首歌。
- Since you like **singing**, let's go to the KTV tonight.
  既然你喜歡唱歌，那我們今天晚上就去 KTV 吧!

6. **singer**
[`sɪŋɚ]

n. [C] 歌手

- The **singer**'s first CD was popular with many young girls.
  這名歌手的第一張雷射唱片受到很多年輕女孩的歡迎。

7. **sir**
[sɝ]

n. [C] 先生；長官；老師

- May I help you, **sir**?
  我能為您服務嗎，先生?
- "Don't question my order." "Yes, **sir**."
  「不要質疑我的命令。」「是的，長官。」

注意

sir 是「稱謂語」，其他稱謂語還有 Dr. (醫生；博士)、Mr. (先生)、Ms. (小姐；女士 = Miss)、Mrs. (太太) 等。

8. **sister**
[`sɪstɚ]

n. [C] 姊妹；姊姊；妹妹

- I have two **sisters** and one little brother.
  我有兩個姊妹跟一個弟弟。

9. **sit**
[sɪt]

過去式	過去分詞	現在進行式
sat [sæt]	sat [sæt]	sitting [ˋsɪtɪŋ]

v.i. 坐；坐下 (+ on)

- Tera is **sitting** on the sofa and watching TV.
  泰拉正坐在沙發上看電視。
- "Good morning, sir." "Good morning. Please *sit down*."
  「老師早安。」「早安，請坐下。」

sit down
坐下

v.i. （建築物）座落於～；位於～

- My house **sits** in the downtown of the city.
  我家座落在城市的商業區。

10. **size**
[saɪz]

n. [C][U] 尺寸；大小

- There are skirts and dresses of all **sizes** at the shop.
  這間店裡有所有尺寸的裙子和洋裝。

n. [C] 型；號；尺碼

- "What is your **size**?" "S."
  「你的型號是什麼?」「小號。」

注意

衣服的型號一般分為 XL(extra large)（特大）、L(large)（大號）、M(medium)（中號）、S(small)（小號）這四種。

Exercise 1

I. 字彙翻譯

1. 唱歌 _____
2. 先生 _____
3. 坐下 _____
4. 尺寸 _____
5. 旁邊 _____

II. 字彙填充

_____ 1. I have loved the music s_____e I first listened to it.

_____ 2. I can answer that s_____e question without thinking.

_____ 3. My s_____r wants me to bring her some food when I go home.

_____ 4. You should not ride your bicycle on the s_____k.

_____ 5. Jay is a famous s_____r; he made a lot of money by his CD's.

III. 字彙選擇

( ) 1. There are cars running on the road, so it is safer to walk on the _____.

(A) sidewalk   (B) side   (C) singer   (D) sister

( ) 2. I have two brothers but only one _____.

(A) sidewalk   (B) sister   (C) shoulder   (D) sir

( ) 3. You had better _____ on the chair if you are tired.

(A) sing   (B) sit   (C) size   (D) side

( ) 4. Nelly _____ a beautiful song to her mother on her birthday party.

(A) sale   (B) said   (C) sat   (D) sang

( ) 5. Sorry, _____, but you can't smoke here.

(A) singer   (B) size   (C) sir   (D) side

S

11. **skirt**
[skɝt]

miniskirt
迷你裙

n. [C] 裙子

- Tina wears a long **skirt** today and looks very beautiful.
  今天蒂娜穿了一件長裙，看起來很漂亮。
- Joanna could be very hot if she puts on a **miniskirt**.
  裘安娜也可以很辣，如果她穿上迷你裙的話。

12. **sky**
[skaɪ]

n. 天空

- The **sky** is clear and the air is fresh. It is great for a picnic.
  天空晴朗，空氣又清新，天氣非常適合野餐。

S

13. **sleep**
[slip]

過去式	過去分詞	現在進行式
slept [slɛpt]	slept [slɛpt]	sleeping [ˋslipɪŋ]

go to sleep/bed
睡覺
sleep late
睡過頭

v.i. 睡覺

- You look tired. Didn't you **sleep** well last night?
  你看起來很疲倦。昨天晚上沒睡好嗎?
- I get up at 6:00 a.m. and *go to **sleep**/bed* at 10:00 p.m.
  我都早上六點起床，晚上十點睡覺。
- I ***slept** late* this morning, so I could not go to school on time.
  我今天早上睡過頭了，所以沒辦法準時到學校。

注意
　　sleep late 指的是早上睡過頭，而不是晚上很晚才睡覺。

n. [U] 睡眠

- It is important for teenagers to have enough **sleep** every night.
  每天晚上有充足的睡眠，對青少年來說很重要。

14. **slow**
[slo]

slow down
減速；緩慢下來

adj. 緩慢的 ↔ fast [fæst] 快的

- I was late because my watch is five minutes **slow**.
  我遲到是因為我的錶慢了五分鐘。

v.t. v.i. 放慢；變慢

- It is raining now, so all the drivers ***slow** down* their cars.
  現在正在下雨，所以所有的駕駛人都把車速放慢了。

15. small

[smɔl]

small talk
聊天；閒談

adj. 小的 ↔ big [bɪg] 大的

· The shoes are too **small** for me; please give me a bigger pair.
這雙鞋對我而言太小了，請給我一雙大一點的。

· It is not good to have *small talk* in class.
在上課中聊天是不好的。

16. smart

[smɑrt]

adj. 聰明的；伶俐的；機警的 ↔ stupid [`stjupɪd] 笨的

· Danny is a **smart** boy; he learns things very fast.
丹尼是個聰明的男孩，他學東西很快。

· It was **smart** of you to call the police in time.
你很機警，能夠及時打電話給警察。

注意

smart 跟 wise 都可以解釋為「聰明的」，但前者指的是「靈敏、反應快」這種與生俱來的聰明，而後者指的則是由經驗、歷練所累積出來的「智慧」，所以我們通常不會用 wise 來形容聰明的小孩子，也不會用 smart 來形容歷練豐富的老人家。

17. smell

[smɛl]

sense of smell
嗅覺

n. [C][U] 氣味；香味；臭味

· The **smell** of the meat is bad. You should never eat it.
那些肉的味道聞起來很糟。你絕不應該吃它。

· Dogs have better *sense of smell* than people do.
跟人比起來，狗有更好的嗅覺。

v.t. v.i. 聞；聞起來

過去式	過去分詞	現在進行式
smelt [smɛlt]	smelt [smɛlt]	smelling [`smɛlɪŋ]

· The dish **smells** good. May I taste it?
這道菜聞起來好香。我可以嚐嚐看嗎?

v.t. v.i. 發出臭味

- When did you clean your room last time? It **smells**.
  你上次清理房間是什麼時候? 它都發出臭味了。

S

18. **smile** [smaɪl]
smile at + sb
對某人微笑

v.i. 微笑

- The girl I like a lot is **smiling** *at* me.
  那個我很喜歡的女孩正在對著我笑。

n. [C] 笑容

- She welcomed us with a sweet **smile**.
  她以甜美的笑容歡迎我們。

19. **smoke**
[smok]

v.t. v.i. 抽煙

- My grandpa likes to **smoke** a pipe after he finishes his dinner.
  我爺爺喜歡在吃完晚餐之後抽煙斗。

give up smoking
戒煙

- My dad *gave up smoking* twenty years ago.
  我爸在二十年前戒煙了。

v.i. 冒煙

- The house is **smoking**. Maybe it is on fire.
  那棟房子正在冒煙。它可能著火了。

n. [C][U] 煙; 煙霧

- There's no **smoke** without fire.
  [諺語] 無風不起浪。

second-hand smoke
二手煙

- Nobody likes the smell of *second-hand* **smoke**.
  沒有人喜歡二手煙的味道。

20. **snack**
[snæk]

n. [C] 點心

- "Do you want an ice cream for a **snack** after dinner?" "Sure."
  「你晚餐後想吃個冰淇淋當點心嗎?」「當然。」

Exercise 2

I. 字彙翻譯

1. 天空 _____   2. 緩慢的 _____   3. 小的 _____

4. 點心 _____   5. 聰明的 _____

II. 字彙填充

_____ 1. What's the s _____l? Is something burning?

_____ 2. Lisa always wears a sweet s _____e on her face.

_____ 3. Mr. Wang gave up s _____king finally after trying several times.

_____ 4. Ariel doesn't like to wear a s _____t. She always wear pants.

_____ 5. It is very late, and most people are s _____ping now.

III. 字彙選擇

( ) 1. What are you cooking? It _____ so good.

(A) smiles   (B) smells   (C) smokes   (D) smarts

( ) 2. Jim is a very _____ boy, so it is easy to teach him.

(A) smoke   (B) slow   (C) smart   (D) small

( ) 3. People feel time passes _____ when they are in hard times.

(A) snack   (B) sky   (C) smart   (D) slow

( ) 4. "Do you want some cake?" "I am almost full, so just give me a _____ piece."

(A) smart   (B) small   (C) smoke   (D) snack

( ) 5. Please keep quiet. Mother is _____ in her bedroom.

(A) sleeping   (B) smiling   (C) shopping   (D) smoking

S

Unit 37

S

1. snake
[snek]

n. [C] 蛇

· Susan cried out on seeing the **snakes**.

蘇珊看到那些蛇的時候，馬上就大哭出來。

2. snow
[sno]

v.i. 下雪

· It is **snowing** outside. Let's make a snowman in the park.

外面下雪了，我們到公園去做雪人吧。

n. [U] 雪

· I want to play in the clean and white **snow**, but it is too cold.

我想在又白又乾淨的雪裡玩，不過實在太冷了。

3. so
[so]

conj. 所以

· It's raining heavily outside, **so** we decide to stay at home.

外面下大雨，因此我們決定留在家裡。

adv. 如此地

· I'm **so** happy to see you again.

能再見到你我真／是如此地高興。

so +Adj/Adv+ that
如此～以致於～

· Jack is **so** excited *that* he could not sleep at night.

傑克如此興奮，以致於晚上睡不著覺。

adv. 也如此；也一樣（置於句首）

· "I love ice cream cakes." "**So** do I."

「我愛冰淇淋蛋糕。」「我也一樣。」

4. sock
[sɑk]

n. [C] 短襪；半筒襪

· It might hurt your feet if you wear your shoes without **socks**.

如果你穿鞋子的時候不穿襪子，腳可能會痛。

注意

sock 一字跟 shoe 一樣，通常都是複數（socks [sɑks]）。跟 socks 相對應的字是 stockings [ˋstɑkɪŋz]（長襪）。

5. sofa
[`sofə]

n. [C] 沙發；長椅

- It is much more comfortable to sit on the **sofa** than on a chair.
  坐在沙發上比坐在椅子上要舒服多了。

6. some
[sʌm]

adj. 一些

- Do you want **some** ice tea? It could make you feel cooler.
  你想喝一些冰茶嗎？它可以讓你涼快點。

pron. 一些

- **Some** of these books are funny, but others are very boring.
  這些書裡面有些蠻有趣，不過其他的就很無聊了。

adj. 某一個

- I know Sandy likes **some** boy, but I don't know who he is.
  我知道仙蒂喜歡某個男孩子，不過我不知道是誰。

7. someone
[`sʌm͵wʌn]

pron. 某人；有人 = somebody [`sʌm͵bɑdɪ]

- **Someone** told me you love seeing movies, too. Is that true?
  有人告訴我你也喜歡看電影。那是真的嗎?

- It must be **someone** here who called me, but who?
  一定是這裡的某人打了電話給我，不過是誰呢?

n. 重要人物

- Mr. Jones used to be **someone** in the office.
  瓊斯先生曾是這個辦公室裡的重要人物。

8. something
[`sʌm͵θɪŋ]

pron. 某事

- There must be **something** wrong, but I don't know what it is.
  一定有某件事不對勁，不過我不知道是什麼事。

or something
諸如此類的什麼

- You look hungry. Do you want a sandwich *or something*?
  你看起來好像餓了。需要一個三明治或諸如此類的什麼嗎?

n. 重要的人、事或物

- The ring is really **something** to me; it was from my mother.
  這個戒指對我真的是很重要的東西，那是我母親給我的。

S

9. sometimes

[ˋsʌmˌtaɪmz]

adv. 有時候

· **Sometimes** I play basketball, but most time I study.

有時候我會打籃球，但大部分時間我都在唸書。

注意

頻率副詞的比較請參考 Unit 2 的 always。

10. somewhere

[ˋsʌmˌhwɛr]

adv. 在某處

· The boy hid the toy **somewhere** in the living room.

男孩將玩具藏在客廳的某處。

S

休息一下喔！

Exercise 1

I. 字彙翻譯

1. 所以 _____   2. 短襪 _____   3. 某人 _____

4. 蛇 _____   5. 一些 _____

II. 字彙填充

_____ 1. I couldn't find my car key, but I think it must be s_____e in my room.

_____ 2. Sitting on the s_____a is really comfortable.

_____ 3. Please listen to me. There is s_____g important I have to tell you.

_____ 4. The weather is so cold; I think it might s_____w tonight.

_____ 5. I usually ride my bike to school, but s_____s I go there by bus.

III. 字彙選擇

( ) 1. Some kids believe that Santa Claus would put presents in his _____ on Christmas Eve.

    (A) sofas   (B) socks   (C) snows   (D) shows

( ) 2. I will have a test tomorrow, _____ I can't see a movie with you tonight.

    (A) snow   (B) slow   (C) so   (D) show

( ) 3. Don't put your hands into the bag, the _____ might bite you.

    (A) smell   (B) smoke   (C) snack   (D) snake

( ) 4. _____ took my umbrella, but I don't know who did it.

    (A) Some   (B) Someone   (C) Sofa   (D) Something

( ) 5. _____ students are playing outside, and others stay in the classroom.

    (A) Some   (B) Somewhere   (C) Sometimes   (D) Someone

S

11. **son**

[sʌn]

n. [C] 兒子

· Mr. Lin has three **sons** but no daughter.

林先生有三個兒子，但沒有女兒。

son-in-law

女婿

· After you marry my daughter, you would be my **son-in-law**.

你在娶了我女兒以後，就是我的女婿了。

12. **song** [sɔŋ]

popular songs

流行歌曲

n. [C] 歌曲；歌謠

· Those girls like to sing *popular songs* in KTV after work.

那些女孩子喜歡在下班後到 KTV 裡唱流行歌曲。

13. **soon**

[sun]

adv. 不久；很快地

· The famous singer is coming **soon**, so everybody is so excited.

那個有名的歌手不久就要來了，所以每個人都很興奮。

as soon as possible

儘快

· My boss asked me to finish the job *as soon as possible*.

我的老闆要求我儘快完成這項工作。

as soon as + S + V,

S + V　一～就～

· *As soon as* Tony leaves school, he goes to play basketball.

湯尼一離開學校，馬上就跑去打籃球了。

14. **sorry**

[`sɔrɪ]

adj. 對不起

· I'm **sorry**, but I didn't mean it.

很抱歉，我不是有意的。

· I'm **sorry** for hitting you in the face.

很抱歉我打到你的臉。

adj. 感到遺憾的；感到難過的

be/feel sorry to + V/

for + N/that + 子句

為～遺憾或難過

· I *feel sorry to* hear the bad news.

我聽到這個壞消息感到很難過 / 遺憾。

· I *am sorry that* you can't come to our party.

很遺憾你不能來參加我們的宴會。

15. **sound**

[saʊnd]

n. [C][U] 聲音

· You should not make **sound** when eating. It's not polite.

你在吃飯的時候不應該發出聲音。那不禮貌。

v.i. 聽起來

- "Do you want to play basketball now?"
  "That **sounds** good. Let's go."
  「你現在想不想去打籃球?」
  「聽起來不壞。我們走吧。」
- Cindy's voice **sounds** sad. What's wrong with her?
  辛蒂的聲音聽起來很傷心。她怎麼啦?

16. **soup**
[sup]

n. [C] 湯

- I'd like to order a chicken **soup**.
  我要點一份雞湯。
- I eat the **soup** which my mom cooked for me.
  我喝了我媽媽為我煮的湯。

注意

英文「喝湯」用的動詞可不是 drink,而是 eat 或 have,這是因為大部分的湯裡有肉或菜,並不像飲料一樣只有液體而已。

17. **south**
[sauθ]

in/on the south of
在〜的南部
to the south of
在〜以南

n. 南方 (the south)

- The birds would fly from the north to the **south** in winter.
  鳥兒在冬天會從北方飛往南方。
- Pingtung is *in/on the **south*** of Taiwan.
  屏東在臺灣的南部。
- America is *to the **south*** of Canada.
  美國在加拿大以南。

adj. 南方的;在南方的

- The **south** wind is not cool at all.
  這南風一點都不涼爽。

adv. 往南方

- We drive **south** to the warm beach.
  我們往南方開,開到一個溫暖的海灘。

S

18. space
[spes]

n. [C][U] 空間；位置

- I bought a house with a parking **space** last year.
  我去年買了一棟附停車位的房子。
- There is not enough **space** in this room to put one more table.
  這房間沒有足夠的空間再擺進一張桌子。

n. [U] 太空

- No one really knows how big the **space** is.
  沒有人確切知道太空有多大。

spaceman
太空人

- I dream to be a **spaceman** and go to the Mars when I grow up.
  我夢想在長大後成為一個太空人，並前往火星。

space ship
太空船

- The *space ship* landed the moon for the first time in 1969 A.D.
  西元一九六九年，太空船首次登陸月球。

19. speak
[spik]

過去式	過去分詞	現在進行式
spoke [spok]	spoken [`spokən]	speaking [`spikɪŋ]

v.t. v.i. 說～（語言）

- Willy can **speak** good English.
  威利英語說的很好。

v.t. v.i. 說話；談話；談論

speak to/with + sb
與某人說話

- Sue is still angry, so she doesn't want to *speak* to Peter.
  蘇還在生氣，所以她不想跟彼得說話。

注意

   say, speak, talk, tell 四者的比較請參閱 Unit 34 的 say。

20. special
[`spɛʃəl]

adj. 特別的

- I have something **special** for you.
  我有個特別的東西要給你。

Exercise 2

I. 字彙翻譯

1. 兒子 ＿＿＿＿＿＿＿＿＿＿　　2. 湯 ＿＿＿＿＿＿＿＿＿＿　　3. 不久 ＿＿＿＿＿＿＿＿＿＿

4. 歌謠 ＿＿＿＿＿＿＿＿＿＿　　5. 感到抱歉的 ＿＿＿＿＿＿＿＿＿＿

II. 字彙填充

＿＿＿＿＿＿＿＿＿＿ 1. It made a big s＿＿＿＿d when the glass fell on the ground.

＿＿＿＿＿＿＿＿＿＿ 2. Thank you for giving me such a s＿＿＿＿l present. I am very happy.

＿＿＿＿＿＿＿＿＿＿ 3. I can s＿＿＿＿k a little English.

＿＿＿＿＿＿＿＿＿＿ 4. The bus is full. There is no other s＿＿＿＿e for one more man to get on.

＿＿＿＿＿＿＿＿＿＿ 5. The airplane flies s＿＿＿＿h to a warmer place.

III. 字彙選擇

(　　) 1. "Do you want to see a movie with me?" "That ＿＿＿＿＿ good. Let's go."

　　　　(A) snows　　　　(B) smells　　　　(C) speaks　　　　(D) sounds

(　　) 2. I'm so ＿＿＿＿＿ to break your glasses. I'll pay for it.

　　　　(A) special　　　　(B) sorry　　　　(C) song　　　　(D) south

(　　) 3. I have tasted the ＿＿＿＿＿. It is really delicious.

　　　　(A) soup　　　　(B) song　　　　(C) south　　　　(D) son

(　　) 4. There is nothing ＿＿＿＿＿ happening today. Everything is as usual.

　　　　(A) south　　　　(B) special　　　　(C) soon　　　　(D) some

(　　) 5. I can't hear your voice. Please ＿＿＿＿＿ louder.

　　　　(A) speak　　　　(B) sleep　　　　(C) shop　　　　(D) smoke

S

Unit 38

1. spell
[spɛl]

v.t. （用英文字母）拼；拼字

- There are some **spelling** mistakes in this sentence.
  這句子裡有一些拼字上的錯誤。
- Do you know how to **spell** the English word "television"?
  你知道「電視」這個英文字怎麼拼嗎?

2. spend
[spɛnd]

spend ＋ 金錢／時間 ＋ (in) Ving/on ＋ N
把錢／時間花在～上面

過去式	過去分詞	現在進行式
spent [spɛnt]	spent [spɛnt]	spending [`spɛndɪŋ]

v.t. 花費（錢；時間）

- Mary *spent* a lot of money *buying* clothes.
  瑪莉花了很多錢在買衣服上。
- Larry has *spent* one hour *on* his homework.
  賴瑞已經花了一小時的時間在功課上。

注意

(1) spend 跟 cost 的比較請參考 Unit 10 的 cost。
(2) spend ＋ 金錢／時間之後可以接動名詞 (Ving) 跟 on ＋ N，但不可接不定詞 (to ＋ V)。

v.t. 渡過（時間）

- We decide to **spend** this weekend in Nantou.
  我們決定在南投度週末。

3. spoon
[spun]

be born with a silver spoon in one's mouth　出生富貴

n. [C] 湯匙；一湯匙的量

- Put one more **spoon** of sugar to the coffee, please.
  請再放一湯匙的糖到這咖啡裡。
- I had my soup with a **spoon**.
  我用湯匙喝湯。
- Lily's father is a rich man, so she *was born with a silver spoon in her mouth*.
  莉莉的爸爸是有錢人，所以她算是啣著銀湯匙出生的。

4. sport
[sport]

play sports
做運動

n. [C][U] 運動（常用複數 sports [sports]）
- Jogging is a good **sport**. It could keep you healthy.
  慢跑是個不錯的運動，它可以讓你保持健康。
- Sam spends at least an hour *playing sports* every day.
  山姆每天花至少一小時的時間做運動。

5. spring
[sprɪŋ]

hot spring
溫泉

n. [C][U] 春天
- If winter comes, can **spring** be far away?
  冬天來了，春天還會遠嗎?

n. [C][U] 泉；泉水
- Taking a *hot spring* bath could make you more beautiful.
  泡溫泉可以讓你變的更美麗。

6. square
[skwɛr]

n. [C] 正方形；方塊物
- It is easy to draw a **square** with a ruler.
  有一把尺就可以輕易的畫出正方形。

n. [C] 廣場
- I will meet you at the town **square** at 10:00 a.m.
  早上十點，我和你在市政廣場碰面。
- Times **Square** is one of the most famous places in New York.
  時代廣場是紐約最著名的地方之一。

7. stand
[stænd]

stand up
起立；站起來
stand + sb + up
放某人鴿子

過去式	過去分詞	現在進行式
stood [stʊd]	stood [stʊd]	standing [`stændɪŋ]

v.i. 站立；站著
- The class *stood up* when the teacher came.
  老師來的時候，全班同學都站了起來。
- Why did you *stand* me *up* last night? I waited for an hour.
  你昨晚為何放我鴿子? 我等了一個小時。

v.t. 容忍；忍受（較常用於否定句及疑問句）
- I can't **stand** any noise when I study.
  在我唸書的時候，我不能忍受任何噪音。

8. star
[stɑr]

shooting star
流星

n. [C] 星星
- There are hundreds of thousands of **stars** in the sky.
  在天上有成千上萬顆星星。
- Look! There is a *shooting star*. Make a wish quickly.
  看！有顆流星。快許個願望。

n. [C] 明星
- Jackie Chan is now a famous movie **star** all over the world.
  成龍現在是世界知名的電影明星。

S

9. start [stɑrt]
start + to V/Ving
開始～

v.t. v.i. 開始 = begin [bɪˋgɪn] 開始
- I **started** *to learn/learning* English when I was ten.
  我從十歲開始學英文。

v.t. v.i. 發動；啟動；使運轉（機器；引擎等）
- The driver **started** the car and then drove away.
  駕駛人發動車子，然後把車開走了。

10. station
[ˋsteʃən]

police station
警察局

n. [C] 車站
- The train will arrive at the **station** at 10:45 a.m.
  火車會在早上十點四十五分抵達車站。

n. [C] （各種機構的）站；所；局；署
- You must call the *police station* if you can't find your son.
  如果你找不到你兒子，一定要打電話給警察局。

Exercise 1

I. 字彙翻譯

1. 春天 _____

2. 廣場 _____

3. 開始 _____

4. 星星 _____

5. 運動 _____

II. 字彙填充

_____ 1. "Would you please s_____l your name again, sir?"

"Sure. It is M-A-T-T-H-E-W, Matthew."

_____ 2. I s_____t my weekend at the beach. That was really great.

_____ 3. The teacher asked Tim to s_____d up because he said the wrong answer.

_____ 4. There are so many people in the Taipei Main S_____n on holidays.

_____ 5. I need a s_____n to have the soup.

III. 字彙選擇

( ) 1. My favorite movie _____ is Tom Cruise.

(A) station (B) square (C) start (D) star

( ) 2. Paul is a strong and healthy man because he plays _____ every day.

(A) springs (B) sports (C) squares (D) spoons

( ) 3. "How much money did you _____ on this jacket?" "About 2,000 dollars."

(A) spend (B) spring (C) spell (D) stand

( ) 4. My favorite season is _____; I don't like winter at all.

(A) sport (B) spring (C) square (D) station

( ) 5. I have to _____ the machine first and then I can work.

(A) star (B) spring (C) start (D) stand

11. **stay**
[ste]

v.t. v.i. 待；停留 ↔ leave [liv] 離開

- I don't want to go on a picnic. May I **stay** home tomorrow?
  我不想去野餐。明天我可以待在家裡嗎?

- Don't go away. Just **stay** here, and I will be back soon.
  別走開。就待在這裡,我很快就回來。

v.i. 繼續；保持

- You must exercise if you want to **stay** healthy.
  如果你想保持健康的話,你必須運動。

n. 停留

- I want to visit more places during my **stay** in America.
  在我停留在美國的時間裡,我想多參觀一些地方。

12. **steak**
[stek]

steak house
牛排館

n. [C][U] 牛排；排餐

- Do you want some salad before the **steak**?
  在吃牛排之前,你想先吃些沙拉嗎?

- I don't want to eat Chinese food, so I go to the *steak house*.
  我不想吃中國菜,所以就跑去了牛排館。

注意

　　steak 一般是指牛排。但如果前面加其他名詞,便可以指其他的排餐,如 fish steak（魚排）、pork steak（豬排）、chicken steak（雞排）,當然牛排也可以說成 beef steak。

13. **still**
[stɪl]

keep still
保持靜止不動

adv. 仍然；還；仍舊

- It has rained for three days, and it is **still** raining now.
  雨已經下了三天了,而且現在仍然還在下雨。

adv. 還要～；更～（強調比較級）

- Two men can't do this job; I need **still** more people to help.
  兩個男人是做不了這項工作的,我需要更多人來幫忙。

adj. 靜止的；不動的

- The kid *keeps still* on his bed. He is sleeping now.
  那孩子躺在床上靜止不動。他現在正在睡覺。

14. stomach

[ˋstʌmək]

on an empty
stomach　空胃

stomachache
胃痛；腹痛

have no stomach for
對～沒胃口

n. [C] 胃

- You should not take medicine *on an empty stomach*.
  你不應該在空胃的時候吃藥。
- I had a **stomachache**, and I couldn't eat anything all day.
  我胃痛，一整天都沒辦法吃任何東西。

n. 食慾；胃口

- I *have no stomach* for that cake; I think it is too sweet.
  我對那個蛋糕沒什麼興趣，我覺得它太甜了。

15. stop

[stɑp]

過去式	過去分詞	現在進行式
stopped [stɑpt]	stopped [stɑpt]	stopping [ˋstɑpɪŋ]

v.t. v.i. 停止

- The rain **stopped** in the afternoon.
  下午的時候，雨停了。

stop to + V
停下動作去做～

stop + Ving
停下～動作

- Mary *stopped to work* when she saw the boss coming.
  在看到老闆過來的時候，瑪莉停下原本的動作，開始工作。
- Mary *stopped working* when it was five thirty p.m.
  在晚上五點半的時候，瑪莉就停止了工作。

v.t. 阻止；阻擋

stop + sb + from
阻止某人做某事

- I must *stop* you *from* doing anything stupid.
  我必須阻止你做出任何愚蠢的事。
- The rain *stopped* them *from* coming to the party on time.
  這場雨使得他們不能準時參加派對。

n. [C] 停車站

bus stop
公車站

- I waited for the bus at the *bus stop*.
  我在公車站等公車。

16. store

[stor]

n. [C] 商店 = shop [ʃɑp]

- My father runs a small **store** in the country.
  我父親在鄉下經營一家小商店。

S

| convenience store
便利商店
drugstore
雜貨店，藥房 | · *Convenience **stores** are almost everywhere in Taiwan.*
臺灣幾乎到處都有便利商店。
· I bought some salt in the **drugstore**.
我在雜貨店裡買了些鹽。

v.t. 貯存
· The typhoon is coming, so many people **store** food at home.
颱風即將來臨，所以很多人都在家裡貯存食物。 |

S

17. **story** [`storɪ]

| bedtime story
床邊故事

ghost story
鬼故事

another story
另一回事 | *n.* [C] 故事
· I ask Mother to tell a *bedtime **story*** before I sleep.
我要求媽媽在我睡覺前說一個床邊故事。
· The kids are afraid to hear *ghost **stories***.
那些孩子害怕聽鬼故事。

· This idea sounds good for me, but for him, it is quite *another **story***.
這主意我覺得很不錯，但對他而言，就完全是另一回事了。

n. [C] 樓層
· I live on the second **story** of that apartment.
我住在那棟公寓的二樓。 |

18. **strange** [strendʒ]

|

feel strange
覺得不舒服

be strange to + N
對～而言是陌生的 | *adj.* 奇怪的
· It is **strange** to wear a shirt to play basketball.
穿著襯衫打籃球很奇怪。
· I have a **strange** cat. It is afraid of mice.
我有一隻奇怪的貓。牠居然怕老鼠。
· I *felt **strange*** this morning, so I didn't go to work.
我今天早上覺得不太舒服，所以就沒去工作了。
adj. 陌生的；不熟悉的
· The job *is **strange** to* me. I have to spend more time learning.
這工作對我而言是陌生的，我得多花點時間學習。 |

19. **stranger**
[`strendʒɚ]

n. [C] 陌生人
- Kids should not talk to any **stranger**.
  小孩子不應該跟任何陌生人交談。

n. [C] 初到者
- I am a **stranger** in this city.
  在這個城市，我算是個<u>外地人</u>／<u>初到者</u>。

n. [C] 生手

a stranger to + N
對～外行

- Jack is *a stranger to* computers.
  傑克對電腦一竅不通。

20. **street**
[strit]

n. [C] 街；街道
- You should not play ball on the **street**. It is very dangerous.
  你不應該在街道上玩球，很危險。
- Peter and I live on different **streets**.
  彼得和我住在不同街。

S

Exercise 2

I. 字彙翻譯

1. 仍然 ＿＿＿＿＿＿＿＿

2. 牛排 ＿＿＿＿＿＿＿＿

3. 陌生的 ＿＿＿＿＿＿＿＿

4. 商店 ＿＿＿＿＿＿＿＿

5. 停留 ＿＿＿＿＿＿＿＿

II. 字彙填充

＿＿＿＿＿＿＿＿ 1. The movie we saw last night is based on（根據）a true s＿＿＿＿y.

＿＿＿＿＿＿＿＿ 2. You should s＿＿＿＿p smoking now, or it might make you sick.

＿＿＿＿＿＿＿＿ 3. The mother told her kids to keep away from s＿＿＿＿rs.

＿＿＿＿＿＿＿＿ 4. Don't take any exercise on a full s＿＿＿＿h.

＿＿＿＿＿＿＿＿ 5. It is late now. All the stores on the s＿＿＿＿t are closed.

III. 字彙選擇

(　　) 1. I want to have a fish ＿＿＿＿＿. Thank you.

(A) story　　　(B) steak　　　(C) stranger　　　(D) stomach

(　　) 2. I don't understand him, and sometimes I think he is a ＿＿＿＿＿ person.

(A) strange　　　(B) stomach　　　(C) stranger　　　(D) street

(　　) 3. How long are you going to ＿＿＿＿＿ here?

(A) start　　　(B) still　　　(C) stay　　　(D) spring

(　　) 4. I am going to the convenience ＿＿＿＿＿. Do you want me to buy anything for you?

(A) store　　　(B) story　　　(C) stop　　　(D) stomach

(　　) 5. I am not angry with you. Of course we are ＿＿＿＿＿ friends.

(A) stay　　　(B) still　　　(C) steak　　　(D) store

Unit 39

1. strong
[strɔŋ]

adj. 強壯的 ↔ weak [wik] 弱的
- If you can keep exercising, you would be a **strong** person.
  如果你能持續運動，你就會成為一個強壯的人。

adj. （飲料）強烈的
- The coffee is too **strong** for teenagers to drink.
  這種咖啡對青少年而言太強烈，他們不應該喝。

2. student
[`stjudn̩t]

n. [C] 學生
- A good **student** should not be late for school.
  好學生上學不應該遲到。

3. study
[`stʌdɪ]

過去式	過去分詞	現在進行式
studied [`stʌdɪd]	studied [`stʌdɪd]	studying [`stʌdɪɪŋ]

v.t. v.i. 研讀；學習；研究
- Keep quiet. Your sister is **studying** English.
  保持安靜。你姊姊正在讀英文呢。

n. [C][U] 學習；調查；研究（複數：studies [`stʌdɪz]）
- Amy spends a lot of time on her English **studies**.
  愛咪在她的英語學習上花了許多的時間。
- Willy is interested in the **study** of birds.
  威利對鳥類調查感到有興趣。

under study
在研究中
- The plan to Mars is still *under* **study**.
  到火星的計畫尚在研究中。

n. [C] 書房
- You can find the book you want in my **study**.
  你可以在我的書房找到你要的書。

4. stupid
[`stjupɪd]

adj. 笨的 ↔ smart [smɑrt] 聰明的
- Don't be a **stupid** man. You must learn to be smarter.
  別當個笨蛋。你必須學著聰明一點。

- You are **stupid** to believe what he said.

  = It's **stupid** of you to believe what he said.

  你真蠢，居然會相信他的話。

S

5. **successful**

[sək`sɛsfəl]

be successful in + N/
Ving

在～方面成功

adj. 成功的

- The **successful** businessman makes lots of money.

  那個成功的商人賺了許多錢。

- Steven *is **successful** in* running a bank.

  史蒂芬成功的經營一家銀行。

6. **sugar** [`ʃʊgɚ]

sugar free

無糖的

a lump of sugar

一塊方糖

n. [U] 糖

- The milk is ***sugar** free*. It is not sweet.

  這牛奶是無糖的。它不甜。

- I always put *two lumps of **sugar*** in my coffee.

  我總是在咖啡裡放兩塊方糖。

7. **summer**

[`sʌmɚ]

summer camp

夏令營

summer vacation

暑假

n. [C][U] 夏天

- It is hot and wet in **summer** here.

  這裡的夏天又熱又濕。

- I learned how to make a fire in the ***summer** camp*.

  我在夏令營裡學會如何生火。

- I spent my ***summer** vacation* at the beach.

  我在海邊渡過我的暑假。

8. **sun**

[sʌn]

bathe in the sun

做日光浴

sunglasses

太陽眼鏡

n. [C][U] 太陽；陽光

- After raining for days, the **sun** finally shows up.

  連下了好幾天雨後，太陽總算露出臉來。

- There is nothing new under the **sun**.

  [諺語] 太陽底下無鮮事。

- I enjoy *bathing in the **sun*** at the beach.

  我喜歡在沙灘上做日光浴。

- The sun is bright so I put on my **sunglasses**.

  陽光刺眼，所以我戴上我的太陽眼鏡。

9. **sunny**

[ˋsʌnɪ]

adj. 有陽光的；暖和的

- I like to play basketball outside when it is **sunny**.
  天氣暖和的時候，我喜歡到室外打籃球。
- If it is **sunny** tomorrow, I will go picnicking with my family.
  如果明天有陽光的話，我就會跟我家人一起去野餐。

10. **supermarket**

[ˋsupɚˏmɑrkɪt]

n. [C] 超市

- I bought some vegetables and drinks in the **supermarket**.
  我在超市買了些蔬菜和飲料。

S

休息一下喔！

Exercise 1

I. 字彙翻譯

1. 糖 ＿＿＿＿＿＿＿　2. 學習 ＿＿＿＿＿＿＿　3. 強壯的 ＿＿＿＿＿＿＿

4. 太陽 ＿＿＿＿＿＿＿　5. 笨的 ＿＿＿＿＿＿＿

II. 字彙填充

＿＿＿＿＿＿＿ 1. It was a s＿＿＿y day in the morning, but it's raining now.

＿＿＿＿＿＿＿ 2. I have no food and drinks now. I will go shopping in the s＿＿＿t.

＿＿＿＿＿＿＿ 3. It is really a hot s＿＿＿r. I want to go swimming.

＿＿＿＿＿＿＿ 4. Jimmy is a s＿＿＿l leader. Everyone loves him and believes him.

＿＿＿＿＿＿＿ 5. My teacher says that a s＿＿＿t should do his homework before he plays.

III. 字彙選擇

( ) 1. The ＿＿＿＿ falls in the west at about six thirty p.m.

(A) student　(B) sugar　(C) sun　(D) study

( ) 2. To pass the test, I ＿＿＿＿ late last night.

(A) studied　(B) stupid　(C) stopped　(D) student

( ) 3. That is a ＿＿＿＿ cat. It can not understand what you say.

(A) strong　(B) summer　(C) sugar　(D) stupid

( ) 4. I am sixteen, and I am a senior high school ＿＿＿＿.

(A) station　(B) summer　(C) student　(D) supermarket

( ) 5. I drink too much ＿＿＿＿ coffee, so I could not sleep at night.

(A) strong　(B) stupid　(C) sunny　(D) street

11. sure [ʃur]

be sure of + N
對～非常確信
for sure
確切地
make sure
確定；設法確定

adj. 確信的

- I *am **sure** of* his success in the future.
  我確信他未來會成功。
- I can't remember what he said *for **sure***. You should ask him.
  我不能確切地記得他說過的話。你應該去問他。
- *Make **sure*** that you turn off the light before you leave.
  在你離開之前，要確定你有關掉燈了。

adv. 當然

- "Could you give me a hand?" "**Sure**. What should I do?"
  「能請你幫我個忙嗎？」「當然，我要做什麼？」

S

12. surprise
[sə`praɪz]

surprise party
驚喜派對

to one's surprise
出乎某人的意料

v.t. 使驚訝；使驚喜；使感到意外

- Anne **surprised** me by kissing me on the face.
  安在我臉上親了一下，讓我感到很驚喜。

n. [C][U] 驚奇；訝異

- Tim gave me a big **surprise** by asking me to marry him.
  提姆要求我嫁給他，給了我一個大大的驚喜。
- We held a *surprise* party for Joanna on her birthday.
  我們在喬安娜生日那天，為她舉辦了一個驚喜派對。
- *To my **surprise***, the crazy dog didn't bite me.
  出乎我意料之外，那隻瘋狗居然沒有咬我。

13. surprised
[sə`praɪzd]

be/feel surprised at
對～感到驚訝

adj. 感到驚訝的

- I was **surprised** that the teacher called off the test today.
  對於老師今天取消考試，我感到很驚訝。
- Father *is **surprised** at* my good grades in math.
  爸爸對我數學的好成績感到驚奇。

注意
情緒動詞的詳細用法請參閱附錄。

14. sweater

[`swɛtɚ]

n. [C] 毛衣

· It was cold, so Jack put on his **sweater** before going out.
天氣很冷，所以傑克在出門前穿上了他的毛衣。

15. sweet

[swit]

adj. 甜的

· The bananas taste **sweet**. Do you want to eat some?
香蕉嘗起來很甜。你要吃一些嗎?

adj. 親切的，和藹的

· It's so **sweet** of you to send me a birthday gift.
= You are so **sweet** to send me a birthday gift.
你真是親切，還送生日禮物給我。

16. swim

[swɪm]

過去式	過去分詞	現在進行式
swam [swæm]	swum [swʌm]	swimming [`swɪmɪŋ]

v.i. 游泳

· It is great to **swim** on a hot summer day.
在炎熱的夏天去游泳是很棒的。

補充

(1) 泳姿：動詞用 swim，如 swim freestyle。
· backstroke　仰式　　· breaststroke　蛙式
· freestyle　自由式
(2) 泳裝：通稱為 swimming suit 或 swimwear。
· swimsuit [`swɪmsʊt]　女生泳衣
· swimming trunks [trʌŋks]　男生泳褲
(3) 游泳池則為 swimming pool [pul]。

17. table

[`tebl̩]

set the table
在餐桌上擺置碗筷

n. [C] 桌子；餐桌

· Please pass me the salt on the **table**.
請把桌子上的鹽巴傳給我。

· Mother is cooking, and she wants us to *set the table* first.
媽媽正在煮飯，她要我們先把餐桌上的碗筷擺好。

table 與 desk 的比較請見 Unit 11 的單字 desk。

18. **take**
[tek]

過去式	過去分詞	現在進行式
took [tʊk]	taken [`tekən]	taking [`tekɪŋ]

v.t. 拿；拿走

· He **took** my notebook without telling me.

　他沒告知我就拿了我的筆記本。

v.t. 花費（金錢；時間等）

it takes + sb + 時間 ／金錢 + to V
花了時間／金錢～

· It ***took*** me three hours *to* clean my bedroom.

　我花了三個小時整理我的寢室。

sth + takes + sb + 時間／金錢
某事物花了某人～

· This beautiful sweater ***took*** me about two thousand dollars.

　這件漂亮的毛衣花了我大概兩千塊。

v.t. 服～；吃～（藥）

take medicine
吃藥

· If you want to get better, you must ***take*** medicine on time.

　如果你想要病情好轉，你就必須準時服藥。

19. **talk** [tɔk]

talk to/with + sb + about + sth
與某人討論某事

v.i. 說話

· Mom is ***talking*** *to* my teacher *about* my life at school.

　媽媽正在和我的老師討論我在學校的生活。

· Money **talks**.

　[諺語] 有錢能使鬼推磨。

talk back to
對～頂嘴；反駁

· You should not ***talk*** *back to* your teacher like that.

　你不應該那樣跟你的老師頂嘴。

say, speak, talk, tell 的比較請參閱 Unit 34 的單字 say。

n. [C][U] 交談

· I had a nice **talk** with my classmates last night.

　我昨晚和我的同學聊得很愉快。

small talk 閒聊；聊天	· I had a *small **talk*** with John when we waited for the bus. 在等公車的時候，我跟約翰聊天。

20. **tall**
[tɔl]

adj. （身高）高的；身材高大的 ↔ short [ʃɔrt] 矮小的

· "How **tall** are you?" "I am six feet **tall**."
「你身高多高?」「我六呎（約 183 公分）高。」

注意

tall 與 high 的比較請見 Unit 19 的單字 high。

T

休息一下喔！

Exercise 2

I. 字彙翻譯

1. 游泳 _____

2. 拿取 _____

3. 身材高大的 _____

4. 當然 _____

5. 感到驚訝的 _____

II. 字彙填充

_____ 1. Don't t_____k to me. I'm busy now.

_____ 2. The kids hide behind the door to give their mother a s_____e.

_____ 3. Boys like Grace because of her s_____t smile.

_____ 4. Put on your s_____r and coat. It is very cold outside.

_____ 5. Don't sit on the t_____e. It is not polite.

III. 字彙選擇

( ) 1. Don't forget to _____ your medicine before you go to bed.

    (A) tall   (B) table   (C) take   (D) talk

( ) 2. My teacher is _____ to my parents about my poor grades.

    (A) taking   (B) talking   (C) surprising   (D) swimming

( ) 3. I like to go _____ on hot summer days.

    (A) swimming   (B) surprising   (C) sweatering   (D) sweeting

( ) 4. My watch is slow, so I don't know what time it is for _____.

    (A) sugar   (B) sun   (C) sure   (D) surprise

( ) 5. All my family sit at the _____, and eat our dinner.

    (A) surprise   (B) sweater   (C) tall   (D) table

T

<h1 style="text-align:center">Unit 40</h1>

1. tape
[tep]

a video tape
錄影帶

n. [C] 磁帶（可泛指錄音帶或錄影帶）
- Listen to the **tape** carefully and repeat after it.
  仔細聽錄音帶並跟著它重複唸一次。
- I didn't go to the movies, but I watched some *video tapes*.
  我沒去看電影，不過倒是看了一些錄影帶。

n. [C][U] 膠帶；膠布
- I sealed the paper box with **tape**.
  我用膠布把紙箱封起來。

2. taste
[test]

have a taste for + N
愛好～

v.t. v.i. 吃起來；嚐起來
- The cake **tastes** really good. Can I have one more?
  這蛋糕嚐起來味道真好。我可以再來一塊嗎?

n. [C][U] 味覺；味道
- The milk got a funny **taste**; it may have gone bad.
  這牛奶的味道怪怪的；可能已經壞掉了。

n. [C][U] 品味；愛好
- You like cakes and he loves pies. You have different **tastes**.
  你喜歡蛋糕而他愛餡餅。你們有不同的愛好。
- Matthew *has a taste for* comic books.
  馬修愛看漫畫書。

3. taxi [ˋtæksɪ]
by taxi
搭計程車

n. [C] 計程車
- I go to the meeting *by taxi* because I am going to be late.
  我搭計程車去參加會議，因為我快要遲到了。

4. tea
[ti]

n. [C][U] 茶
- I can't sleep at night because I drink too much **tea**.
  我因為喝了太多茶，所以晚上睡不著。

注意

　　tea（茶）的種類有許多種，較常見的「紅茶」英文叫做 black tea，「綠茶」就叫做 green tea。

T

5. teach
[titʃ]

過去式	過去分詞	現在進行式
taught [tɔt]	taught [tɔt]	teaching [`titʃɪŋ]

v.t. 教，教導

· My mother **teaches** me how to cook a fish.
我媽媽教我如何烹煮一條魚。

· Irene **teaches** English at school.
艾琳在學校教英文。

v.i. 教學；教書；當老師

· Kevin **teaches** in a senior high school.
凱文在一所高中教書。

注意

teach 的字尾是 ch，所以在與第三人稱單數主詞搭配時，後面是加 es 而非 s。

6. teacher
[`titʃɚ]

n. [C] 老師

· Holly is a good **teacher**; all her students love her.
荷莉是個好老師，她的所有學生都喜愛她。

· Miss Lin is my math **teacher** at school.
林小姐是學校的數學老師。

homeroom teacher
導師

· My *homeroom teacher* is kind to every student.
我的導師對每個學生都很親切。

7. team
[tim]

n. [C] 隊伍；小組；團隊

· We are a **team**, so we have to work together.
我們是一個小隊，所以我們必須一起工作。

a school team
校隊

· I practice hard to join the *school* basketball *team*.
為了要加入籃球校隊，我努力地練習。

teammate
隊友，同隊隊員

· You are **teammates**, so you should help each other.
你們是同隊隊員，所以應該互相幫助。

teamwork
團隊合作

· It needs **teamwork** to finish this job.
要完成這項工作就必須團隊合作。

8. teenager

[`tin͵edʒɚ]

n. [C] 青少年

· Many **teenagers** can't get along well with their parents.
許多青少年和父母相處不好。

9. telephone

[`tɛlə͵fon]

talk on the telephone
講電話

telephone number
電話號碼

n. [C] 電話

· I don't want to *talk on the telephone*. I must meet you.
我不想在電話上談。我必須見你一面。

· My *telephone number* is 02-2500-6600. Please call me back.
我的電話號碼是 02-2500-6600，請回電給我。

telephone 可簡稱為 phone [fon]。另外跟 telephone 相關的字還有 cell phone（手機）、phone book（電話簿）等等。

v.t. 跟～講電話；打電話給～

· Mary asks her husband to **telephone** her every day.
瑪莉要求她老公每天打電話給她。

10. television

[`tɛlə͵vɪʒən]

watch television/TV
看電視

a television/TV set
電視機

n. [C] 電視（常用縮寫 TV [`ti`vi]）

· Mother won't let me *watch TV* before I do my homework.
在我做功課之前，媽媽不准我看電視。

· LCD *TV sets* are more and more popular these days.
有液晶螢幕的電視機現今越來越普遍了。

注意

「看」電視用的動詞是 watch [watʃ]（看），可不要跟其他的動詞 (see, look) 搞混喔！

Exercise 1

I. 字彙翻譯

1. 隊伍 _____
2. 教導 _____
3. 計程車 _____
4. 茶 _____
5. 錄音帶 _____

II. 字彙填充

_____ 1. T_____rs are persons who are between 13 and 19 years old.

_____ 2. Watching too much t_____n is bad for your eyes.

_____ 3. Nelson is on the t_____e now. Do you want to talk to him?

_____ 4. The pizza with the beef t_____es really good.

_____ 5. My English t_____r is very kind to us.

III. 字彙選擇

( ) 1. Please give me a cup of ice _____. Thanks.

    (A) team   (B) tape   (C) tea   (D) taxi

( ) 2. Now people don't watch video _____; they watch DVD's.

    (A) tapes   (B) teams   (C) taxis   (D) tastes

( ) 3. Tammy is a couch potato. He watches _____ at least ten hours every day.

    (A) television   (B) teenager   (C) telephone   (D) teacher

( ) 4. Can I use your _____? I must call my sister right now.

    (A) teacher   (B) teenager   (C) television   (D) telephone

( ) 5. There is no bus going there. You'd better take a _____.

    (A) tape   (B) tea   (C) taxi   (D) team

11. tell

[tɛl]

過去式	過去分詞	現在進行式
told [told]	told [told]	telling [`tɛlɪŋ]

v.t. 告訴；說

- I **told** you not to break the rules, didn't I?
  我告訴過你不要犯規了，不是嗎?

tell + sb + about
告訴某人關於～

- Please **tell** me more *about* the news.
  請再多告訴我一些有關那則新聞的事。

tell a lie/the truth
說謊／實話

- If you really want to help him, you have to **tell** him *the truth*.
  如果你真的想幫助他，就必須告訴他實話。

tell a story
說故事

- Joe **told** a sad *story* and made all the girls cry.
  喬說了一個很傷心的故事，讓女孩們都哭了。

注意

　　say, speak, talk, tell 的比較請參閱 Unit 34 的單字 say。

v.t. v.i. 識別；辨別

- I can't **tell** which bag is mine. They look all the same.
  我分辨不出來那個袋子是我的。它們看起來都一樣。

tell A from B
分辨 A 與 B

- Paul looks like his brother. It's hard to **tell** one *from* the other.
  保羅跟他的弟弟長的很像。要分辨誰是誰很難。

12. tennis

[`tɛnɪs]

n. [U] 網球（運動）

- Judy likes to play **tennis**; she wants to be a **tennis** player.
  茱蒂喜歡打網球，她希望將來能成為一個網球選手。

注意

　　球類運動的動詞用的都是 play。

補充

　　網球場叫做 tennis court [`tɛnɪs,kort]，網球拍叫做 tennis-racket [`tɛnɪs,rækɪt]，網球則叫做 tennis-ball [`tɛnɪs,bɔl]。跟網球在英文用法上比較相關的有 table tennis（桌球），它也可以叫做 pingpong [`pɪŋpɔŋ] 乒乓球。

13. **test**
[tɛst]

n. [C] 小考

· There will be a math **test** next Tuesday.
下星期二將有一個數學小考。

 補充

· test [tɛst] 小考

· examination [ɪɡ͵zæmə`neʃən] = exam [ɪɡ͵zæm] 大考

n. [C] 測試；檢驗

· Sandy was asked to have a DNA **test**.
仙蒂被要求作 DNA 檢驗。

v.t. 測驗；檢驗；檢查

· If you can't see things clearly, you should have your eyes **tested**.
如果你看東西看不清楚,那你應該要去檢查眼睛了。

14. **than**
[ðæn]

would rather + V₁ +
than + V₂
寧願～也不要～

conj. 比（與比較級連用）

· Peter is taller/more serious **than** me/I am.
彼得比我高／嚴肅。

· I'*d rather* stay home ***than*** go shopping with those girls.
我寧願待在家,也不要和那些女孩去購物。

prep. 超過（後接計量數目）

· Matt works more **than** eight hours a day.
馬特每天工作超過八小時。

 補充

than（比）與 then（當時；然後）在拼法和發音上都相當類似,但意義和用法則完全不同,請注意。

15. **thank**
[θæŋk]

v.t. 謝謝

· **Thanks**. = **Thank** you.
謝謝。

T

thank + sb + for
因～而感謝某人

- **Thank** you very much.
  非常謝謝你。
- *Thank* you *for* your help.
  感謝你的幫忙。
- Neo *thanks* me *for* giving him a ride.
  尼歐謝謝我載他一程。

n. 感謝；謝意 (～s)

- Many **thanks**. = A thousand **thanks**. = **Thanks** a lot.
  非常感謝。／感激不盡。（較通俗且口語化的用法）

thanks to + N
幸虧～；由於～

- *Thanks* to your help, I wasn't late for school.
  幸虧有你的幫忙，我上學才沒有遲到。

16. **that**
[ðæt]

art. 那，那個

- Pass me **that** pen on the desk, please.
  請把書桌上的那隻筆傳給我。

pron. 那，那個；那人；那東西；那件事 (代替出現過的名詞)

- Do you see the kid over there? **That**'s my boy.
  你有看到在那裡的男孩嗎？那是我兒子。

pron. 代替關係代名詞 who 或 which

- The man who sent me to the station is my father.
  = The man **that** sent me to the station is my father.
  送我到車站的那個人是我爸爸。
- I bought a present which cost five hundred dollars for Mary.
  = I bought a present **that** cost five hundred dollars for Mary.
  我買了一個價值五百元的禮物給瑪莉。

conj. （引導名詞子句，做為動詞的受詞或名詞的同位語）

- Don't you know **that** the new teacher is coming today?
  你不知道今天新老師要來嗎？
- I have a dream **that** I can become a doctor one day.
  我有一個夢想，就是希望我有一天能成為一個醫生。

conj. （引導副詞子句，用以表示原因或理由）

- Paul is sad **that** he lost his favorite toy yesterday.
  保羅很傷心，因為他昨天把他心愛的玩具弄丟了。

so that
以便

- I turned on the light *so **that*** I could read my book.
  我打開燈，以便於我能讀書。

17. **theater**
[ˋθɪətɚ]
movie theater
電影院

n. [C] 劇場；電影院；戲院

- I went to the *movie **theater*** to see a movie.
  我去電影院看電影。

18. **then** [ðɛn]
then = at that time
那時；當時

adv. 那時，當時

- You were short and fat **then**, but you look pretty now.
  當時妳又矮又胖，但現在妳看起來很漂亮。

adv. 然後

- Turn right on the next street, and **then** you'll see the theater.
  在下一條街右轉，然後你就會看到電影院了。

19. **there**
[ðɛr]

adv. 在那裡；到那裡；向那裡

- We had a good time **there**.
  我們在那裡玩得很愉快。
- I want to go **there** to buy some ice cream.
  我想去那裡買些冰淇淋。

adv. 瞧，你看（用於引起注意或加強語氣）

- **There** comes the train.
  你看，火車來了。

pron. 有（與 be 動詞連用）

- **There** are five books on the desk.
  書桌上有五本書。

20. **these**
[ðiz]

art. 這些的

- **These** pens are mine, and those are yours.
  這些筆是我的，那些是你的。

these

pron. 這些

· Do you see the candies on the table? All of **these** are yours.
你看到桌上的這些糖果嗎? 這些全是你的。

T

休息一下喔!

Exercise 2

I. 字彙翻譯

1. 網球 _____
2. 那個 _____
3. 這些 _____
4. 比 _____
5. 然後 _____

II. 字彙填充

_____ 1. T_____e are five people on the bus.

_____ 2. We went to the t_____r to see the movie of Steve Spielberg.

_____ 3. T_____k you for everything you did for me.

_____ 4. "Have you prepared for the math t_____t today?"

"Yes. I studied until ten o'clock last night."

_____ 5. The bad kid likes to t_____l a lie to his teacher.

III. 字彙選擇

( ) 1. It's hard to _____ if Johnny lies.

　　(A) tell 　　　(B) thank 　　　(C) tape 　　　(D) teach

( ) 2. "What are _____?" "They are all my birthday presents."

　　(A) there 　　　(B) then 　　　(C) these 　　　(D) tennis

( ) 3. Did you see the rabbit _____? It is so cute.

　　(A) than 　　　(B) there 　　　(C) that 　　　(D) thank

( ) 4. _____ to the good weather, we had lots of fun at the playground.

　　(A) Thanks 　　　(B) Tests 　　　(C) These 　　　(D) There

( ) 5. I play _____ every week. That is my favorite sport.

　　(A) tennis 　　　(B) these 　　　(C) test 　　　(D) theater

T

Unit 41

1. thin
[θɪn]

adj. 瘦的 ↔ fat [fæt] 胖的

- I was fat before, but now I am **thinner**.
  我以前胖胖的，不過現在我比較瘦。

adj. 薄的

- The book is light and **thin**.
  這本書又輕又薄。

adj. 細的

- Pan drew a **thin** red line to mark the key words.
  潘畫一條細細的紅線，標示出關鍵字。

adj. 稀疏的

- My father's hair is **thin**.
  我爸爸的頭髮很稀疏。

adj. 稀薄的

- The air is **thin** in the high mountains.
  高山上的空氣很稀薄。

2. thing
[θɪŋ]

n. [C] 物品；東西；事情

- Remember to bring all the **things** I told you.
  記得把我告訴你要帶的東西全都帶著。

- I have lots of **things** to do today.
  我今天有一大堆事情要做。

3. think
[θɪŋk]

過去式	過去分詞	現在進行式
thought [θɔt]	thought [θɔt]	thinking [`θɪŋkɪŋ]

v.t. v.i. 想；思考

- Peter **thought** for a long time before he decided to leave.
  彼得在下定決心要離開之前，思考了很長一段時間。

think of + N
想起～

- The doll makes me *think* of my little daughter.
  這洋娃娃讓我想起我的小女兒。

| think about + N
考慮～ | • "Do you want to see a movie?"<br>"I am **thinking** about it."
「你想要看電影嗎?」
「我正在考慮。」 |
| | *v.t. v.i.* 認為
• I don't **think** this is a good idea.
我不認為這是個好主意。
• I **think** you should take more exercise.
我認為你應該多做點運動。 |

4. thirsty
[`θɝstɪ]

be thirsty for + N
渴望～

adj. 口乾的, 渴的
• I felt quite **thirsty** after jogging for an hour.
慢跑一小時後，我覺得非常口渴。

adj. 渴望的
• Rick is **thirsty** for the new bicycle.
瑞克渴望擁有那部新腳踏車。

5. this
[ðɪs]

art. 這; 這個
• **This** doll belongs to me.
這個洋娃娃是屬於我的。

pron. 這; 這人; 這東西; 這件事
• After reading so many books, I find **this** is my favorite.
在讀過這麼多書之後，我發現這本才是我的最愛。
(this 代替之前出現過的名詞 book)
• **This** is my second time to go to Hong Kong.
這次是我第二次去香港。

6. those
[ðoz]

adj. 那些
• **Those** books are mine, not yours.
這些書是我的，不是你的。
• **Those** clothes over there are all for sale.
放在那邊的那些衣服全是要賣的。

T

pron. 那些；那些人；那些東西；那些事

those who + V
那些～的人

- Don't eat the dishes on the desk. **Those** are all my dinner.
  別吃桌上的菜，那些全是我的晚餐。
- God helps *those* *who* help themselves.
  [諺語] 天助自助者。
- This theater is open for *those* *who* like special movies.
  這家戲院是為了那些喜愛特別電影的人而開設的。

7. **though**
[ðo]

conj. 雖然；儘管 = although [ɔl`ðo]

- **Though** the kid doesn't like vegetables, he eats them all.
  雖然那孩子並不喜歡蔬菜，但他還是把它們吃光了。
- **Though** I am your friend, I can't help you cheat.
  儘管我是你朋友，我還是不能幫你作弊。

8. **thousand**
[`θauzənd]

thousands of + Ns
數以千計的～

n. [C][U] （一）千

- The new pair of shoes cost me five **thousand** dollars.
  這雙新鞋花了我五千塊錢。
- *Thousands* of people work in the big factory.
  數以千計的人在這個大工廠裡工作。

注意

thousand 只有在跟 of 連用，表示「數以千計的～」時，後面才會加 s，在一般的情況之下是不加的。例如：「兩千元」應該是 two thousand dollars 而不是 two thousands dollars。

9. **ticket**
[`tɪkɪt]

ticket for/to + N
～的票

n. [C] 票（車票、門票、電影票等），入場券

- You can't get on the train without a **ticket**.
  沒車票你就不能上火車。
- I got two **tickets** *for/to* the basketball game for free.
  我免費拿到兩張籃球比賽的票。

n. [C] 罰單

- Jason got a **ticket** for parking in the wrong place.
  傑森收到一張罰單，是罰他隨便亂停車。

10. **tiger**
[ˋtaɪgɚ]

n. [C] 老虎

· Don't be close to the **tiger**. It is very dangerous.
別靠近那隻老虎，那很危險。

· The baby **tiger** is like a cat.
小老虎看起來像一隻貓。

休息一下喔！

T

Exercise 1

I. 字彙翻譯

1. 思考 _____
2. 東西 _____
3. 這個 _____
4. 老虎 _____
5. 瘦的 _____

II. 字彙填充

_____ 1. If you want to see the movie, you have to buy t_____ts first.

_____ 2. He plays basketball very well t_____h he's not tall.

_____ 3. He was so t_____y that he drank a bottle of water.

_____ 4. T_____e who like to exercise are usually more strong and healthy.

_____ 5. T_____ds of people came to Taipei for the movie festival.

III. 字彙選擇

(　　) 1. What is the _____ you want most? Health, money or love?

    (A) though   (B) thing   (C) thin   (D) think

(　　) 2. You are too _____ now; you should eat more meat.

    (A) though   (B) thing   (C) think   (D) thin

(　　) 3. I _____ of my mother when I saw the old woman.

    (A) thanked   (B) thousand   (C) though   (D) thought

(　　) 4. Jogging for three miles makes me hungry and _____.

    (A) thirsty   (B) ticket   (C) think   (D) though

(　　) 5. I spent fifty _____ dollars to buy a computer, and I have no money now.

    (A) thousand   (B) ticket   (C) though   (D) thirsty

11. **time**

[taɪm]

it's time for sb to V
該是～的時候了

(at) any time
任何時候；隨時

at the same time
同時

have a good time
玩的很愉快

in time
及時（剛好來得及）

kill time
消磨時間

on time
準時

n. [U] 時間

- "What **time** is it now?" "It is twelve thirty."
  「現在幾點鐘啦?」「十二點三十分。」
- "Do you have the **time**?" "It's four o'clock."
  「現在幾點?」「四點。」
- "Do you have **time**?" "Yes."
  「你現在有空嗎?」「有啊。」
- Hurry up! We don't have **time** to wait.
  快一點，我們沒時間等了。
- **Time** is money.
  [諺語] 時間就是金錢。
- *It's **time** for* you *to* wake up and eat breakfast.
  你該起床吃早餐了。
- You can come to play *any **time***.
  你隨時都可以過來玩。
- It is dangerous to drive and talk on the phone *at the same **time***.
  同時開車和講電話是很危險的。
- "I will go to the zoo with my family tomorrow."
  "*Have a good **time**.*"
  「明天我要跟我家人去動物園。」「祝你玩的愉快。」
- We *had a good **time*** at the beach last weekend.
  上週末我們在海灘上玩的很高興。
- I arrived at the airport *in **time***. I was almost late.
  我及時趕到機場，差一點就遲到了。
- If I have nothing to do, I will read some books to *kill **time***.
  如果我沒事做的話，我就會唸點書來消磨時間。
- You should go to school *on **time***.
  你應該準時到校。

n.[C] 次數

- Lily goes swimming three **times** a week.
  莉莉每週游泳三次。

12. tired
[taɪrd]

adj. 疲倦的

· After doing all the work, I feel very **tired**.
做完所有工作後，我感到非常疲倦。

adj. 厭倦的，厭煩的

be tired of + N/Ving
對～感到厭倦

· I *am* ***tired*** *of* watching TV all day.
我對於一整天看電視感到厭煩。

13. today
[tə`de]

adv. 今天

· We really had a good time at the beach **today**.
我們今天在海邊真地玩得很愉快。

n. [U] 今天

· "What date is **today**?" "May tenth."
「今天幾月幾號?」「五月十號。」

adv. 在現今；在當代

· **Today** we have much better life than years ago in Taiwan.
跟數年前比起來，在現今的台灣，我們有更好的生活。

14. together
[tə`gɛðɚ]

adv. 一起；共同

· Diana and I did some shopping **together** last Sunday.
上個禮拜天黛安娜跟我一起去採購。

· Every family will get **together** on Chinese New Year's Eve.
在農曆除夕每個家庭會相聚在一起。

15. tomato
[tə`meto]

n. [C] 蕃茄（複數：tomatoes [tə`metoz]）

· Is a **tomato** a kind of vegetable or fruit?
蕃茄是一種蔬菜還是一種水果?

16. tomorrow
[tə`mɔro]

n. [U] 明天

· **Tomorrow** will be my birthday, and I'll hold a party.
明天是我生日，我會辦個派對。

the day after
tomorrow　後天

· Today is Friday, and *the day after* ***tomorrow*** would be Sunday.
今天禮拜五，那麼後天就是禮拜天。

後天的說法是 the day after tomorrow，大後天則是 two days after tomorrow，其餘依此類推。

adv. 明天

· See you **tomorrow**.
　明天見。

---

17. **tonight**
[tə`naɪt]

adv. 今晚

· I drank too much coffee; I don't think I can sleep **tonight**.
　我喝了太多咖啡，我想今晚我是睡不著了。

n. [U] 今晚

· Did you watch **tonight**'s news on TV?
　你看到今晚電視上的新聞了嗎?

T

18. **too**
[tu]

adv. 太～; 過份

· It's **too** cold today. I don't want to go out at all.
　今天太冷了。我一點也不想出門。

· You are **too** much. You should say sorry to her.
　你太過份了，你應該向她道歉。

too + Adj/Adv + to
+ V　太～而不能～

· Hank is **too** tired *to* work any more.
　漢克太累，所以不能再繼續工作了。

adv. 也; 還; 而且

· "I like that movie." "I like it, **too**."
　「我喜歡那部電影。」「我也喜歡。」

---

19. **tooth**
[tuθ]

n. [C] 牙齒（複數: teeth [tiθ]）

· Remember to check your **teeth** once a year.
　記得要一年檢查一次你的牙齒。

bad tooth
蛀牙; 齲齒

· When Adam's *bad **tooth*** was pulled out, he cried out loudly.
　當亞當的蛀牙被拔掉時，他大聲的哭叫出來。

brush one's teeth
刷牙

· Do you *brush your **teeth*** after every meal?
　你每餐飯後都有刷牙嗎?

20. **touch**
[tʌtʃ]

v.t. 接觸，觸摸，碰

· You should not **touch** the art works in the museum.
你不該去碰那些博物館裡的藝術作品。

v.t. 感動

· I was **touched** by that movie. I cried when I saw it.
我被那部電影感動了。在看這部電影的時候我哭了。

n. [U] 聯繫；接觸

keep in touch with
與～保持聯繫

· I still *keep in **touch** with* my classmates in elementary school.
我仍然與小學的同班同學保持聯繫。

T

休息一下喔！

Exercise 2

I. 字彙翻譯

1. 今天 _____

2. 時間 _____

3. 疲倦的 _____

4. 今晚 _____

5. 也 _____

II. 字彙填充

_____ 1. I need some t_____oes to make salad.

_____ 2. What date is t_____w?

_____ 3. Kevin and I went out t_____r several times.

_____ 4. "How often do you brush your t_____h?" "Two times a day."

_____ 5. People are all t_____hed by Mother Teresa's story.

III. 字彙選擇

(   ) 1. Molly is _____ after doing all the homework.

     (A) tomato   (B) tired   (C) time   (D) together

(   ) 2. Fanny is _____ angry to speak any word.

     (A) tooth   (B) too   (C) touch   (D) tonight

(   ) 3. The weather is very good _____. Let's play basketball outside.

     (A) together   (B) tomato   (C) today   (D) tomorrow

(   ) 4. Don't _____ that machine. You might get hurt.

     (A) touch   (B) tooth   (C) too   (D) tomorrow

(   ) 5. We don't have much _____ left. Please hurry up.

     (A) tooth   (B) time   (C) tomato   (D) tiger

T

Unit 42

1. towel
[ˋtauəl]

n. [C] 毛巾；手巾；紙巾

· I clean the table and chairs with a **towel**.
我用一條毛巾把桌子跟椅子擦乾淨。

2. town
[taun]

n. [C] 鎮，城鎮

· My family moved to the **town** from the country last month.
我家上個月從鄉下搬到鎮上去。

downtown
商業區

· My sisters are going to shop in **downtown**.
我的姊姊們正要去商業區購物。

3. toy
[tɔɪ]

n. [C] 玩具

· Those kids are playing with their **toys**.
那些孩子們正在玩他們的玩具。

adj. 作為玩具的

· The boy asks his father to buy a **toy** train for him.
那男孩要求他爸爸買個玩具火車給他。

4. traffic
[ˋtræfɪk]

n. [U] 交通

· There is much **traffic** in the rush hour.
尖峰時段行人和車輛（交通）很多。

heavy traffic
交通擁擠；塞車

· David was late because of the *heavy **traffic***.
大衛因為塞車而遲到了。

a traffic light
紅綠燈

· It is safe to go when the ***traffic** light* turns green.
交通號誌燈變綠的時候，就可以安全通過了。

traffic rules
交通規則

· You have to follow the ***traffic** rules* any time.
你必須隨時遵守交通規則。

5. train
[tren]

n. [C] 火車

· I will go to Taipei by **train** tomorrow morning.
我明天早上要搭火車到台北。

get on/off the train 上／下火車	• Hurry up, or we'll miss the **train**. 　快點兒，否則我們就趕不上火車了。 • We'll *get off the train* at the next station. 　我們要在下一站下（火）車。
	v.t. 訓練；培養 • The teacher **trains** us to speak English. 　老師訓練我們說英文。 • The boy was **trained** to be a basketball player. 　那男孩被培養為一個籃球選手。

6. **tree**
[tri]

grow a tree
種植／栽培樹木

n. [C] 樹，樹木
• We had a picnic under the **tree** in the park.
　我們在公園裡的樹下野餐。
• Grandpa *grew* some *trees* in the garden.
　爺爺在花園裡種了幾棵樹。

7. **trip** [trɪp]

take a trip to + N
到～去旅行

on a business trip
出差

n. [C] 旅行；遠足
• I plan to *take a trip to* America this summer.
　我計畫在這個夏天到美國去旅行。
• I come to Hong Kong *on a business trip*.
　我是到香港來出差的。
• My boss asked me to go *on a business trip* to Japan next week.
　我老闆要求我下禮拜到日本去出差。

8. **trouble**
[`trʌbl̩]

have trouble + Ving
做～有困難

ask/look for trouble
自找麻煩

n. [C][U] 麻煩
• You have a big **trouble**.
　你有大麻煩了。
• Many people *have **trouble** speaking* in public.
　許多人在公開演講方面感到有困難。
• You are *asking for **trouble***.
　你是在自找麻煩。

get into trouble 惹麻煩	· "Don't *get into* **trouble** at school," my mother said. 我媽媽說：「不要在學校惹麻煩。」
	n. [U] 故障 (+ with)
	· There are some **troubles** with my truck. I can't start it. 我的卡車有點故障。我無法發動它。
	v.t. 使煩惱／憂慮
	· The math test tomorrow really **troubles** me. 明天要舉行的數學小考真的讓我很煩惱。

9. truck
[trʌk]

a truck driver
卡車司機

n. [C] 卡車

· These desks will be sent to the school by **truck**.
這些書桌會用卡車載到學校去。

· As *a **truck** driver*, I drive a **truck** around Taiwan every day.
身為一名卡車司機，我每天開著卡車繞著臺灣跑。

10. true
[tru]

a dream come true
夢想實現

adj. 真的；真實的

· Everything I said is **true**. I didn't lie to you.
我說的每件事都是真的，我沒有對你說謊。

· The man in the **true** story is still living in the world.
這真實故事裡的那個人現在還活在這個世界上。

· Your *dream* will *come **true*** if you work hard.
如果你努力的話，你的夢想一定會實現的。

Exercise 1

I. 字彙翻譯

1. 旅行 _____   2. 卡車 _____   3. 玩具 _____

4. 樹木 _____   5. 城鎮 _____

II. 字彙填充

_____ 1. The fast t_____n to Taipei will arrive at 9:56 a.m.

_____ 2. I dried my body with a big t_____l after I took a bath.

_____ 3. The policeman stopped the car because the driver didn't follow the t_____c rules.

_____ 4. Do you have t_____e answering this question?

_____ 5. Is that t_____e? I can't believe it.

III. 字彙選擇

(　　) 1. I am _____ my dog to sit down.

    (A) troubling　　(B) training　　(C) tripping　　(D) truing

(　　) 2. If we keep cutting _____, we will have no fresh air in the future.

    (A) toys　　(B) trips　　(C) trees　　(D) trucks

(　　) 3. I have some _____ now. Can you help me?

    (A) troubles　　(B) trucks　　(C) towels　　(D) traffics

(　　) 4. I know you can drive a car, but it doesn't mean you can drive a _____, too.

    (A) trouble　　(B) traffic　　(C) trip　　(D) truck

(　　) 5. You have to stop if the _____ light is red.

    (A) traffic　　(B) trouble　　(C) true　　(D) train

T

11. try
[traɪ]

過去式	過去分詞	現在進行式
tried [traɪd]	tried [traɪd]	trying [ˋtraɪɪŋ]

v.t. v.i. 嘗試

- **Try** this cookie. It is really delicious.
  試試這塊餅乾，真的很好吃。
- I **tried** to move the table by myself but I couldn't.
  我試著自己搬過那張桌子，但我搬不動。

try on + N
試穿～

- You had better **try** *on* the shoes before you buy them.
  你在買下鞋子之前，最好先試穿過。

n. [C] 嘗試

give it a try
嘗試一次

- Don't give up before you *give it a try*.
  不要在嘗試過一次之前就放棄。

worth a try
值得一試

- Though it may not work, it's still *worth a* **try**.
  雖然可能行不通，但仍值得一試。

12. turn [tɝn]

turn right/left
右轉／左轉

v.t. v.i. 轉，轉動

- You should **turn** *left* if you want to go to the park.
  如果你是要去公園的話，應該要左轉。
- **Turn** *right* at the next street and you'll see the theater.
  在下一條街右轉，你就會看到那家戲院了。

turn on/off + N
打開／關上～

- Please **turn** *off* the light when you leave.
  在你離開的時候，請把燈關掉。

turn in + N
交出／交上～

- My teacher asked me to **turn** *in* my homework on time.
  我的老師要求我準時交出作業。

v.t. v.i. 使變得，使成為

turn (from N) to N
（從～）變為～

- After ten years, Helen **turned** *from* a girl *to* a woman.
  十年過後，海倫從一個女孩轉變為一個女人。

n. [C] （輪流時的）一個班次；一次機會

- It is your **turn** to do the dishes.
  輪到你洗碗了。

13. typhoon
[taɪ`fun]

n. [C] 颱風

- The **typhoon** will bring strong wind and heavy rain.

  那個颱風將會帶來強風和豪雨。

- **Typhoons** usually come in July and August in Taiwan.

  在臺灣，颱風通常在七、八月來襲。

14. umbrella
[ʌm`brɛlə]

n. [C] 雨傘

- It might rain today, so don't forget to bring your **umbrella**.

  今天可能會下雨，所以別忘了帶傘。

15. uncle
[`ʌŋkl̩]

n. [C] 叔叔；伯伯；大叔；姨父；舅舅；姑丈

- My **uncle** and aunt will come to visit us this weekend.

  這個週末，我叔叔跟阿姨要來拜訪我們。

U

16. under
[`ʌndɚ]

prep. 在～下面

- There's a cat **under** your chair.

  你的椅子底下有隻貓。

adv. 小於～；低於～；未滿～

- It is so cold. It is **under** 10°C today.

  好冷。今天氣溫低於 10°C。

- Children **under** eighteen can't see this movie.

  未滿十八歲的孩子不能看這部電影。

17. understand
[ˌʌndɚ`stænd]

過去式	過去分詞	現在進行式
understood [ˌʌndɚ`stʊd]	understood [ˌʌndɚ`stʊd]	understanding [ˌʌndɚ`stændɪŋ]

v.t. v.i. 明白；瞭解；理解

- Do you **understand** what I am saying?

  你了解我在說什麼嗎？

- Why did you do this to me? I don't **understand**.

  為什麼你要對我這麼做？我不明白。

18. **unhappy**
[ʌn`hæpɪ]

adj. 不高興的 ↔ happy [`hæpɪ] 高興的
- Dad was **unhappy** about my poor grades.
  父親對我糟糕的成績感到很不高興。

19. **uniform**
[`junə,fɔrm]

n. [C] 制服
- Students have to wear **uniforms** at school.
  學生在學校必須穿制服。

20. **until** [ən`tɪl]
not...until...
直到～才～

prep. 直到
- I did*n't* go to bed *until* 10:00 p.m.
  直到晚上十點我才上床睡覺。

conj. 直到
- I forgot to do my homework **until** my mother told me to.
  直到媽媽告訴我，我才想起來要寫作業。

注意

　　在英文的句子裡，not...until... 的句型是寫成「某人沒有做某事，一直到某時間」，但在翻譯成中文時，則應該翻成「某人一直到某時間，才去做某事」，這是在遇到這種句型時所特別需要注意的。

U

Exercise 2

I. 字彙翻譯

1. 制服 _____
2. 直到 _____
3. 嘗試 _____
4. 叔叔 _____
5. 在～下面 _____

II. 字彙填充

_____ 1. What's wrong with you? You look u_____y.

_____ 2. I ask my teacher because I don't u_____d the question.

_____ 3. The weather is fine, so I don't think I need an u_____a.

_____ 4. We don't have to go to school today because of the t_____n.

_____ 5. You should t_____n on the light when you read a book.

III. 字彙選擇

( ) 1. Jeff didn't get married _____ he is thirty five.

    (A) uniform   (B) uncle   (C) under   (D) until

( ) 2. My cat likes to hide _____ the bed.

    (A) understand   (B) under   (C) uncle   (D) unhappy

( ) 3. My _____ runs a shoes store in the town.

    (A) uncle   (B) uniform   (C) umbrella   (D) until

( ) 4. The _____ of mailmen is green.

    (A) umbrella   (B) uncle   (C) uniform   (D) typhoon

( ) 5. I _____ on the radio to listen to music.

    (A) trouble   (B) train   (C) turn   (D) try

U

Unit 43

1. up [ʌp]

get up
起床

stand up
起立；站起來

wake up
醒來

be up to + sb
取決於某人

what's up
發生什麼事了?

adv. 向上 ↔ down [daun] 向下

- Jack goes to bed and *gets up* early every day.
  傑克每天都早睡早起。
- Everyone *stands up* when the boss walks into the office.
  當老闆走進辦公室的時候，所有人都站了起來。
- I *woke up* in 2:00 a.m. for a bad dream.
  因為做了惡夢，我在凌晨兩點醒了過來。
- Where you want to go *is up* to you. Don't ask me.
  你想去哪裡取決於你自己。不要問我。
- *What's up*? Why does everyone here look sad?
  怎麼了? 為什麼這裡的每個人看起來都很傷心?

U

2. use

[juz]

used to + V
過去常常～

be used to + Ving
習慣於～

make use of + N
利用；使用

there is no use +
Ving　做～沒有用

v.t. v.i. 用；使用

- I **used** all my money to buy a new toy.
  我用我所有的錢買了一個新的玩具。
- You should learn to **use** your time well.
  你得學著好好使用你的時間。
- I *used to read* before I sleep, but now I am too tired to do it.
  我以前常常在睡前閱讀，但現在我太累就不這麼做了。
- Father *is used to smoking* after dinner.
  爸爸習慣在晚飯後抽煙。

n. [C][U] 使用

- Mary *made use of* the bottles to grow flowers.
  瑪莉利用那些瓶子來種花。
- *There's no use* crying over spilled milk.
  [諺語] 覆水難收。

3. useful

[`jusfəl]

adj. 有用的 ↔ useless [`juslɪs] 沒用的

- It is always **useful** to read more books.
  多讀點書總是有用的。

· This book gives me much **useful** knowledge.
這本書給了我很多有用的知識。

---

4. **usually**
[`juʒəlɪ]

adv. 經常；通常

· What do you **usually** do after work?
你下班後通常做什麼？

注意
頻率副詞的比較請參考 Unit 2 的單字 always。

---

5. **vacation**
[ve`keʃən]

summer/winter vacation
暑／寒假

n. [C][U] 假期

· "How did you spend the long **vacation**?"
"I took a trip to America."
「你的長假是怎麼渡過的?」
「我到美國去旅行了。」

· I almost went swimming every day in the *summer **vacation***.
我暑假幾乎每一天都去游泳。

注意
vacation 與 holiday（假日）的比較請參閱 Unit 19 的單字 holiday。

---

6. **vegetable**
[`vɛdʒətəbl̩]

grow vegetables
種植蔬菜

n. [C] 蔬菜

· Green **vegetables** are rich in vitamin C.
綠色蔬菜富含維它命 C。

· The farmer *grows* rice and ***vegetables*** on his farm.
那個農夫在他的田裡種植稻米和蔬菜。

---

7. **very**
[`vɛrɪ]

adv. 非常地，很

· Sara is **very** friendly to everyone she knows.
莎拉對她所認識的每個人都非常地友善。

· "I have done my homework." "**Very** good."
「我已經寫完回家作業了。」「很好。」

V

8. video
[`vɪdɪ,o]

n. [C] 錄影機；錄影帶

· Norman watched the tape with his **video**.
  諾曼用他的錄影機看那捲帶子。

adj. 電視的

a video game
電動遊戲

· Most boys love to play *video* games.
  大多數的男孩喜歡玩電動遊戲。

9. visit [`vɪzɪt]
visit + sb
拜訪某人
visit + some place
參觀某地

v.t. 拜訪；參觀

· I *visited* my teacher in senior high school last weekend.
  我上週末去拜訪了我的高中老師。

· This is his first time to *visit* the museum.
  這是他第一次參觀這家博物館。

10. voice
[vɔɪs]

n. [U] 聲音

· Vanessa has a beautiful **voice**. She wants to be a singer.
  凡妮莎有很美的聲音。她想成為一個歌手。

Exercise 1

I. 字彙翻譯

1. 非常地 _____
2. 聲音 _____
3. 向上 _____
4. 錄影機 _____
5. 使用 _____

II. 字彙填充

_____ 1. Eating green v_____es is good for you.

_____ 2. I went to several countries during my summer v_____n.

_____ 3. I u_____y play basketball in my free time, but sometimes I go swimming.

_____ 4. I think this book is u_____l for those who want to learn English.

_____ 5. My friend, Diana, is going to v_____t me this weekend.

III. 字彙選擇

( ) 1. I won't get _____ until noon on Sundays.

　　(A) use 　　(B) voice 　　(C) video 　　(D) up

( ) 2. This _____ game is so interesting. I always forget time when I play it.

　　(A) useful 　　(B) video 　　(C) very 　　(D) usually

( ) 3. He speaks in a low _____ because he doesn't want anyone to hear him.

　　(A) voice 　　(B) video 　　(C) vacation 　　(D) vegetable

( ) 4. Thank you _____ much. You really helped a lot.

　　(A) very 　　(B) video 　　(C) voice 　　(D) visit

( ) 5. I don't know how to _____ this machine. Can you teach me?

　　(A) under 　　(B) visit 　　(C) use 　　(D) video

V

11. **wait** [wet]

wait for + N
等待～

v.i. 等待

- I have **waited** *for* the bus for half an hour.
  我已經等公車等了半個小時了。

12. **waiter**

[`wetɚ]

n. [C] （男）侍者；服務生

- I tell the **waiter** that I can order now.
  我告訴那個侍者，現在我可以點餐了。

13. **waitress**

[`wetrɪs]

n. [C] 女服務生

- My sister works as a **waitress** at the high-class restaurant.
  我姐在這家高級餐廳當女服務生。

14. **wake**

[wek]

過去式	過去分詞	現在進行式
woke [wok]	woken [`wokən]	waking [`wekɪŋ]

v.i. 醒來

wake up
醒來

- When I **woke** up, the party was over and everyone had left.
  當我醒來的時後，派對已經結束，所有人也都已經離開了。

v.t. 喚醒

wake + sb + up
叫醒某人

- Don't **wake** her *up*. Let her sleep for more time.
  別叫醒她。讓她多睡點。

15. **walk**

[wɔk]

v.i. 走路；散步

- I have to **walk** to school when I don't catch the bus.
  我沒趕上公車時，就得走路去上學。

v.t. 蹓～（寵物）

- I usually **walk** my dog in the park.
  我通常在公園裡蹓我的狗。

n. [C] 走路；散步

take a walk
散步

- Grace likes to *take a* **walk** under the moonlight.
  葛蕾絲喜歡在月光下散步。

W

16. wall [wɔl]

on the wall
在牆上

n. [C] 牆壁；圍牆

- Peter is looking at the picture *on the wall*.
  彼得正在看牆上掛著的那幅畫。

17. want [wɑnt]

v.t. 想要；要

- Sandy **wants** a big butter cake on her birthday.
  仙蒂在她的生日想要一個好大的奶油蛋糕。
- What on earth do you **want** me to do?
  你到底想要我做什麼？

18. warm [wɔrm]

keep + sb + warm
讓某人保持溫暖

warm up
暖身；做準備

adj. 溫暖的 ↔ cool [kul] 涼快的

- It's **warm** in spring and cool in autumn.
  春天很溫暖，秋天很涼爽。
- The sweater would *keep* you **warm** in the winter.
  這件毛衣可以讓你在冬天的時候保持溫暖。

v.t. 使溫暖 (+ up)

- A cup of hot coffee will **warm** you up on the cold days.
  在寒冷的日子裡，一杯熱咖啡會使你暖和起來。
- The players are *warming* up before the game starts.
  這些選手在比賽開始前做暖身運動。

19. wash [wɑʃ]

v.t. 清洗；洗滌；洗

- Remember to **wash** your hands before eating.
  吃飯前要記得洗手。
- Father **washed** his car last Sunday.
  爸爸上禮拜天洗了他的車。

20. watch [wɑtʃ]

v.t. 看著

- I went bird **watching** with my father in the mountains.
  我跟父親去山上賞鳥。
- I don't like to **watch** TV; I usually read in my free time.
  我不喜歡看電視。我空閒時間通常都用來讀書。

W

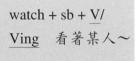

watch

watch + sb + <u>V</u>/
<u>Ving</u>　看著某人～

- Monica **watches** her son get on the school bus every day.
  莫妮卡每天看著她兒子坐上校車。

注意

　　look, see, watch 三者的比較請參考 Unit 24 的單字 look。

n. [C] 手錶

- My **watch** is three minutes slow.
  我的手錶慢了三分鐘。

休息一下喔！

W

Exercise 2

I. 字彙翻譯

1. 想要 _____   2. 醒來 _____   3. 女侍者 _____

4. 走路 _____   5. 牆壁 _____

II. 字彙填充

_____ 1. We called the w_____r and told him what we ordered.

_____ 2. It is sunny and w_____m, so we decide to have a picnic outside.

_____ 3. I think you should w_____h your car; it looks very dirty.

_____ 4. You can go first. Don't w_____t for me.

_____ 5. I don't know what time it is; I don't wear a w_____h.

III. 字彙選擇

( ) 1. The clock on the _____ tells us what time it is.

    (A) wall   (B) waiter   (C) watch   (D) walk

( ) 2. It is good for you to _____ for minutes after a meal.

    (A) want   (B) wait   (C) walk   (D) wake

( ) 3. I _____ the kids playing with toys in the living room.

    (A) watched   (B) walked   (C) wanted   (D) warmed

( ) 4. Peter said he doesn't _____ to see that movie, so we shall go ourselves.

    (A) walk   (B) want   (C) wait   (D) wash

( ) 5. My father is going to be back from America; I can't _____ to see him.

    (A) want   (B) walk   (C) wake   (D) wait

Unit 44

1. water
[ˋwɔtɚ]

n. [U] 水

· I drink some **water** after exercising.

在運動過後，我喝了一些水。

v.t. 澆水；灌溉

· I have to **water** my flowers three times a week.

我一星期必須替我的花澆三次水。

2. way
[we]

n. [C] 路；道路

· "Where are you now?" "I am on my **way**."

「你現在在哪兒?」「我在路上了。」

on the way to + N
在到某地去的路上

· *On the **way** to* school yesterday, I met an old friend.

昨天在上學途中，我遇到一個老朋友。

n. [C] 方式；方法

· I can't think of any other **way** to help you.

我想不出其他的方法可以幫你了。

by the way
順道一提

· *By the **way***, can you buy me some milk after work?

順道一提，你可以在下班後幫我買些牛奶嗎?

no way
決不

· "Can you come to work this Sunday?" "*No **way**.*"

「你這禮拜天可以來工作嗎?」「決不。」

n. [C] 方面；點

· They see the same question in different **ways**.

他們以不同的觀點來看相同的問題。

3. weak
[wik]

adj. 身體虛弱的 ↔ strong [strɔŋ] 強壯的

· Grandmother is too **weak** to stand up.

祖母太虛弱以至於無法站起來。

adj. 能力差的

· Hanson is good in math, but **weak** in English.

韓森的數學能力很好，不過英文能力就差了。

364

4. **wear**
[wɛr]

過去式	過去分詞	現在進行式
wore [wor]	worn [worn]	wearing [ˋwɛrɪŋ]

v.t. 穿～

• Alice **wore** a beautiful dress to the party tonight.
   愛麗絲今天晚上穿了一件漂亮的衣服參加宴會。

v.t. 戴～

• Ray looks very different when he **wears** a pair of glasses.
   雷戴眼鏡的時候，看起來非常不一樣。

• I **wore** a hat to keep my head warm.
   我戴了頂帽子，以保持我頭部的溫暖。

v.t. 帶著～（表情）

• Joan **wore** a smile on her face when she saw us.
   當瓊看到我們的時候，臉上帶著微笑。

5. **weather**
[ˋwɛðɚ]

weatherman
氣象播報員

n. [U] 天氣

• If the **weather** is fine tomorrow, we will go to the beach.
   如果明天天氣好的話，我們就要去海灘。

• The **weatherman** says it will rain tomorrow.
   氣象播報員說明天會下雨。

6. **week**
[wik]

weekday　工作天
（指週一到週五）

n. [C] 週；星期；禮拜

• We are going to have a math test on Wednesday this **week**.
   我們這禮拜的禮拜三將會有一個數學小考。

• The students have to turn in their homework next **week**.
   學生們下禮拜就必須交出他們的家庭作業。

n. [C] 一週；一星期；一個禮拜

• We have spent several **weeks** on this plan, so we must make it.
   我們已經花了好幾週在這個計畫上，所以一定要成功。

• People work hard on **weekdays** and rest on weekends.
   人們在工作天努力工作，然後在週末休息。

7. weekend

[ˋwikˋɛnd]

on the/this weekend
在這個週末

on weekends
每逢週末

n. [C] 週末

- How do you spend your **weekend**.
  你如何過你的週末?

- We plan to go shopping *on the* **weekend**.
  我們計畫在這個週末去購物。

- My father usually goes fishing *on* **weekends**.
  我爸爸週末通常都去釣魚。

8. welcome

[ˋwɛlkəm]

v.t. 歡迎

- We held a party to **welcome** the new classmate.
  我們辦了一個宴會歡迎新來的同學。

adj. 受歡迎的

- The handsome boy is very **welcome** at school.
  那個帥帥的男生在學校很受歡迎。

- "Thank you." "You are **welcome**."
  「謝謝。」「不客氣。」

interj. 歡迎

- **Welcome** to my new home.
  歡迎來到我的新家。

9. well

[wɛl]

as well
也;同樣地

as well as
和;也

adj. 健康的;安好的

- "How do you feel now?" "Very **well**."
  「你現在覺得如何?」「很好。」

adv. 很好地

- The American speaks Chinese very **well**.
  這美國人中文講得很好。

- I will go fishing this Sunday, and Dad will go *as **well***.
  我這禮拜天要去釣魚,而且爸爸也會去。

- Laura loves cakes *as **well** as* ice cream.
  蘿拉喜歡蛋糕,也喜歡冰淇淋。

W

10. west

[wɛst]

n. 西方 (the west)

· The farm is in the **west** of my home.
那個農場在我家的西方。

adv. 向西方地；在西方地

· The airplane is flying **west**.
這架飛機正朝著西方飛行。

休息一下喔！

Exercise 1

I. 字彙翻譯

1. 方式 _____ 2. 一週 _____ 3. 安好的 _____

4. 穿戴 _____ 5. 西方 _____

II. 字彙填充

_____ 1. Everyone drives slowly because of the bad w_____r.

_____ 2. I will spend my w_____d on the beautiful beach.

_____ 3. Grain has to take care of his grandma because she is too w_____k now.

_____ 4. The waiter gave me a cup of lemon w_____r and the menu.

_____ 5. W_____e to the playground, and hope you can enjoy yourselves here.

III. 字彙選擇

( ) 1. We have to work five days every _____.

    (A) weekend   (B) week   (C) weak   (D) weather

( ) 2. I think studying hard is the only _____ to pass the test.

    (A) week   (B) water   (C) weather   (D) way

( ) 3. I don't know if I can go fishing tomorrow. It's up to the _____.

    (A) weather   (B) week   (C) west   (D) weekend

( ) 4. The food from the _____ is very different from the Chinese food.

    (A) water   (B) west   (C) week   (D) way

( ) 5. I feel a little cold because I forgot to _____ my jacket.

    (A) weak   (B) wear   (C) week   (D) well

11. wet
[wɛt]

原級	比較級	最高級
wet [wɛt]	wetter [`wɛtɚ]	wettest [`wɛtɪst]

adj. 濕的；潮濕的 ↔ dry [draɪ] 乾的

· His coat was all **wet** after the heavy rain.

經過這場大雨，他的外套全濕了。

12. what
[hwɑt]

adj. 什麼（疑問詞）

· "**What** date is today?" "Today is May 2nd."

「今天是幾月幾號?」「今天是五月二號。」

adj. 多麼；何等（用於感嘆句）

· **What** a cute child she is! = How cute the child is!

這是個多麼可愛的小孩呀! = 這個小孩是多麼地可愛呀!

pron. 什麼（疑問代名詞）

· **What** is that thing on the table?

放在桌子上的那個東西是什麼呀?

· "**What** does your father do?" "A police officer."

「你父親是做什麼的?」「警官。」

pron. 什麼（關係代名詞）

· I don't know **what** the man is thinking about.

我不知道那男人在想什麼。

注意

　　what 當關係代名詞時，不需要有先行詞。

13. when
[hwɛn]

adv. 何時，什麼時候（疑問副詞）

· **When** will you turn in your homework?

你什麼時候才會交出作業呀?

adv. 當～時候（關係副詞，引導關係子句）

· I don't remember those years **when** I was a kid.

我已經不記得當我還是小孩子時候的那些年了。

w

conj. 當～時候
- The girl cried out **when** other kids laughed at her.
  當其他的孩子取笑她的時候，那女孩大聲哭了出來。

14. **where**
[hwɛr]

adv. 何地，在哪兒（疑問副詞）
- **Where** is my umbrella?
  我的雨傘在哪兒呀?

adv. 在哪裡；往哪兒（關係副詞）
- I don't know **where** to go.
  我不知道該往哪兒去。

conj. 在～地方
- I found my dog **where** I usually walked it.
  我在我平常溜狗的地方找到了我的狗。

pron. 哪裡，什麼地方
- **Where** do you come from?
  你來自什麼地方啊?

15. **whether**
[ˋhwɛðɚ]

conj. 是否
- I don't know **whether** it would be sunny (or not).
  我不知道明天天氣是否會晴朗。
- You must go to school **whether** you like it or not.
  不管喜不喜歡，你都必須上學。

16. **which**
[hwɪtʃ]

adj. 哪一個／些（疑問形容詞）
- **Which** bicycle do you like, the white one or the blue one?
  你喜歡哪一輛腳踏車，白色這輛還是藍色這輛?

pron. 哪一個／些（疑問代名詞）
- **Which** do you like? A cute doll or a toy train?
  你喜歡哪一個? 是可愛的洋娃娃還是玩具火車?

pron. 那一個／些（關係代名詞）
- I like the book **which** has a rabbit on the cover.
  我喜歡那一本封面上有一隻兔子的書。

17. white
[hwaɪt]

adj. 白色的
- There is nothing painted on the **white** paper.
  白紙上什麼都還沒畫上去。

n. [U] 白色
- **White** is the color of snow.
  白色是雪的顏色。

18. who
[hu]

pron. 誰，什麼人（疑問代名詞）
- **Who** are you? Do I know you?
  你是誰？我認識你嗎？

pron. ～的人（限定關係代名詞）
- My sister **who** lives in California is a teacher.
  我住在加州的那一個姊姊是一個老師。（不只一個姊姊）

pron. 他；她；他們；她們（非限定關係代名詞）
- My sister, **who** lives in California, is a teacher.
  我姊姊，她住在加州，是一個老師。（只有一個姊姊）

19. whose
[huz]

pron. 誰的；哪個人的（疑問代名詞）
- **Whose** money is there on the table?
  在桌子上的錢是誰的？

pron. 那個／些人的（關係代名詞）
- The man **whose** hair is gray is Bill's boss.
  那個頭髮是灰色的男人是比爾的老闆。

20. why
[hwaɪ]

adv. 為何，為什麼（疑問副詞）
- **Why** didn't you call me last night?
  為什麼昨天晚上你沒打電話給我？

adv. 為何，為什麼（關係副詞）
- I don't know **why** they don't like me.
  我不知道為什麼他們不喜歡我。

W

Exercise 2

I. 字彙翻譯

1. 哪一個 _____
2. 濕的 _____
3. 誰 _____
4. 為什麼 _____
5. 什麼 _____

II. 字彙填充

_____ 1. It won't matter w_____r you come or not tomorrow.

_____ 2. W_____e is my cat? I cannot find it.

_____ 3. Does anybody know w_____e pencil this is?

_____ 4. I was studying English w_____n Mary called me last night.

_____ 5. My face turned w_____e as I heard the bad news.

III. 字彙選擇

( ) 1. The dog fell into the river and got all _____.
   (A) why   (B) wet   (C) white   (D) what

( ) 2. _____ did you cheat on the exam? I don't understand.
   (A) When   (B) What   (C) Who   (D) Why

( ) 3. The woman _____ talks with the teacher is my mother.
   (A) who   (B) whose   (C) what   (D) why

( ) 4. I don't know _____ candy tastes better. They look all the same.
   (A) which   (B) where   (C) whose   (D) when

( ) 5. Mary never told me _____ she does, but I guess she is a waitress.
   (A) where   (B) when   (C) what   (D) who

Unit 45

1. wife
[waɪf]

n. [C] 妻子，老婆（複數：wives [waɪvz]）
- I work outside, and my **wife** takes care of our kids at home.
  我在外面工作，而我老婆在家裡照顧小孩。

2. will
[wɪl]

aux. 將；將會（表示單純的未來）（過去式：would [wʊd]）
- There **will** be a great program on TV tonight.
  今天晚上電視會播出一個很棒的節目。

aux. 願意；將要；將會（表示意志，意願）
- I **will** go shopping with my mother tomorrow.
  明天我將要跟我媽媽去逛街購物。
- What **would** you do if you were me?
  如果你是我的話，你會怎麼做？

n. [C][U] 意志；自制力

free will
自由意志

- Everyone has *free* **will** to decide what he/she wants.
  每個人都有自由意志，可決定他／她要什麼。

3. win
[wɪn]

過去式	過去分詞	現在進行式
won [wʌn]	won [wʌn]	winning [ˋwɪnɪŋ]

v.t. 在～中獲勝；贏得～ ↔ lose [luz] 輸掉
- I was surprised that my favorite team **won** the game last night.
  我最喜愛的隊昨天贏得了比賽，我很驚喜。

v.i. 勝利；贏 ↔ lose [luz] 輸
- You must practice hard if you want to **win**.
  如果你想要贏，就必須要努力練習。

4. wind
[wɪnd]

n. [C][U] 風
- I feel cool when the **wind** blows.
  當風吹的時候，我覺得很涼快。
- Put on your coat; there is too much **wind** outside.
  穿上你的外套，外面風很大。

W

5. window
[ˈwɪndo]

n. [C] 窗戶
- Would you mind opening the **window** for me?
  你介意幫我開窗嗎？
- Eyes are the **windows** of the souls.
  眼睛是靈魂之窗。

n. [C] （電腦）視窗
- Don't open several **windows** once when using a computer.
  在使用電腦的時候，不要一次開好幾個視窗。

6. windy
[ˈwɪndɪ]

adj. 刮風的；風大的
- The typhoon is coming, so it would be **windy** tomorrow.
  颱風要來了，所以明天風會很大。

7. winter
[ˈwɪntɚ]

winter vacation
寒假

n. [C][U] 冬天
- Animals save food to get through the cold **winter**.
  動物們儲存食物，以渡過寒冬。
- Schools are closed during the *winter* vacation.
  在寒假期間，學校是關閉（不開放）的。

8. wise
[waɪz]

adj. 聰明的；有智慧的
- It is **wise** of you to decide to give up smoking.
  你決定戒煙這件事很有智慧。
- A **wise** man knows what he should do at this moment.
  有智慧的人懂得此時該做什麼事。

9. wish
[wɪʃ]

v.t. v.i. 希望；想要
- Lily **wishes** to travel around the world.
  莉莉想要環遊世界。
- Jenny **wishes** she were a movie star.
  珍妮希望她自己是個電影明星。

make a wish
許下願望

注意

　　wish 後面如果加的是與現實相反的幻想或希望，後面的子句就必須使用假設語氣（如本例句）。wish 跟 hope 的比較請參見 Unite 19 的 hope。

n. [C] 願望

· I *made* three *wishes* on my birthday.
　我在我生日那天許下了三個願望。

10. **woman**
[`wumən]

n. [C] 女人（複數：women [`wɪmən]）

· Every mother is a great **woman**.
　每一個媽媽都是偉大的女人。

· Men and **women** are different in many ways.
　男人和女人在很多方面都不一樣。

休息一下喔！

Exercise 1

I. 字彙翻譯

1. 風 _____ 2. 妻子 _____ 3. 聰明的 _____

4. 獲勝 _____ 5. 刮風的 _____

II. 字彙填充

_____ 1. I w_____h I could go to the movies with you, but I am too busy.

_____ 2. Mother asks me to close the w_____ws before I go to bed, because it is a little cold tonight.

_____ 3. I don't think Lily w_____l like your idea to make fun of her.

_____ 4. During this w_____r vacation, I will go to America for two weeks.

_____ 5. Old people think that men should work outside and w_____e should take care of the family.

III. 字彙選擇

( ) 1. It is so easy for me to _____ the game.

(A) will　　　　(B) win　　　　(C) wish　　　　(D) wise

( ) 2. I feel a little cold because it is _____ today.

(A) wind　　　　(B) wish　　　　(C) wise　　　　(D) windy

( ) 3. My first _____ is that everyone in this world is happy.

(A) wish　　　　(B) wind　　　　(C) will　　　　(D) wife

( ) 4. The old _____ is very happy because all her kids are good to her.

(A) winter　　　　(B) woman　　　　(C) window　　　　(D) wish

( ) 5. In some countries, men could get married to more than one _____.

(A) window　　　　(B) wind　　　　(C) wife　　　　(D) winter

11. wonderful
[ˋwʌndɚfəl]

adj. 極好的；奇妙的；美好的

- I had a very **wonderful** vacation in America.
  我在美國渡過一個非常美好的假期。
- Life is **wonderful**, isn't it?
  人生是美好的，不是嗎?

12. word
[wɝd]

n. [C] 字

- I wrote a book of fifty thousand **words**.
  我寫了一本五萬字的書。

n. [C] 話；說詞

- I don't believe your **words**.
  我不相信你的話。

have one's word
獲得某人的承諾

- Now you *have my* **word**. I will bring a present back to you.
  現在你有我的承諾。我將帶禮物回來給你。

keep/break one's word
遵守／未遵守某人的承諾

- To be an example to your kids, you must *keep your* **word**.
  為了要成為你孩子的榜樣，你必須遵守你的承諾。
- I can't believe him because he always *break his* own **word**.
  我無法相信他，因為他總是不遵守他自己的承諾。

in a word
簡言之

- *In a* **word**, I can't help you now.
  簡言之，現在我沒辦法幫你。

13. work
[wɝk]

v.i. 工作

- James **works** as a doctor in a small town.
  詹姆士現在在一個小鎮裡當醫生。
- The father **works** hard to keep his family.
  那位父親努力工作以扶養家庭。

work on + N
致力於～

- The doctor has *worked* on this plan for many years.
  那位博士已經致力於這項計畫好多年了。

v.i. 起作用；行的通

- Your way doesn't **work**. We must think of another idea.
  你的方法行不通，我們得另外想一個主意。

n. [C][U] 工作；勞動

- It will take lots of **work** and time to build this bridge.
  要蓋這座橋將會耗費許多的勞力和時間。

at work
工作中
out of work
失業

- My father is still *at work* at ten p.m.
  我爸爸晚上十點仍然在工作。

- Linda is *out of work* and looking for a new job.
  琳達失業了，她正在找新的工作。

注意

work 與 job 的比較請參見 Unit 21 的單字 job。

n. [C][U] 著作；作品（通常用複數）

- I am studying on Hemingway's **works**.
  我正在研究海明威的作品。

- Van Gogh made this famous art **work** in 1889.
  梵谷在一八八九年畫了這個著名的藝術作品。

14. **workbook**
[`wɝk͵bʊk]

n. [C] 習作簿；練習簿

- Our teacher asked us to write the **workbook** at home.
  我們的老師要我們在家裡寫習作簿。

15. **worker**
[`wɝkɚ]

n. [C] 工人；勞動者

- There are two hundred **workers** in this factory.
  在這家工廠裡有兩百個工人。

16. **world**
[wɝld]

n. 世界 (the world)

- Those stars live in a different **world** from us.
  那些明星與我們生活在不同的世界裡。

in the world
在這世界上
in the world
到底（用於疑問句）
the end of the world
世界末日

- She is the most beautiful woman *in the world*.
  她是這世界上最美麗的女人。

- What *in the world* do you want me to do?
  你到底要我做什麼？

- Take it easy. This is not *the end of the world*.
  放輕鬆點，這又不是世界末日。

17. worry

[ˋwɝɪ]

過去式	過去分詞	現在進行式
worried [ˋwɝɪd]	worried [ˋwɝɪd]	worrying [ˋwɝɪɪŋ]

v.i. 擔心

- Don't **worry**. Everything will be fine.
  別擔心了，每件事都會順利的。
- You don't have to *worry* about me. I will be fine.
  你不用擔心我，我會很好的。
- Tina *is **worried** about* her grades on the math test.
  蒂娜擔心她那次數學測驗的成績。

worry about
= be worried about
擔心～

18. write

[raɪt]

過去式	過去分詞	現在進行式
wrote [rot]	written [ˋrɪtn̩]	writing [ˋraɪtɪŋ]

v.t. 寫；寫作

- The teacher asks me to **write** the word for ten times.
  老師要我把這個字寫十遍。
- The doctor has **written** five books so far.
  那位博士到目前為止已經寫了五本書。

v.i. 寫；寫作

- The man **writes** to make a living.
  那男人以寫作維生。

v.i. 寫信

- I **wrote** to my mother every week when I was in America.
  我在美國的時候，每個禮拜都寫信給我媽媽。

19. writer

[ˋraɪtɚ]

n. [C] 作家

- She is a famous **writer**. She made much money by her books.
  她是個著名的作家，她靠她的書賺了很多錢。

20. wrong

[rɔŋ]

adj. 錯誤的 ↔ right [raɪt] 正確的

- It is **wrong** to cheat on the test.
  在考試的時候作弊是錯誤的。

W

wrong

there's something
wrong with + N
某物故障；出問題

- Sorry, you have the **wrong** number.
  抱歉，你打錯電話了。
- We think *there's something **wrong** with* this computer.
  我們認為這台電腦故障了。

n. [U] 錯誤
- It is not always clear between right and **wrong**.
  在正確與錯誤之間的界線並不總是那麼明顯。

n. [C] 壞事，不法行為，不道德行為
- He was finally caught after doing so many **wrongs**.
  在做過那麼多壞事之後，他總算被逮到了。

W

休息一下喔！

Exercise 2

I. 字彙翻譯

1. 字 _____
2. 工作 _____
3. 練習簿 _____
4. 工人 _____
5. 寫作 _____

II. 字彙填充

_____ 1. It is w_____l to have you as my friend.

_____ 2. Don't w_____y about your kids. I will take care of them.

_____ 3. Nothing in the w_____d can change your parents' love for you.

_____ 4. The first book of that w_____r is about a smart kid and a pet dog.

_____ 5. Your answer is w_____g, but I can give you a second chance.

III. 字彙選擇

( ) 1. It is your _____ to clean the bathroom today, and I will wash the clothes.

    (A) worry   (B) world   (C) word   (D) work

( ) 2. Janet didn't go home last night, and her parents were very _____ about her.

    (A) worried   (B) worker   (C) wrong   (D) written

( ) 3. I have to write my _____ this afternoon, so I can't play with you.

    (A) word   (B) workbook   (C) wonderful   (D) world

( ) 4. Mike is a _____ and his job is to put toys into little boxes.

    (A) worry   (B) wrong   (C) writer   (D) worker

( ) 5. This is an important _____, and you should keep it in your mind.

    (A) world   (B) work   (C) word   (D) wrong

w

21. **year**

[jɪr]

數字 + years old =
數字 + years of age
～歲大
year after year
每年；年復一年

n. [C] 年；歲數

· The writer spent five **years** and six months writing the book.
那位作家花了五年六個月的時間寫這本書。

· I am twenty nine **years** old.

= I am twenty nine **years** *of age*.
我二十九歲。

· These birds fly back to the south **year** *after* **year**.
這些鳥每年都會飛回南方。

22. **yellow**

[`jɛlo]

adj. 黃色的

· You should stop on seeing the traffic light turning **yellow**.
看到紅綠燈變黃色，你就應該停下來了。

n. [U] 黃色

· **Yellow** is the color of bananas and taxies.
黃色是香蕉和計程車的顏色。

23. **yesterday**

[`jɛstɚ͵de]

adv. 昨天

· I didn't go to school **yesterday** because I caught a cold.
我昨天沒去上學，因為我感冒了。

n. [U] 昨天

· Sometimes I wish I could go back to **yesterday**.
有時候我希望我能夠回到昨天。

24. **yet**

[jɛt]

adv. 尚未（用於否定句）

· It's 11:00 p.m., but Helen hasn't come home **yet**.
現在是晚上十一點了，但是海倫還沒回家。

adv. 現在；已經（用於疑問句）

· Have you finished your homework **yet**?
你已經做完你的家庭作業了嗎？

25. **young**

[jʌŋ]

adj. 年輕的 ↔ old [old] 老的

· You are too **young** to work; you should study in school now.
你出來工作還太年輕，你現在應該在學校唸書。

Y

26. **ZOO**
[zu]

n. [C] 動物園

· There are many kinds of animals in the **zoo**.
在動物園裡有許多種的動物。

休息一下喔！

Z

Exercise 3

I. 字彙翻譯

1. 年 _____   2. 尚未 _____   3. 動物園 _____

II. 字彙填充

_____ 1. The cooked rice will turn y _____w and hard if you don't eat it soon.

_____ 2. Why didn't you come to the party y _____y? We had lots of fun.

_____ 3. Many y _____g men think it is cool to smoke and drink, but it is wrong.

III. 字彙選擇

(　　) 1. Are you 18 _____? If you are not, you can't see this movie.

　　(A) year　　　　(B) yet　　　　(C) young　　　　(D) yesterday

(　　) 2. I don't think there are polar bears（北極熊）in this _____.

　　(A) zoo　　　　(B) video　　　　(C) way　　　　(D) yet

(　　) 3. "How old are you?" "I am twenty eight _____ old."

　　(A) young　　　　(B) years　　　　(C) yet　　　　(D) yellows

Z

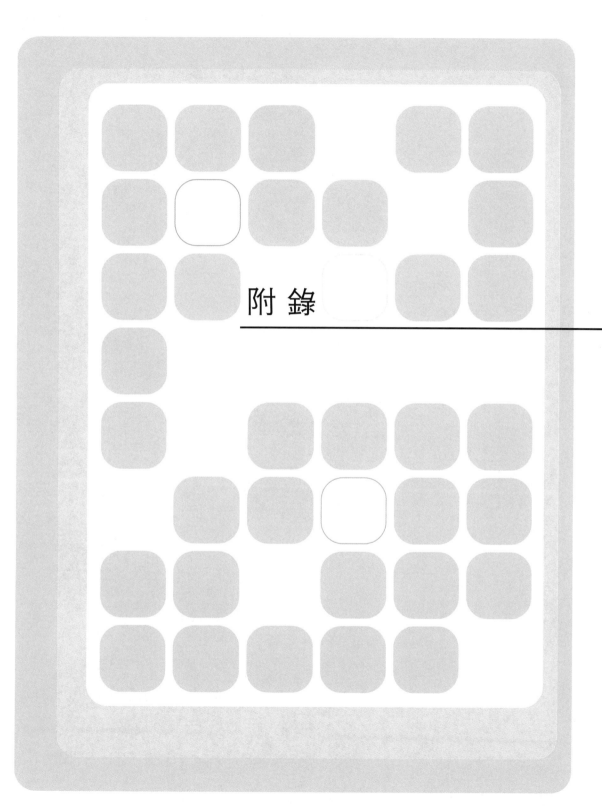

附 錄

一、人稱代名詞

◎主格

	第一人稱	第二人稱	第三人稱
單數	I [aɪ] 我	you [ju] 你	he [hi] 他 she [ʃi] 她 it [ɪt] 它 / 牠
複數	we [wi] 我們	you [ju] 你們	they [ðe] 他們

◎受格

	第一人稱	第二人稱	第三人稱
單數	me [mɪ] 我	you [ju] 你	him [hɪm] 他 her [hɚ] 她 it [ɪt] 它 / 牠
複數	us [ʌs] 我們	you [ju] 你們	them [ðɛm] 他們

· Ken gave **me** a birthday present.
　肯送我一個生日禮物。

◎反身代名詞

	第一人稱	第二人稱	第三人稱
單數	myself [maɪ`sɛlf] 我自己	yourself [juɚ`sɛlf] 你自己	himself [hɪm`sɛlf] 他自己 herself [hɚ`sɛlf] 她自己 itself [ɪt`sɛlf] 它 / 牠自己
複數	ourselves [ˌaur`sɛlvz] 我們自己	yourselves [jur`sɛlvz] 你們自己	themselves [ðəm`sɛlvz] 他們自己

· I walked home (by) **myself**.
　我獨自一人走路回家。

二、人稱所有格

	第一人稱	第二人稱	第三人稱
單數	my [maɪ] 我的	your [jʊr] 你的	his [hɪz] 他的 her [hɝ] 她的 its [ɪts] 它 / 牠的
複數	our [aʊr] 我們的	your [jʊr] 你們的	their [ðɛr] 他們的

◎所有格代名詞

	第一人稱	第二人稱	第三人稱
單數	mine [maɪn] 我的東西	yours [jʊrs] 你的東西	his [hɪz] 他的東西 hers [hɝz] 她的東西 its [ɪts] 它 / 牠的東西
複數	ours [aʊrs] 我們的東西	yours [jʊrs] 你們的東西	theirs [ðɛrz] 他們的東西

· This is **my** book, not **yours**.

　這是我的書，不是你的。

三、BE 動詞變化
◎現在式:

	原形	第一人稱	第二人稱	第三人稱
單數	be [bi]	am [æm]	are [ɑr]	is [ɪz]
複數		are [ɑr]	are [ɑr]	are [ɑr]

◎過去式:

	第一人稱	第二人稱	第三人稱
單數	was [wɑz]	were [wɝ]	was [wɑz]
複數	were [wɝ]	were [wɝ]	were [wɝ]

◎完成式：

	第一人稱	第二人稱	第三人稱
單數		been [bɪn]	
複數			

四、介系詞

along [ə`lɔŋ]	*prep.* 沿著，順著
	• I walked **along** the street. 我沿著街道走。
around [ə`raʊd]	*prep.* 周圍
	• I looked **around** the room. 我環視房間周圍。
	prep. 附近
	• The store is not **around** here. 那家商店不在這附近。
at [æt]	*prep.* 在～地點
	• I took a walk **at** the park. 我在公園散步。
	prep. 在～時刻
	• I go to bed **at** ten o'clock. 我在十點就寢。
behind [bɪ`haɪnd]	*prep.* 在～後面
	• I stand **behind** my mother. 我站在我媽媽的後面。
beside [bɪ`saɪd]	*prep.* 在～旁邊
	• There is a river **beside** the school. 在學校旁邊有一條河。
between [bɪ`twin]	*prep.* 在～之間（通常指兩者之間）
	• The house is **between** the hill and the river. 那房子位在丘陵與河流之間。
by [baɪ]	*prep.* 經由～（用於被動語態）
	• The book is written **by** a famous writer. 這本書是由一個著名作家所寫的。
during	*prep.* 在～期間

基本 1000 單字書

[`djʊrɪŋ]	• I went to America **during** the winter vacation. 我在寒假期間去了一趟美國。
except [ɪk`sɛpt]	*prep.* 除了～之外
	• All of us will go to the party **except** Tom. 除了湯姆之外，我們所有的人都會去參加派對。
for [fɔr]	*prep.* 為了～
	• I made a cake **for** my teacher. 我為我的老師做了一個蛋糕。
from [frɑm]	*prep.* 從～（時間）
	• I studied **from** eight o'clock to ten o'clock. 我從八點唸書念到十點。
	prep. 從～（地點）
	• I walked **from** home to the park. 我從家裡走路到公園。
	prep. 從～（人）
	• I got a package **from** my mother. 我從我媽媽那兒拿到一個包裹。
into [`ɪntu]	*prep.* 到～裡面
	• I put the book **into** the bag. 我把書放到袋子裡。
of [ɑv]	*prep.* ～的
	• The door **of** the room is closed. 房間的門是關著的。
to [tu]	*prep.* 到～
	• I walked **to** the school yesterday. 昨天我走路到學校。
with [wɪð]	*prep.* 用～（工具）
	• I write down my name **with** a pencil. 我用鉛筆寫下我的名字。
	prep. 和～（人）
	• I went shopping **with** my sister. 我和我姊姊去逛街。
without [wɪ`ðaʊt]	*prep.* 不用～；沒有～
	• I can do this job **without** your help. 不用／沒有你的幫忙我也可以做這個工作。

五、基數

一	二	三	四	五
one [wʌn]	two [tu]	three [θri]	four [fɔr]	five [faɪv]
六	七	八	九	十
six [sɪks]	seven [`sɛvn̩]	eight [et]	nine [naɪn]	ten [tɛn]
十一	十二	十三	十四	十五
eleven [ɪ`lɛvn̩]	twelve [twɛlv]	thirteen [`θɝ`tin]	fourteen [`for`tin]	fifteen [`fɪf`tin]
十六	十七	十八	十九	二十
sixteen [`sɪks`tin]	seventeen [ˌsɛvn̩`tin]	eighteen [`e`tin]	nineteen [`naɪn`tin]	twenty [`twɛntɪ]
三十	四十	五十	六十	七十
thirty [`θɝtɪ]	forty [`fɔrtɪ]	fifty [`fɪftɪ]	sixty [`sɪkstɪ]	seventy [`sɛvn̩tɪ]
八十	九十	一百	一千	一萬
eighty [`etɪ]	ninety [`naɪntɪ]	hundred [`hʌndrəd]	thousand [`θauzn̩d]	ten thousand
十萬	一百萬	一千萬		
one hundred thousand	million	ten million		

- There are **fifty four** students in my class.

我班上有五十四個學生。

注意

　　基數的變化有其規則可循，瞭解規則可以幫助記憶，也可以省去許多功夫。

數字	規則	特例
13–19	數字 3–9 的字尾加 teen，發音為 [tin]	(1) thirteen、fifteen 為不規則變化。 (2) eighteen 因字尾已有 t，所以只加 een。
20–90 （10 的倍數）	數字 3–9 的字尾加 ty，發音為 [tɪ]	(1) twenty、forty 為不規則變化。 (2) thirty、fifty、eighty 的變化規則同 13–19。

六、序數

第一	第二	第三	第四	第五
first [fɝst]	second [ˋsɛkənd]	third [θɝd]	fourth [forθ]	fifth [fɪfθ]
第六	第七	第八	第九	第十
sixth [sɪksθ]	seventh [ˋsɛvn̩θ]	eighth [etθ]	ninth [naɪnθ]	tenth [tɛnθ]
第十一	第十二	第十三	第十四	第十五
eleventh [ɪˋlɛvn̩θ]	twelfth [twɛlfθ]	thirteenth [ˋθɝˋtinθ]	fourteenth [ˋforˋtinθ]	fifteenth [ˋfɪfˋtinθ]
第十六	第十七	第十八	第十九	第二十
sixteenth [ˋsɪksˋtinθ]	seventeenth [͵sɛvn̩ˋtinθ]	eighteenth [ˋeˋtinθ]	nineteenth [ˋnaɪnˋtinθ]	twentieth [ˋtwɛntɪɪθ]
第三十	第四十	第五十	第六十	第七十
thirtieth [ˋθɝtɪɪθ]	fortieth [ˋfɔrtɪɪθ]	fiftieth [ˋfɪftɪɪθ]	sixtieth [ˋsɪkstɪɪθ]	seventieth [ˋsɛvn̩tɪɪθ]
第八十	第九十	第一百	第一千	
eightieth [ˋetɪɪθ]	ninetieth [ˋnaɪntɪɪθ]	hundredth [ˋhʌndrədθ]	thousandth [ˋθaʊzn̩dθ]	

注意

　　從基數到序數的變化除了少數特例之外，基本上是呈規則變化的，變化的公式以以下之表格呈現。

數字	規則	特例
1–19	基數字尾加 th，發音為 [θ]	(1) first, second, third, fifth, twelfth 為不規則變化。 (2) eighth 因字尾已有 t，所以只加 h。
20–90 (10 的倍數)	基數去掉字尾 y，加 ieth，發音為 [ɪθ]	
百、千	基數字尾加 th，發音為 [θ]	

◎當序數超過十九，且不為十的倍數時，就會變為兩個數字的組合，此時切記「第一個數字仍為基數」，只有「第二個數字才要變成序數」。Ex：第二十一是 twenty first，第五十七是 fifty seventh。
◎序數之前一般都會加定冠詞 the。Ex：第一本書唸成 the first book。

· Paul slept before he counted the **eighty fifth** sheep.

保羅在數到第八十五隻羊之前就睡著了。

七、星期（介系詞用 on）

星期一	星期二	星期三	星期四	星期五
Monday [`mʌnde]	Tuesday [`tjuzde]	Wednesday [`wɛnzde]	Thursday [`θɝzde]	Friday [`fraɪˌde]
星期六	星期日			
Saturday [`sætɚde]	Sunday [`sʌnde]			

· We don't have to go to school on **Sunday**.

我們星期日不用上學。

八、月份（介系詞用 in）

一月	二月	三月	四月	五月
January [`dʒænjuˌɛrɪ]	February [`fɛbruˌɛrɪ]	March [mɑrtʃ]	April [`eprəl]	May [me]
六月	七月	八月	九月	十月
June [dʒun]	July [dʒu`laɪ]	August [`ɔgəst]	September [sɛp`tɛmbɚ]	October [ak`tobɚ]
十一月	十二月			
November [no`vɛmbɚ]	December [dɪ`sɛmbɚ]			

· We have lots of rain in **April** and **May**.

四月和五月雨量很多。

九、日期、年份

(1)日期：

　1.日期的念法是「月份＋序數」。

　2.「在」幾月幾日的介系詞用 on。

　　Ex：一月十日唸成 January tenth；三月二十八日唸成 March twenty-eighth。

Ex：較為特殊的日期的唸法會在日期〈序數〉之前加定冠詞 the，如美國的國慶日七月四日就較常被唸成 July the fourth 而非 July fourth。

· **January first** is a national holiday.

一月一日是個國定假日。

(2)西元年份：

1. 分成兩個十位數的唸法。

Ex：1983 年唸成 nineteen eighty three（十九、八十三）

2. 同一般數字的唸法。

Ex：2005 年唸成 two thousand and five（兩千零五）

3.「在」西元第幾年的介系詞用 in。

· The kid was born in **nineteen ninety four**.

那孩子出生在一九九四年。

· I went to America in **two thousand and four**.

我在二〇〇四年去了美國。

附錄 ② 情緒動詞

一、情緒動詞的共通點在於:

(1)所有的情緒動詞均為及物動詞。

(2)所有的情緒動詞在加 ed 成為形容詞後,均以「人」為主詞,翻譯為「感到～的」。 如果後面有加受詞的話,意思就是「對〈某事／物〉感到～的」,此時不同的情緒 動詞就要搭配不同的介系詞,如 interested 搭配 in,excited 搭配 about。

(3)所有的情緒動詞在加 ing 成為形容詞後,大部份以「物」為主詞,翻譯為「令人感 到～的」。

二、情緒動詞用法與搭配:

bore [bor]	*v.t.* 使～感無聊
	· The meeting **bores** me. 這會議讓我感到無聊。
bored [bord]	*adj.* 感到無聊的(介系詞 with)
	· John is **bored** with his job. 約翰對他的工作感到無聊。
boring [`borɪŋ]	*adj.* 令人感到無聊的;無趣的
	· The **boring** movie made me sleep. 那無趣的電影讓我睡著了。

interest [`ɪntərɪst]	*v.t.* 使～感興趣
	· The toy train **interests** the kid. 這個玩具火車引起了小孩子的興趣。
interested [`ɪntərɪstɪd]	*adj.* 感興趣的(介系詞 in)
	· I am **interested** in collecting kites. 我對收集風箏感到有興趣。
interesting [`ɪntərɪstɪŋ]	*adj.* 令人感興趣的;有趣的
	· This is an **interesting** book to me. 對我而言,這是一本有趣的書。

excite [ɪk`saɪt]	*v.t.* 使～感到興奮，刺激
	· The trip to America **excites** me very much. 美國之旅讓我感到十分的興奮。
excited [ɪk`saɪtɪd]	*adj.* 感到興奮的（介系詞 about）
	· The girl is so **excited** about the winning of her team. 那女孩因為她的隊伍贏得比賽而感到非常興奮。
exciting [ɪk`saɪtɪŋ]	*adj.* 令人興奮的；刺激的
	· I love to play **exciting** games. 我喜歡玩刺激的遊戲。

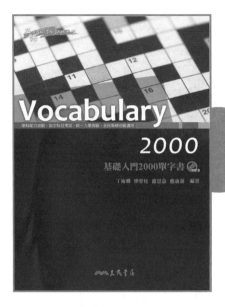

Vocabulary 2000
基礎入門2000單字書

作者：丁雍嫻 邢雯桂 盧思嘉 應惠蕙

- ◆ 依據大考中心所公佈之詞彙分級表，將其第一、二級有系統地收錄其中。
- ◆ 精心編寫大量例句，讓您精確掌握字的用法。常用片語及同、反義字的補充，豐富實用，讓您輕鬆擴大學習範圍。
- ◆ 經專業外籍人士審稿，實用性及準確性兼具，讓您打穩基礎、贏在起跑點。
- ◆ 每章節均附即時評量，讓您隨時檢驗學習成果。
- ◆ 附單字朗讀MP3光碟，讓您加強各單字的唸法，對記憶單字更有莫大的幫助。
- ◆ 不論是高中生，高職生，或是要準備全民英檢的社會人士，熟讀本書，英文內力必定大增，征服各項考試，更加輕鬆寫意。

Vocabulary 2000 隨身讀

- ◆ 最豐富的內容收錄在最迷你的篇幅中，隨身攜帶使用最方便。
- ◆ 補充重要片語及例句，讓您徹底掌握單字用法。
- ◆ 同反義字補充豐富，讓您輕鬆延伸學習範圍。
- ◆ 提供索引功能，讀到衍生字時可快速翻回其字根，反覆練習增加記憶。

初級全民英檢必備

Basic

Vocabulary 1000

嚴雅貞・張淑如　編著

基本1000單字書
練習題解答

三民書局

Unit 1

Exercise 1

I. 1. above 2. a.m. 3. about 4. a few 5. a little

II. 1. afternoon 2. able 3. After 4. lot 5. afraid

III. 1. (B) 2. (C) 3. (D) 4. (A) 5. (A)

Exercise 2

I. 1. air 2. all 3. airplane 4. already 5. age

II. 1. again 2. airport 3. agree 4. Almost 5. ago

III. 1. (A) 2. (B) 3. (D) 4. (D) 5. (C)

Unit 2

Exercise 1

I. 1. American 2. animal 3. always 4. anyone 5. another

II. 1. angry 2. answer 3. America 4. also 5. and

III. 1. (C) 2. (A) 3. (B) 4. (D) 5. (B)

Exercise 2

I. 1. ask 2. appear 3. art 4. arm 5. as

II. 1. apple 2. aunt 3. anything 4. arrive 5. apartment

III. 1. (C) 2. (A) 3. (A) 4. (B) 5. (D)

Unit 3

Exercise 1

I. 1. bakery 2. ball 3. away 4. bad 5. back

II. 1. band 2. banana 3. baby 4. bag 5. autumn

III. 1. (B) 2. (C) 3. (D) 4. (A) 5. (B)

Exercise 2

I. 1. bathroom 2. basketball 3. bath 4. basket 5. bear

II. 1. beach 2. beautiful 3. bank 4. baseball 5. because

III. 1. (B) 2. (D) 3. (D) 4. (B) 5. (D)

Unit 4

Exercise 1

I. 1. believe 2. belong 3. before 4. become 5. bell

II. 1. bed 2. bees 3. beginning 4. beef 5. bedroom

III. 1. (D) 2. (C) 3. (A) 4. (B) 5. (A)

Exercise 2

I. 1. bird 2. bicycle/bike 3. blind 4. belt 5. bite, bit, bitten

II. 1. black 2. bite 3. big 4. blocked 5. blackboard

III. 1. (B) 2. (A) 3. (D) 4. (D) 5. (A)

Unit 5

Exercise 1

I. 1. bookstore 2. book 3. blue 4. blow 5. boring

II. 1. body 2. bored 3. boat 4. borrow 5. born

III. 1. (D) 2. (B) 3. (A) 4. (C) 5. (A)

Exercise 2

I. 1. bread 2. bowl 3. both 4. breakfast 5. break, broke, broken

II. 1. boys 2. box 3. break 4. bottle 5. bottom

III. 1. (C) 2. (D) 3. (A) 4. (B) 5. (A)

Unit 6

Exercise 1

I. 1. brush 2. bus 3. business 4. brown 5. bring, brought, brought

II. 1. building 2. bridge 3. burned 4. bright 5. brothers

III. 1. (A) 2. (B) 3. (B) 4. (B) 5. (C)

Exercise 2

I. 1. camera 2. camp 3. but 4. cake 5. busy

II. 1. bought 2. butter 3. can 4. called 5. businessman

III. 1. (A) 2. (B) 3. (A) 4. (C) 5. (D)

Unit 7

Exercise 1

I. 1. care 2. careful 3. case 4. candy 5. cat

II. 1. cap 2. car 3. carries 4. card 5. catch

III. 1. (B) 2. (B) 3. (D) 4. (A) 5. (C)

Exercise 2

I. 1. chalk 2. celebrate 3. chance 4. change 5. cheap

II. 1. chair 2. cents 3. center 4. cheated 5. cell phone

III. 1. (D) 2. (A) 3. (B) 4. (C) 5. (B)

Unit 8

Exercise 1

I. 1. Chinese 2. check 3. chicken 4. cheese 5. china

II. 1. cheered 2. Christmas 3. chocolate 4. children 5. chopsticks

III. 1. (B) 2. (C) 3. (A) 4. (C) 5. (A)

Exercise 2

I. 1. classroom 2. church 3. city 4. climb 5. clear

II. 1. classmate 2. circle 3. class 4. clean 5. clock

III. 1. (A) 2. (A) 3. (B) 4. (A) 5. (D)

Unit 9

Exercise 1

I. 1. clothes 2. coffee 3. close 4. color 5. cloudy

II. 1. club 2. Coke 3. coat 4. cold 5. collected

III. 1. (C) 2. (D) 3. (B) 4. (A) 5. (A)

Exercise 2

I. 1. cookie 2. comfortable 3. computer 4. come 5. common

II. 1. comic 2. cook 3. copies 4. cool 5. convenient

III. 1. (A) 2. (C) 3. (B) 4. (D) 5. (C)

Unit 10

Exercise 1

I. 1. cousin 2. couch 3. cow 4. correct 5. cost, cost, cost

II. 1. country 2. crazy 3. cross 4. counted 5. covered

III. 1. (D) 2. (B) 3. (C) 4. (B) 5. (A)

Exercise 2

I. 1. daughter 2. cup 3. cry 4. dance 5. cut

II. 1. dark 2. date 3. dangerous 4. day 5. cute

III. 1. (D) 2. (B) 3. (A) 4. (C) 5. (C)

Unit 11

Exercise 1

I. 1. decide 2. different 3. delicious 4. dead 5. department store

II. 1. dear 2. difficult 3. dictionary 4. died 5. desk

III. 1. (D) 2. (C) 3. (A) 4. (A) 5. (B)

Exercise 2

I. 1. dig 2. doll 3. dinner 4. do 5. dining room

II. 1. dishes 2. dogs 3. doctor 4. dirty 5. dollars

III. 1. (B) 2. (A) 3. (C) 4. (D) 5. (A)

Unit 12

Exercise 1

I. 1. down 2. draw 3. dress 4. driver 5. drop

II. 1. drive 2. drink 3. door 4. dozens 5. dream

III. 1. (B) 2. (A) 3. (A) 4. (D) 5. (A)

Exercise 2

I. 1. east 2. egg 3. ear 4. dry 5. eat, ate, eaten

II. 1. Each 2. easy 3. early 4. earth 5. either

III. 1. (C) 2. (A) 3. (D) 4. (A) 5. (B)

Unit 13

Exercise 1

I. 1. elephant 2. enter 3. end 4. eraser 5. e-mail

II. 1. elementary 2. else 3. enough 4. enjoy 5. English

III. 1. (D) 2. (A) 3. (B) 4. (B) 5. (C)

Exercise 2

I. 1. eve 2. every 3. everyone 4. even 5. ever

II. 1. excellent 2. excited 3. example 4. Everything 5. evening

III. 1. (A) 2. (B) 3. (B) 4. (D) 5. (D)

Unit 14

Exercise 1

I. 1. eye(s) 2. face 3. fact 4. experience 5. fall, fell, fallen

II. 1. expensive 2. exercise 3. Excuse 4. exciting 5. factory

III. 1. (B) 2. (A) 3. (A) 4. (D) 5. (C)

Exercise 2

I. 1. fan 2. farm 3. famous 4. father 5. feel, felt, felt

II. 1. family 2. farmer 3. favorite 4. fat 5. fast

III. 1. (B) 2. (C) 3. (D) 4. (C) 5. (A)

Unit 15

Exercise 1

I. 1. few 2. fill 3. first 4. fine 5. fire

II. 1. finished 2. finally 3. find 4. Festival 5. fingers

III. 1. (C) 2. (A) 3. (D) 4. (A) 5. (B)

Exercise 2

I. 1. fisherman 2. food 3. fish 4. fix 5. fly, flew, flown

II. 1. flowers 2. follow 3. floor 4. foot 5. foreign

III. 1. (D) 2. (B) 3. (A) 4. (B) 5. (B)

Unit 16

Exercise 1

I. 1. full 2. fruit 3. foreigner 4. fork 5. friendly

II. 1. free 2. forgot 3. front 4. friends 5. fresh

III. 1. (D) 2. (B) 3. (A) 4. (B) 5. (B)

Exercise 2

I. 1. fun 2. get 3. funny 4. gas 5. girl

II. 1. future 2. gifts 3. garbage 4. games 5. garden

III. 1. (D) 2. (A) 3. (C) 4. (A) 5. (B)

Unit 17

Exercise 1

I. 1. go 2. glass 3. goat 4. glove 5. grandfather

II. 1. grandmother 2. good 3. glad 4. gave 5. grade

III. 1. (B) 2. (C) 3. (A) 4. (D) 5. (A)

Exercise 2

I. 1. grass 2. hair 3. gray 4. grow 5. group

II. 1. green 2. ground 3. great 4. habit 5. guess

III. 1. (D) 2. (A) 3. (A) 4. (B) 5. (D)

Unit 18

Exercise 1

I. 1. hat 2. ham 3. happy 4. handsome 5. hard-working

II. 1. happened 2. hamburgers 3. hands 4. half 5. hard

III. 1. (D) 2. (B) 3. (A) 4. (B) 5. (B)

Exercise 2

I. 1. healthy 2. heavy 3. headache 4. heat 5. have

II. 1. head 2. health 3. hear 4. hate 5. heart

III. 1. (A) 2. (C) 3. (D) 4. (B) 5. (C)

Unit 19

Exercise 1

I. 1. help 2. hide 3. hill 4. hit 5. hold

II. 1. helpful 2. history 3. hobby 4. high 5. here

III. 1. (A) 2. (B) 3. (D) 4. (B) 5. (A)

Exercise 2

I. 1. home 2. horse 3. hope 4. hot 5. hot dog

II. 1. holidays 2. homework 3. hospital 4. honest 5. hotel

III. 1. (A) 2. (C) 3. (D) 4. (B) 5. (C)

Unit 20

Exercise 1

I. 1. hour 2. how 3. hundred 4. hurt 5. ice

II. 1. hungry 2. house 3. husband 4. hurry 5. however

III. 1. (C) 2. (D) 3. (A) 4. (A) 5. (B)

Exercise 2

I. 1. interested 2. ice cream 3. interesting 4. if 5. in

II. 1. interest 2. idea 3. important 4. inside 5. Internet

III. 1. (B) 2. (D) 3. (D) 4. (A) 5. (B)

Unit 21

Exercise 1

I. 1. job 2. join 3. juice 4. jump 5. joy

II. 1. island 2. jogging 3. jeans 4. jacket 5. junior

III. 1. (C) 2. (A) 3. (B) 4. (A) 5. (B)

Exercise 2

I. 1. key 2. kid 3. kind 4. king 5. keep, kept, kept

II. 1. kisses 2. kilograms 3. kicked 4. just 5. kill

III. 1. (D) 2. (A) 3. (B) 4. (C) 5. (B)

Unit 22

Exercise 1

I. 1. knee 2. knock 3. land 4. lake 5. know, knew, known

II. 1. knowledge 2. lamp 3. kitchen 4. knife 5. kite

III. 1. (C) 2. (B) 3. (B) 4. (A) 5. (B)

Exercise 2

I. 1. later 2. language 3. lazy 4. last 5. lead, led, led

II. 1. large 2. laughs 3. late 4. leader 5. learned

III. 1. (C) 2. (D) 3. (B) 4. (A) 5. (A)

Unit 23

Exercise 1

I. 1. leg 2. lemon 3. left 4. lend 5. let, let, let

II. 1. leave 2. letters 3. least 4. lessons 5. less

III. 1. (D) 2. (A) 3. (C) 4. (A) 5. (B)

Exercise 2

I. 1. lion 2. lip 3. list 4. line 5. lie, lay, lain

II. 1. listen 2. light 3. library 4. lives 5. like

III. 1. (C) 2. (B) 3. (A) 4. (B) 5. (D)

Unit 24

Exercise 1

I. 1. live 2. love 3. low 4. living room 5. lose, lost, lost

II. 1. loud 2. lonely 3. Long 4. little 5. Look

III. 1. (C) 2. (B) 3. (D) 4. (A) 5. (B)

Exercise 2

I. 1. mail 2. many 3. make 4. map 5. man, men

II. 1. machine 2. mailman 3. lunch 4. magic 5. lucky

III. 1. (A) 2. (D) 3. (B) 4. (B) 5. (A)

Unit 25

Exercise 1

I. 1. meal 2. mark 3. math 4. may 5. meat

II. 1. market 2. married 3. matter 4. Maybe 5. means

III. 1. (C) 2. (D) 3. (B) 4. (A) 5. (A)

Exercise 2

I. 1. meet 2. menu 3. mile 4. milk 5. medium

II. 1. medicine 2. meeting 3. minute 4. million 5. mind

III. 1. (B) 2. (C) 3. (A) 4. (B) 5. (D)

Unit 26

Exercise 1

I. 1. miss 2. morning 3. more 4. moon 5. moment

II. 1. months 2. modern 3. monkeys 4. money 5. mistake

III. 1. (D) 2. (B) 3. (A) 4. (C) 5. (B)

Exercise 2

I. 1. mother 2. mouth 3. move 4. much 5. mouse, mice

II. 1. museum 2. mountain 3. movie 4. most 5. motorcycle

III. 1. (B) 2. (D) 3. (A) 4. (B) 5. (A)

Unit 27

Exercise 1

I. 1. neck 2. near 3. never 4. new 5. news

II. 1. national 2. named 3. need 4. music 5. must

III. 1. (B) 2. (D) 3. (C) 4. (D) 5. (A)

Exercise 2

I. 1. noodle 2. noon 3. nod 4. next 5. north

II. 1. Nobody 2. nose 3. noise 4. night 5. nice

III. 1. (B) 2. (D) 3. (A) 4. (B) 5. (C)

Unit 28

Exercise 1

I. 1. office 2. off 3. now 4. notebook 5. nurse

II. 1. officer 2. nothing 3. o'clock 4. noticed 5. number

III. 1. (A) 2. (C) 3. (D) 4. (C) 5. (A)

Exercise 2

I. 1. once 2. on 3. OK 4. one 5. or

II. 1. Open 2. old 3. oil 4. often 5. Only

III. 1. (A) 2. (C) 3. (B) 4. (D) 5. (A)

Unit 29

Exercise 1

I. 1. out 2. own 3. pack 4. p.m. 5. over

II. 1. other 2. orange 3. order 4. outside 5. package

III. 1. (A) 2. (C) 3. (D) 4. (A) 5. (B)

Exercise 2

I.   1. park 2. part 3. paint 4. pass 5. party
II. 1. pages 2. pants 3. pair 4. parents 5. paper
III. 1. (B) 2. (C) 3. (A) 4. (A) 5. (D)

Unit 30
Exercise 1
I.   1. pet 2. PE 3. pay 4. pencil 5. pen
II. 1. people 2. piano 3. perhaps 4. past 5. person
III. 1. (A) 2. (B) 3. (D) 4. (B) 5. (A)

Exercise 2
I.   1. piece 2. pie 3. pick 4. pink 5. pig
II. 1. picnic 2. place 3. pizza 4. pictures 5. plan
III. 1. (B) 2. (C) 3. (A) 4. (A) 5. (D)

Unit 31
Exercise 1
I.   1. police 2. player 3. poor 4. please 5. play
II. 1. playground 2. polite 3. popcorn 4. popular 5. points
III. 1. (B) 2. (A) 3. (C) 4. (A) 5. (D)

Exercise 2
I.   1. pork 2. present 3. price 4. possible 5. post office
II. 1. postcard 2. practice 3. pounds 4. prepare 5. pretty
III. 1. (B) 2. (D) 3. (A) 4. (B) 5. (C)

Unit 32
Exercise 1
I.   1. public 2. proud 3. queen 4. question 5. push
II. 1. problem 2. programs 3. purple 4. pulled 5. putting
III. 1. (C) 2. (A) 3. (D) 4. (A) 5. (B)

Exercise 2
I.   1. quiet 2. quite 3. rain 4. rainbow 5. railway
II. 1. radio 2. rabbit 3. quick 4. read 5. rainy
III. 1. (A) 2. (B) 3. (C) 4. (B) 5. (D)

Unit 33
Exercise 1
I.   1. real 2. restroom 3. red 4. restaurant 5. repeat
II. 1. really 2. remember 3. ready 4. refrigerator 5. rest
III. 1. (C) 2. (A) 3. (D) 4. (B) 5. (A)

Exercise 2
I.   1. road 2. river 3. room 4. ride 5. ring, rang, rung
II. 1. rice 2. right 3. rich 4. round 5. roses
III. 1. (B) 2. (B) 3. (A) 4. (D) 5. (C)

Unit 34
Exercise 1
I.   1. sad 2. salt 3. ruler 4. same 5. run, ran, run
II. 1. safe 2. rules 3. sandwich 4. salad 5. sale
III. 1. (D) 2. (B) 3. (A) 4. (C) 5. (B)

Exercise 2
I.   1. season 2. say 3. sea 4. see 5. seat
II. 1. saves 2. school 3. seldom 4. second 5. sell
III. 1. (D) 2. (C) 3. (B) 4. (A) 5. (A)

Unit 35
Exercise 1
I.   1. share 2. shall 3. ship 4. sheep 5. send
II. 1. serious 2. sentence 3. senior 4. Several 5. shape

III. 1. (A) 2. (C) 3. (B) 4. (D) 5. (C)

Exercise 2

I.   1. short 2. shopkeeper 3. shoulder 4. shy 5. sick

II. 1. shirt 2. shop 3. shoes 4. should 5. show

III. 1. (A) 2. (B) 3. (D) 4. (C) 5. (A)

Unit 36

Exercise 1

I.   1. sing 2. sir 3. sit 4. size 5. side

II. 1. since 2. simple 3. sister 4. sidewalk 5. singer

III. 1. (A) 2. (B) 3. (B) 4. (D) 5. (C)

Exercise 2

I.   1. sky 2. slow 3. small 4. snack 5. smart

II. 1. smell 2. smile 3. smoking 4. skirt 5. sleeping

III. 1. (B) 2. (C) 3. (D) 4. (B) 5. (A)

Unit 37

Exercise 1

I.   1. so 2. sock 3. someone 4. snake 5. some

II. 1. somewhere 2. sofa 3. something 4. snow 5. sometimes

III. 1. (B) 2. (C) 3. (D) 4. (B) 5. (A)

Exercise 2

I.   1. son 2. soup 3. soon 4. song 5. sorry

II. 1. sound 2. special 3. speak 4. space 5. south

III. 1. (D) 2. (B) 3. (A) 4. (B) 5. (A)

Unit 38

Exercise 1

I.   1. spring 2. square 3. start 4. star 5. sport

II. 1. spell 2. spent 3. stand 4. Station 5. spoon

III. 1. (D) 2. (B) 3. (A) 4. (B) 5. (C)

Exercise 2

I.   1. still 2. steak 3. strange 4. store 5. stay

II. 1. story 2. stop 3. strangers 4. stomach 5. street

III. 1. (B) 2. (A) 3. (C) 4. (A) 5. (B)

Unit 39

Exercise 1

I.   1. sugar 2. study 3. strong 4. sun 5. stupid

II. 1. sunny 2. supermarket 3. summer 4. successful 5. student

III. 1. (C) 2. (A) 3. (D) 4. (C) 5. (A)

Exercise 2

I.   1. swim 2. take 3. tall 4. sure 5. surprised

II. 1. talk 2. surprise 3. sweet 4. sweater 5. table

III. 1. (C) 2. (B) 3. (A) 4. (C) 5. (D)

Unit 40

Exercise 1

I.   1. team 2. teach 3. taxi 4. tea 5. tape

II. 1. Teenagers 2. television 3. telephone 4. tastes 5. teacher

III. 1. (C) 2. (A) 3. (A) 4. (D) 5. (C)

Exercise 2

I.   1. tennis 2. that 3. these 4. than 5. then

II. 1. There 2. theater 3. Thank 4. test 5. tell

III. 1. (A) 2. (C) 3. (B) 4. (A) 5. (A)

Unit 41

Exercise 1

I.   1. think 2. thing 3. this 4. tiger 5. thin

II. 1. tickets 2. though 3. thirsty 4. Those 5. Thousands

III. 1. (B) 2. (D) 3. (D) 4. (A) 5. (A)

Exercise 2

I.　1. today 2. time 3. tired 4. tonight 5. too

II.　1. tomatoes 2. tomorrow 3. together 4. teeth 5. touched

III.　1. (B)　2. (B)　3. (C)　4. (A)　5. (B)

Unit 42

Exercise 1

I.　1. trip 2. truck 3. toy 4. tree 5. town

II.　1. train 2. towel 3. traffic 4. trouble 5. true

III.　1. (B)　2. (C)　3. (A)　4. (D)　5. (A)

Exercise 2

I.　1. uniform 2. until 3. try 4. uncle 5. under

II.　1. unhappy 2. understand 3. umbrella 4. typhoon 5. turn

III.　1. (D)　2. (B)　3. (A)　4. (C)　5. (C)

Unit 43

Exercise 1

I.　1. very 2. voice 3. up 4. video 5. use

II.　1. vegetables 2. vacation 3. usually 4. useful 5. visit

III.　1. (D)　2. (B)　3. (A)　4. (A)　5. (C)

Exercise 2

I.　1. want 2. wake 3. waitress 4. walk 5. wall

II.　1. waiter 2. warm 3. wash 4. wait 5. watch

III.　1. (A)　2. (C)　3. (A)　4. (B)　5. (D)

Unit 44

Exercise 1

I.　1. way 2. week 3. well 4. wear 5. west

II.　1. weather 2. weekend 3. weak 4. water 5. Welcome

III.　1. (B)　2. (D)　3. (A)　4. (B)　5. (B)

Exercise 2

I.　1. which 2. wet 3. who 4. why 5. what

II.　1. whether 2. Where 3. whose 4. when 5. white

III.　1. (B)　2. (D)　3. (A)　4. (A)　5. (C)

Unit 45

Exercise 1

I.　1. wind 2. wife 3. wise 4. win 5. windy

II.　1. wish 2. windows 3. will 4. winter 5. women

III.　1. (B)　2. (D)　3. (A)　4. (B)　5. (C)

Exercise 2

I.　1. word 2. work 3. workbook 4. worker 5. write

II.　1. wonderful 2. worry 3. world 4. writer 5. wrong

III.　1. (D)　2. (A)　3. (B)　4. (D)　5. (C)

Exercise 3

I.　1. year 2. yet 3. zoo

II.　1. yellow 2. yesterday 3. young

III.　1. (B)　2. (A)　3. (B)

悅讀養成

輕鬆掌握閱讀關鍵
養成優質閱讀能力

本書特色：

1. 特選50篇題材活潑多元之文章，各篇依字數遞增排列，漸進培養閱讀能力。

2. 以初級字彙、句型為主架構文章，奠定基礎閱讀實力。

3. 閱測題目掌握五大閱讀技巧，涵蓋各類考試出題關鍵；訓練綜合運用詞彙、語意、語法知識之能力。

4. Try it! 單元每回精選5組單字或片語，累積字彙助你一臂之力。

5. 翻譯與解析附文章及閱測翻譯、重點試題說明、難字提示，自我評量輕鬆上手。

本書特色

◆ 本書係參考教育部公布之「國民中小學英語最基本一千字詞」
編寫而成，按字母排列，每個單字均附有KK音標、詞性及中文常
用字義。

◆ 本書單字更有精心編寫的例句及相關片語補充，並適時說明字詞的重要
用法，讓讀者不只是會背，更會正確的使用該詞條。

◆ 每十個單字就附有十五題的實戰測試題目，讓讀者隨時測試、加強記憶。

◆ 隨書附贈MP3光碟。